IMAGES
of America

CHEHALIS

I0807676

On the Cover: This photograph shows Chehalis Avenue during the Fourth of July parade in 1915. The parade route passed Giffey Hardware and Fechtner & Sons (jewelers, watchmakers, and bicycle dealers). The festivities featured a baseball game at 3:00 p.m. Leading the parade is Chehalis booster Alva E. Judd, a native of Iowa who had worked as a newspaperman and educator before launching a career in real estate. (Courtesy of the Lewis County Historical Museum.)

IMAGES
of America

CHEHALIS

Julie McDonald Zander

ARCADIA
PUBLISHING

ISBN 978-0-7385-7603-9

Published by Arcadia Publishing
Charleston, South Carolina

Printed in the United States of America

Library of Congress Control Number: 2011925219

For all general information, please contact Arcadia Publishing:
Telephone 843-853-2070
Fax 843-853-0044
E-mail sales@arcadiapublishing.com
For customer service and orders:
Toll-Free 1-888-313-2665

Visit us on the Internet at www.arcadiapublishing.com

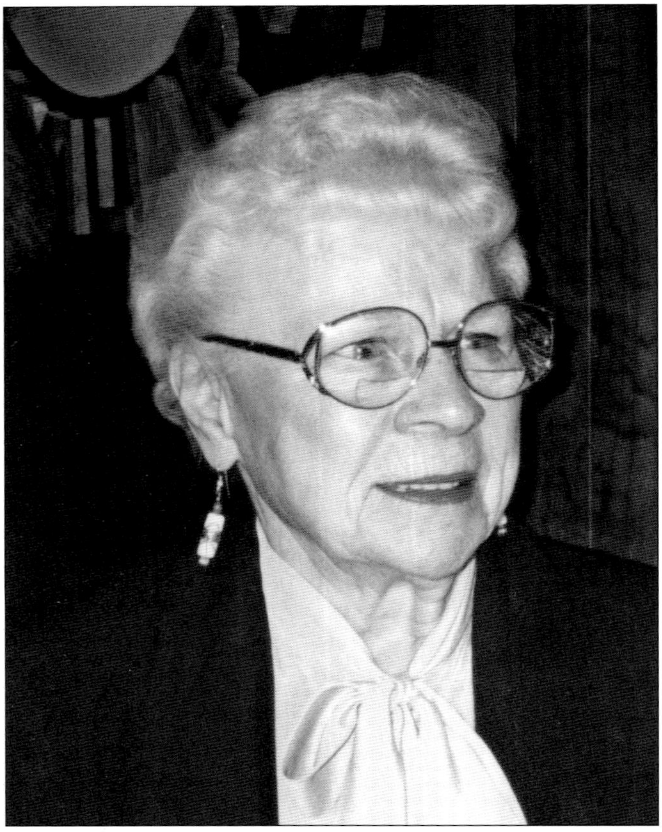

This book is dedicated to Margaret (Shaver) Shields of Centralia, who has helped preserve much of the history stored at the Lewis County Historical Museum as a volunteer there for more than 33 years.

Contents

Acknowledgments		6
Introduction		7
1.	Early Pioneers at Chehalis	9
2.	Claquato Pioneers	15
3.	William West, Creating a City	21
4.	Dawn of a Century	31
5.	Growth in the Teens	55
6.	The Roaring Twenties	71
7.	The Depression Era	87
8.	A World at War	99
9.	Moving Forward	111
Bibliography		127

ACKNOWLEDGMENTS

Many people helped to create this book, especially all the volunteers and employees at the Lewis County Historical Museum. Director Debbie Knapp and the historical society board gave me complete access to all photographs and information. Longtime volunteer Margaret Shields located images for the book so that I could scan them and type the caption cards. She also helped me find the histories and newspaper articles that serve as a foundation for the historical information shared within these pages. Margaret Shields, Debbie Knapp, Edna Fund, and my husband, Larry Zander, helped by selecting the best photographs and reading the information for accuracy. Caryn Foley at the City of Chehalis and Chehalis City Council members helped me update the town's history during the past 30 years. All photographs are courtesy of the Lewis County Historical Museum unless otherwise noted. The *Chronicle* in Centralia, Washington; the Chehalis-Centralia Railroad Association; the City of Chehalis; the Veterans Memorial Museum; the Boeing Company; Eva Perona Hauck; Dorothy McMahan Powell; and Sarah Ciranny Zopolos also shared images for the book.

INTRODUCTION

The history of Chehalis began long before the first white settlers set foot in the lush green countryside nestled between two rivers and surrounded by pristine stands of timber. For centuries, Native Americans from the Upper Chehalis and Taidnapam band of the Cowlitz tribes fished for salmon and steelhead in the Chehalis River, living in cedar longhouses during winters and portable teepees in summer.

The Upper Chehalis and Lower Chehalis, living downstream from present-day Chehalis, spoke a language known as Salish and bartered and intermarried. Men hunted elk and deer and dug clams, while women picked roots and berries and mastered the art of weaving strong baskets to carry and store food and water.

The Chehalis tribes take their name from the native Chi-ke-lis, meaning "shifting sands." The Cowlitz Taidnapam band also lived near the upper Chehalis River at times, although neither tribe seemed to have permanent villages in the Chehalis area, perhaps because it encompasses traditional lands of both tribes. Or maybe because land near the river flooded. Both tribes traveled the Chehalis and Cowlitz Rivers in shallow, stone-chiseled canoes or flat-bottom boats, hauling freight to trade with Yakama Indians on the east side of the Cascade Mountain range.

The first white men to travel near the Cowlitz River were members of the Lewis and Clark expedition that left St. Louis, Missouri, on May 14, 1804, and arrived at the Pacific Ocean in mid-November 1805. Returning home, they camped along the Cowlitz River, which they called the "Cowlitskee," on March 27, 1806.

By 1811, John Jacob Astor had established the Northwest Fur Company's trading post at Fort George on the Columbia River, and a year later, during the war of 1812, the British captured the fort at Astoria. In 1819, Dr. John McLoughlin, who was working for the Hudson's Bay Company, negotiated a merger of the two businesses. By 1824, the Hudson's Bay Company established its headquarters at Fort Vancouver near the confluence of the Columbia and Willamette Rivers.

In late 1818, an employee of the Northwest Fur Company, 18-year-old Quebec native Simon Bonaparte Plomondon, canoed up the Columbia River and paddled upstream on the Cowlitz River to a landing near present-day Toledo, where he was captured by the Cowlitz tribe. Because he was unarmed and spoke several Indian dialects, the Cowlitz chief Scanewa released the tall teenager after several weeks, extracting a promise that he would return with trade goods. Returning with them, Plomondon married one of the chief's daughters, laying a foundation for trade throughout the region. Their first child was born in 1821.

Plomondon shared news of the land with good fishing, plenty of trapping, and an open prairie ready for plowing. The Hudson's Bay Company established Fort Nisqually to the north near Puget Sound in 1833, and Plomondon is said to have helped with the construction. In the late 1830s, Plomondon established the Cowlitz Farm for the company on four square miles of Cowlitz Prairie northeast of present-day Toledo. The farm grew 10,000 bushels of wheat annually and fed 100 head of dairy cattle and more than 500 ewes. Plomondon is also credited with recruiting French-Canadian Catholic missionaries to Cowlitz Prairie. He later became an independent farmer with a brick kiln and sawmill on his property.

Before 1844, the Hudson's Bay Company had allowed only five families to settle north of the Columbia River: James Birnie and George Roberts at Cathlamet and Simon Plomondon, Marcel Bernier, and Antonie Gobar on Cowlitz Prairie. However, by 1844, the dispute over the British-American boundary spawned the presidential campaign slogan "54-40 or fight," referring to the desired northern latitudinal boundary in a controversy that spurred even more wagons to roll west along the Oregon Trail.

A year later, on August 18, 1845, the settlers' provisional government and the Hudson's Bay Company reached a boundary agreement, designating all the land north of the Columbia River as the Vancouver district. Then, on December 21, 1845, that district was divided in two, with all the land west of the Cowlitz River and north to present-day Sitka, Alaska, designated as the Lewis district, after explorer Meriwether Lewis. The Vancouver and Lewis districts were dubbed "counties" the following day. This explains why Lewis County—once so large geographically—has become known as the "mother of all counties."

In June 1846, the British ceded the Vancouver district to the United States, but with all of Vancouver Island remaining under Great Britain's rule, with the boundary established at the 49th parallel. By then, even more Americans had settled north of the Columbia River.

John R. Jackson, a tall, rugged man, settled on a prairie north of the Cowlitz Farm in 1844. German native George Waunch traveled west from Missouri on the Oregon Trail in 1844 at the age of 21 and settled on the northwest bank of the Skookumchuck River, about two miles upstream of its confluence with the Chehalis River, sharing his land with the Upper Chehalis Indians. In 1846, Sidney S. and Nancy Ford, New York natives who had traveled west in 1845 with their five children in an immigration train of 300, settled nearby on what today is called Fords Prairie in northwest Centralia. Joseph Borst, 24 years old and from New York, settled just south of the Fords' home on the same prairie in 1846.

The United States created the Oregon Territory on August 13, 1848. The provisional government ended March 3, 1849, and during the first territorial convention at Oregon City on July 16, 1849, delegates changed the name of Vancouver County to Clark, in honor of Capt. William Clark.

Even more homesteaders followed the Oregon Trail after Congress passed the Donation Land Claim Act on September 27, 1850, granting 320 acres to single men and 640 acres to a man and his wife who lived on and cultivated the land for five years.

Mail service began in the region in 1851, and on September 11, 1852, the region's first newspaper, the *Columbian*, was published in Olympia. Early Lewis County settlers paid for a ferry, warehouse, roads, bridges, and a schoolhouse.

But Lewis County residents in the area of New Market (today known as Tumwater) didn't like having the Lewis County seat so far south at Jackson Courthouse. Traveling there required crossing the swift Skookumchuck River and trudging through swampy bottomland near present-day Chehalis, initially known as Saunders Bottom. The dissatisfaction led to the division of Lewis County, creating Thurston County on January 12, 1852, with its county seat in Olympia. A county created in 1854 and named Chehalis became Grays Harbor County in 1915.

The geographic distance also created dissatisfaction among those living north of the Cowlitz River who didn't like Oregon Territory's seat of government so far away, as it had moved to Salem. At an August 29, 1851, convention, 26 delegates agreed to petition Congress to create the Columbia Territory and build military roads from the Columbia River to Puget Sound and east to Walla Walla. Among the delegates were Ford, Borst, Jackson, and Schuyler Stuart Saunders, founder of Chehalis. They sent another petition during the Monticello convention on November 25, 1852.

Finally, on March 2, 1853, Congress created the Washington Territory, giving settlers what they wanted but changing the proposed name from Columbia to Washington.

One

Early Pioneers at Chehalis

The first settlers in what is Chehalis today were Schuyler S. Saunders, a New York native, and his Irish bride, Eliza.

Saunders, a well-educated farmer born about 1810, married young. After his wife left with their two daughters, he followed them west but never found them. Instead, in a hotel restaurant at Fort Vancouver, he took a shining to a petite 25-year-old waitress, Eliza Tynan, who was born in 1824 in Ireland.

After marrying in 1851, the couple traveled north on the Cowlitz River and settled near the confluence of the Chehalis and Newaukum Rivers. The marshy bottomland soon bore the moniker Saunders Bottom. They built their cabin on higher ground, on the east side of present-day Market Street (now Market Boulevard), and filed a donation land claim for 640 acres (although their measurements proved an acre short, giving them 639 acres).

Shortly after her marriage, Eliza (Tynan) Saunders took the north half of the donation land claim, leaving the southern portion in Schuyler's name. By 1859, the couple had four sons and a daughter. On May 8, 1858, the family established a post office in their log home and called it Saundersville.

The next local settlers were Judge Obadiah McFadden, his wife, Margaret, and their nine children. They bought Schuyler Saunders's 320 acres and built a log cabin in 1859.

While traveling south on business, 47-year-old Schuyler fell ill and died at John R. Jackson's farm. Eliza (Tynan) Saunders later married a man named McGuire, who fathered her daughter, Catherine. He left one night to look for cows and never returned. On July 27, 1865, Eliza married H.F. Basye (sometimes spelled Basey), a saloon keeper who liked to drink, and had two more children, Lucy and Edward, who she later said "trampled on her heart."

Her last husband was John Barrett, another saloon keeper, who had bragged to friends that he would woo and wed Eliza so that her valuable property would be placed on the market and sold. Their marriage ended in divorce after Barrett charged Eliza $25 to sign some legal papers.

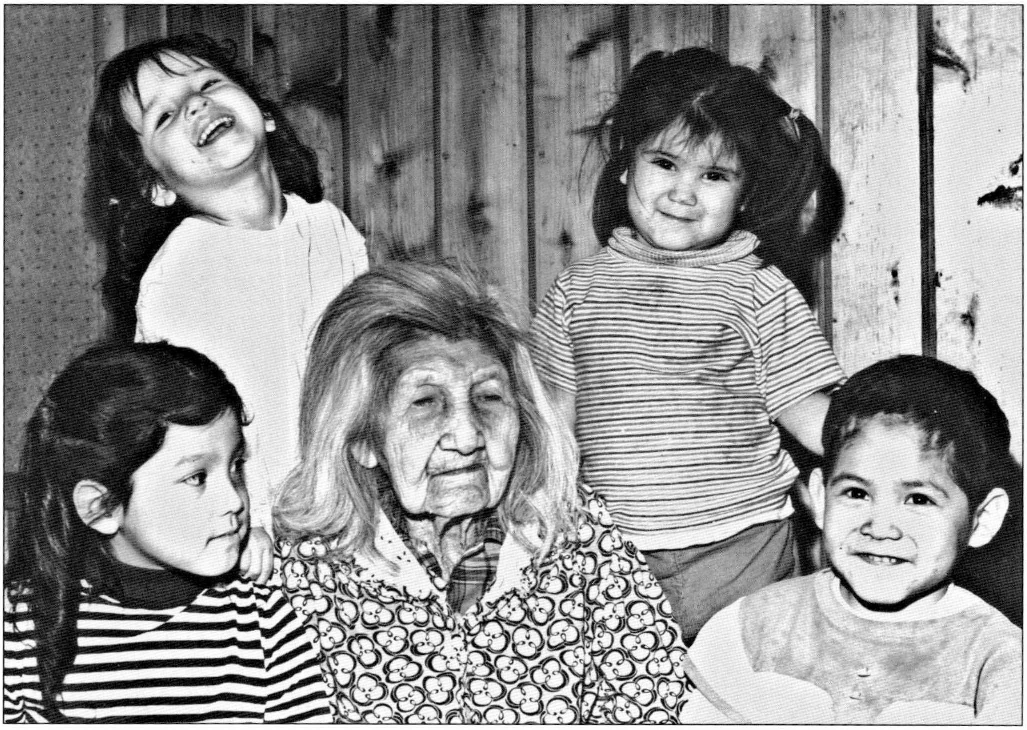

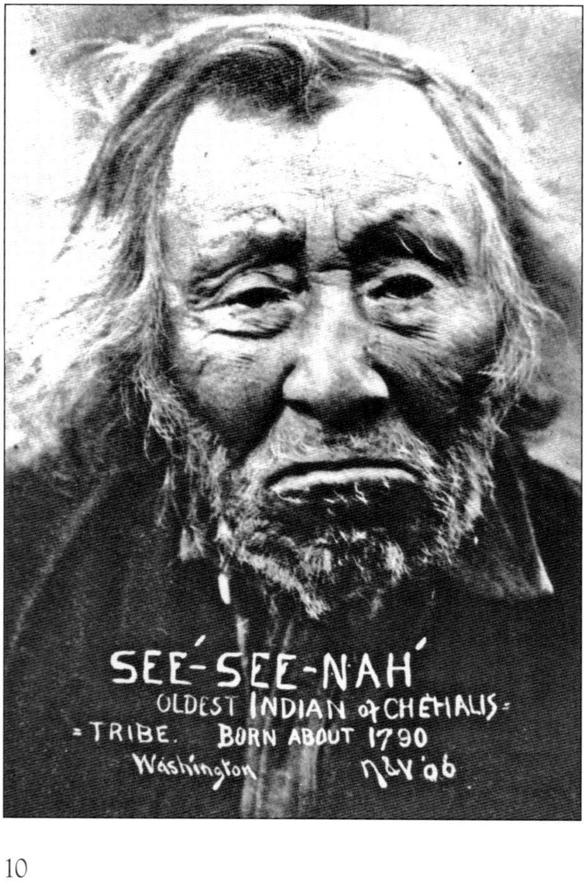

Mary Kiona, a niece of Cowlitz chief Scanewa, is seen in January 1970 with four of her great-great-grandchildren: (from left to right) Magpie, Anna Marie, Joanie, and Raymond Eyle "Junior." The Cowlitz-Yakama Indian, an expert basket weaver, lived to be 115, 118, or 122. The Lewis County Historical Museum features baskets she created and a recording of her speaking in her native tongue about first seeing white people and covered wagons.

This c. 1905 photograph shows See-See-Nah, a Chehalis Indian patriarch born about 1790. His paternal grandfather was a Quinault Indian. His father married a Chehalis woman who owned land along the Chehalis River. Another spelling of his name is Secena.

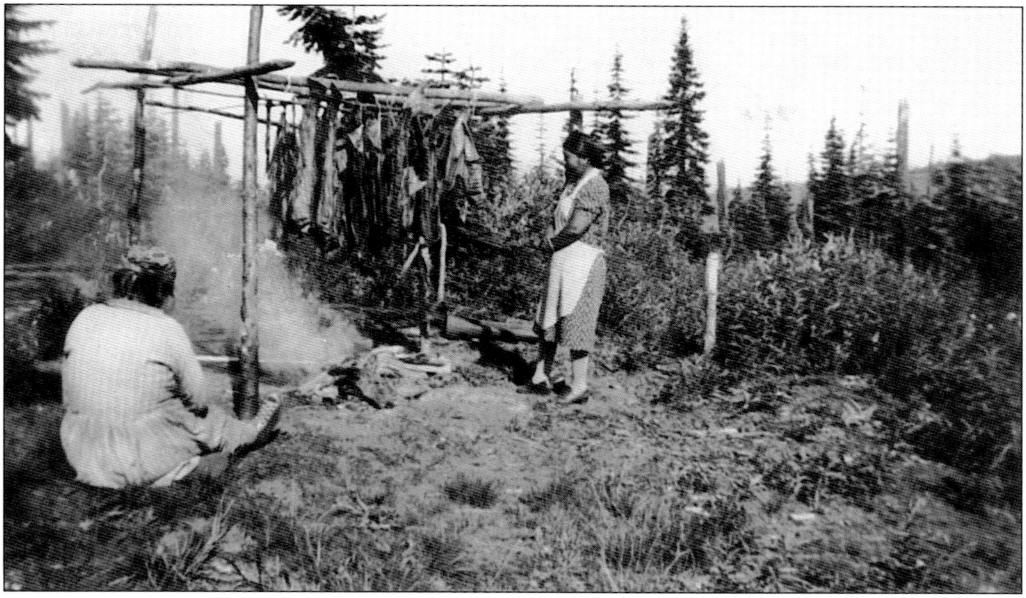

Both the Cowlitz and Chehalis tribes fished for salmon and steelhead in the Chehalis River. This photograph shows two Cowlitz women in print dresses smoking salmon in 1950. The rack and fish carcasses over the fire can be seen.

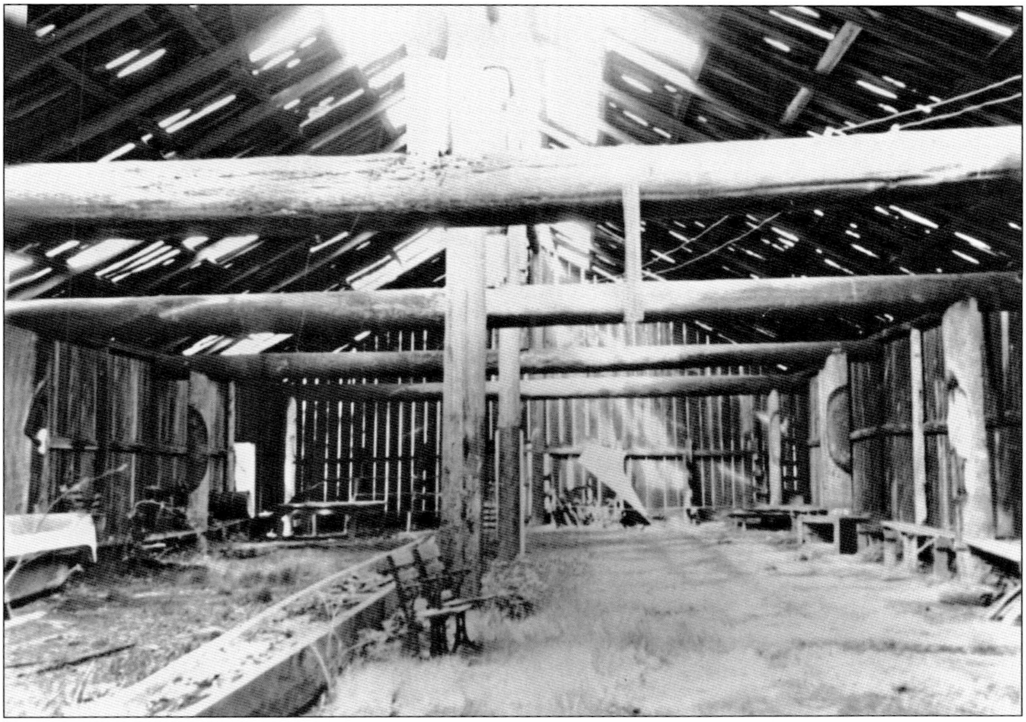

Upper Chehalis and Cowlitz tribes traditionally spent winters in cedar longhouses, usually with the end facing the river. In summer they lived in easily portable teepees fashioned from tightly woven cattail mats wrapped around slanted poles. This photograph shows the interior of a longhouse, location unknown. It was used as a model for an Indian diorama built in 1976 and displayed at the Lewis County Historical Museum.

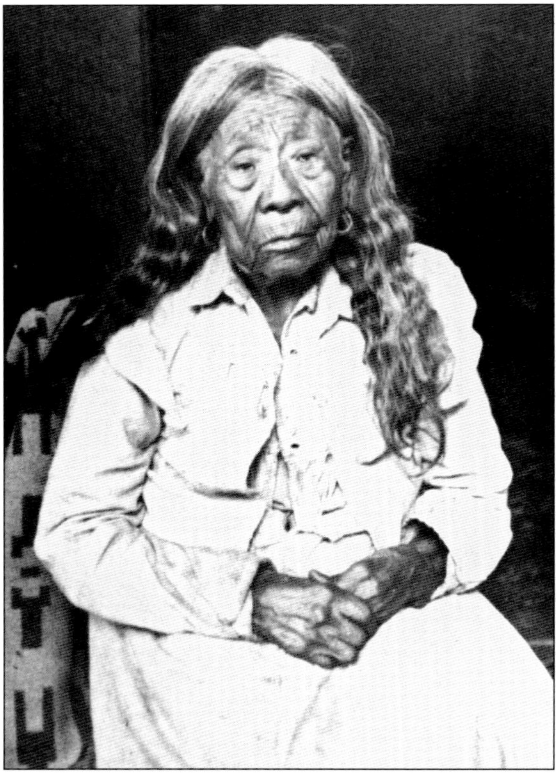

Wyhlenhy, an Indian woman, was 110 years old when this photograph was taken in the late 1800s. She had clear recollections of having seen Meriwether Lewis, Capt. William Clark, and other members of the now-famous Corps of Discovery during their exploration of the Pacific Northwest from 1804 to 1806.

The John R. Jackson home, known as the historic Jackson Courthouse, was built in 1844 along the northern route of the Oregon Trail. The one-and-a-half-story log home with a cedar shake roof and brick chimney features a front porch with a roof supported by round peeled logs. The St. Helens Club in Chehalis later renovated the cabin, where Ulysses S. Grant and Gov. Isaac Stevens and his wife had stopped.

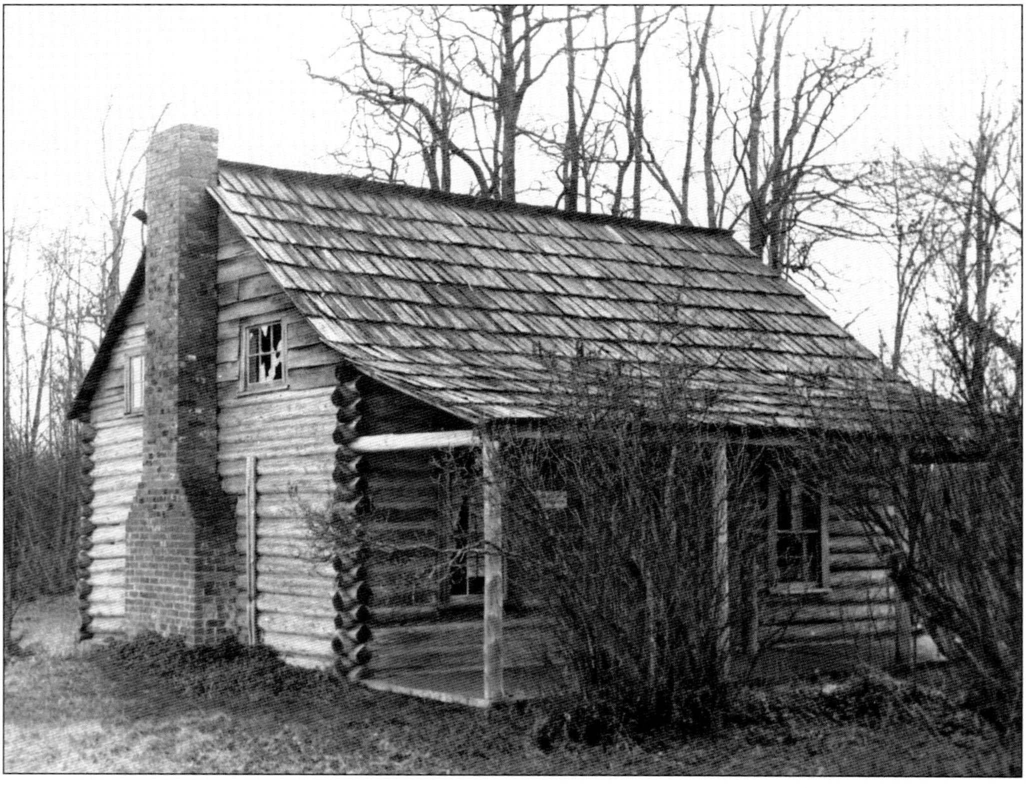

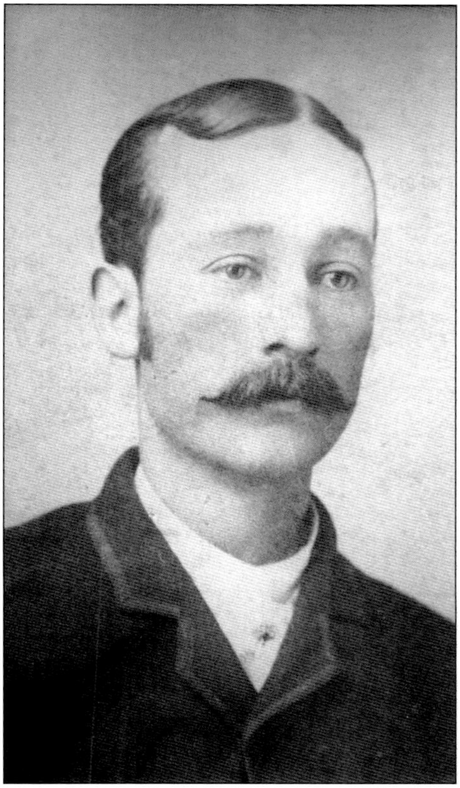

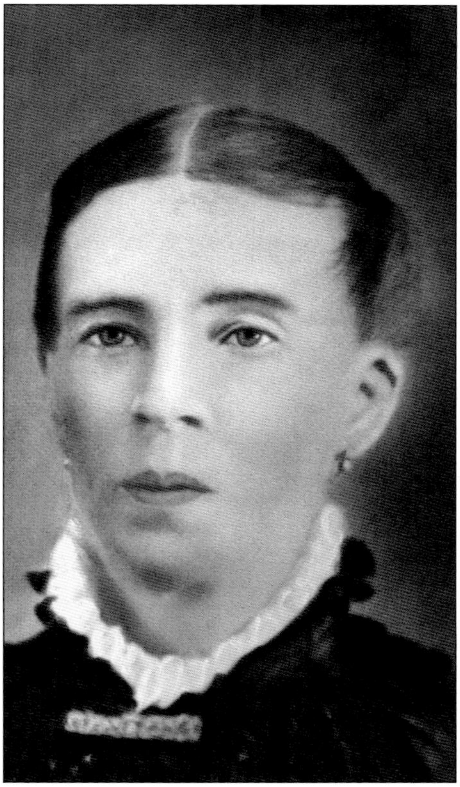

Eliza (Tynan) Saunders McGuire Bayse Barrett, a petite yet feisty Irishwoman, founded Chehalis with her husband, Schuyler S. Saunders, a New York native who traveled west in 1849 to find his runaway wife and two daughters. Schuyler and Eliza homesteaded property described later by Judge Obadiah McFadden as "fit only for a frog pond." However, they built their home (pictured October 1, 1884, at Main and Market Streets) on higher ground, where Eliza lived most of her life. After Schuyler died in 1860, Eliza married and divorced three times. Local businessmen criticized her for refusing to sell her land more quickly, but she couldn't read or write and had been cheated several times. She died May 18, 1900, having given birth to eight children and tamed a wild land. Her surname is misspelled on her headstone as "Barrette."

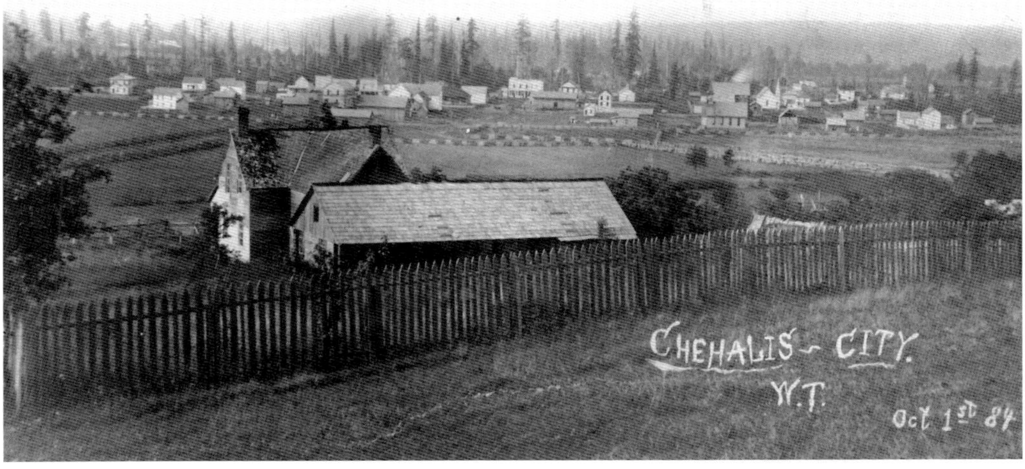

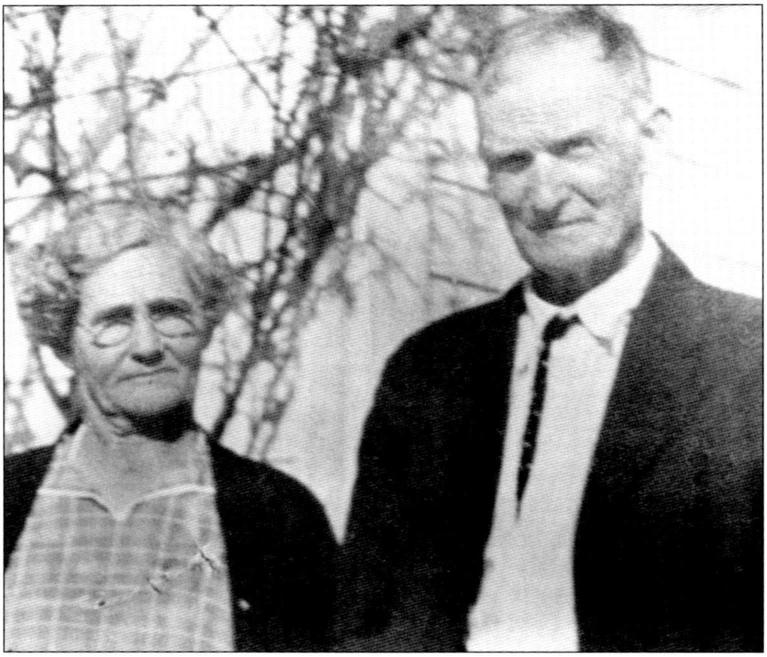

Eliza (Tynan) Saunders's son, Joseph Saunders, is seen with his wife, Sandra (Bishop) Saunders. After Joseph Saunders died January 28, 1952, at the age of 92, editors bemoaned his death as the last link in the chain of Lewis County history. "It isn't often these days that a man has the opportunity of starting life with a community," the editor of the *Chehalis Advocate* wrote on January 31, 1952.

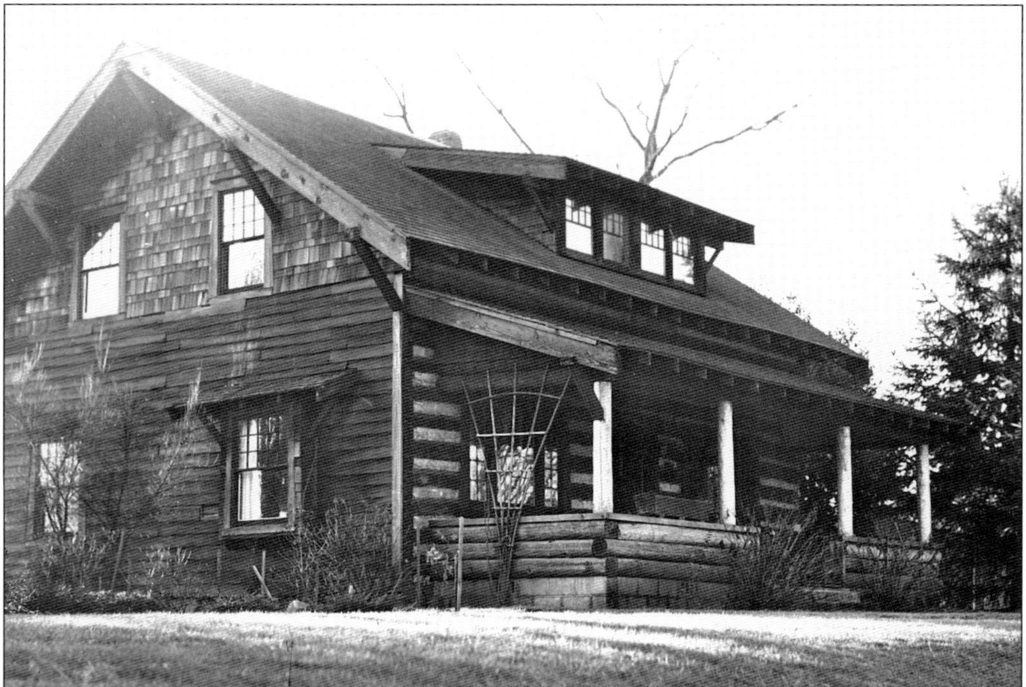

Judge Obadiah McFadden, who was born in 1814, brought his wife, Margaret, and nine children to Chehalis in 1859. McFadden, chief justice of the Territorial Superior Court and later a territorial congressman, paid Schuyler Saunders $1,100 for 320 acres. The McFaddens lived with the Saunders family while building their attractive log home. Today, the 1,595-square-foot home at 475 Southwest Chehalis Avenue is the state's oldest continuously lived in residence. It is listed in the National Register of Historic Places.

Two

Claquato Pioneers

Initially, the Saunders family's nearest neighbors were the Davis family, who settled on the hillside three miles away in 1853 in an area the Indians called Claquato.

Lewis H. Davis, a Vermont native, built a double-log cabin for his family. His son, Levi Adrian Davis, filed a claim on adjoining property.

At the outbreak of the Indian Wars of 1855 and 1856, a friendly Chehalis Indian, John Heyton, rode through the night to warn settlers of impending Indian attacks. The Saunders family and other settlers fled west to the recently built Claquato Fort, a 100-square-foot stockade with blockhouses.

When threats faded in the fall of 1856, the Saunders family returned home to find their house, barn, and fences burned, their stock killed, and everything they owned stolen or destroyed. They started over. Despite the tensions, Cowlitz and Chehalis Indians seemed to like Schuyler Saunders, who preached the gospel and sang hymns. Native Americans named children after him and referred to him as "King George's Man."

In the fall of 1857, L.A. Davis began operating his waterwheel-powered saw- and gristmill. In 1858, Davis sawed the lumber used to build a little church that still stands today—the oldest remaining church in Washington, complete with original pews and pulpit, a bronze bell shipped around Cape Horn from Boston, and wooden spires protruding from the belfry to represent a crown of thorns.

Claquato thrived as a way station for travelers, featuring hotels, blacksmith and carpenter shops, and even a ferry across the Chehalis River. The Davis Prairie post office opened May 10, 1858, and was renamed the Claquato post office September 15, 1858. By 1864, the community had up to 50 residents. In 1862, the legislature agreed to make Claquato the county seat if L.H. Davis donated the land and supplied the courthouse, so he donated a 161-by-250-foot lot and built a two-story courthouse.

When the Northern Pacific Railroad bypassed Claquato in 1874, citizens gradually moved east to Chehalis, leaving the community a ghost town, with only the church and cemetery nestled among large evergreens testifying to its earlier heyday.

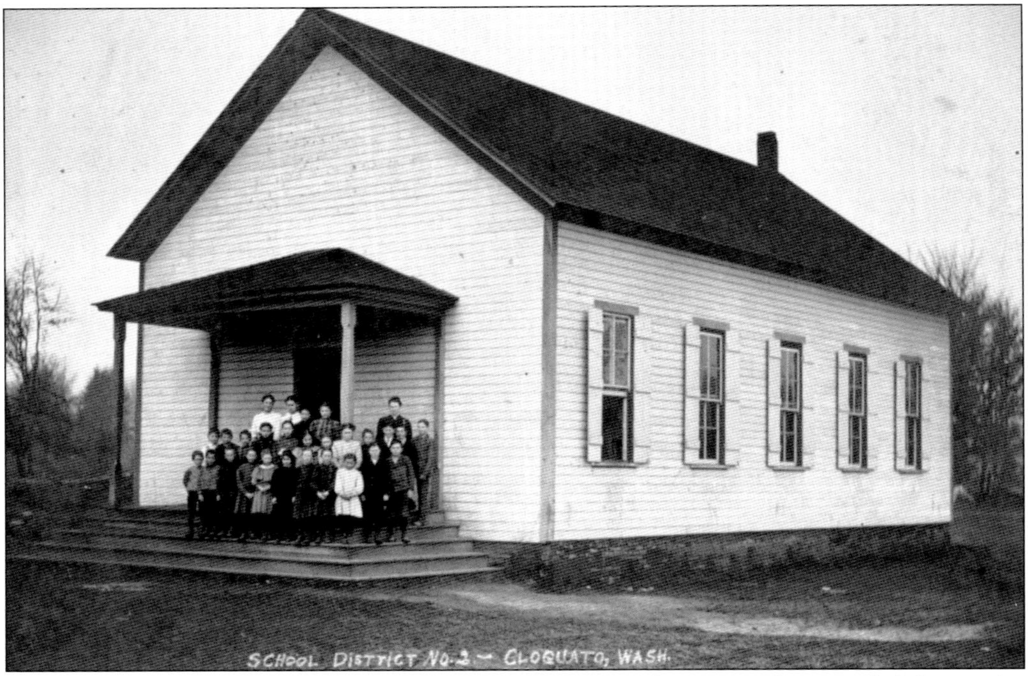

Vermont native Lewis Hawkins Davis left Indiana in 1851 and, two years later, settled three miles west of the Saunders family on a hillside known as Claquato, a Chehalis Indian word meaning "high ground" or "hill." He built a log cabin and a combination grist- and sawmill and donated land for a church. The Claquato Church, built in 1858 with hand-forged nails and local lumber, is among the oldest territorial churches still in its original location. It was the third Protestant church built between the Columbia River and Olympia and features a belfry covered with a symbolic crown of thorns. The bronze bell in the belfry came around Cape Horn from Boston in 1857. The above photograph, taken about 1905, shows Claquato School with students and teachers on the front steps. The image below shows children outside the Methodist-Episcopal Church about 1900.

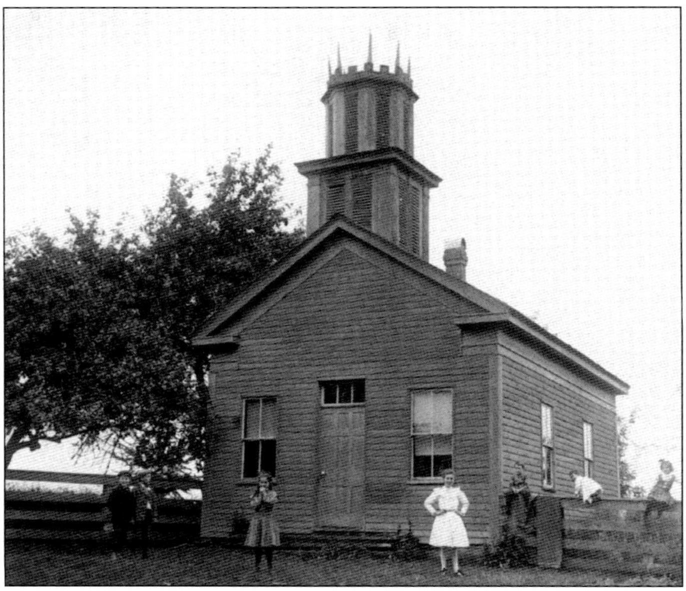

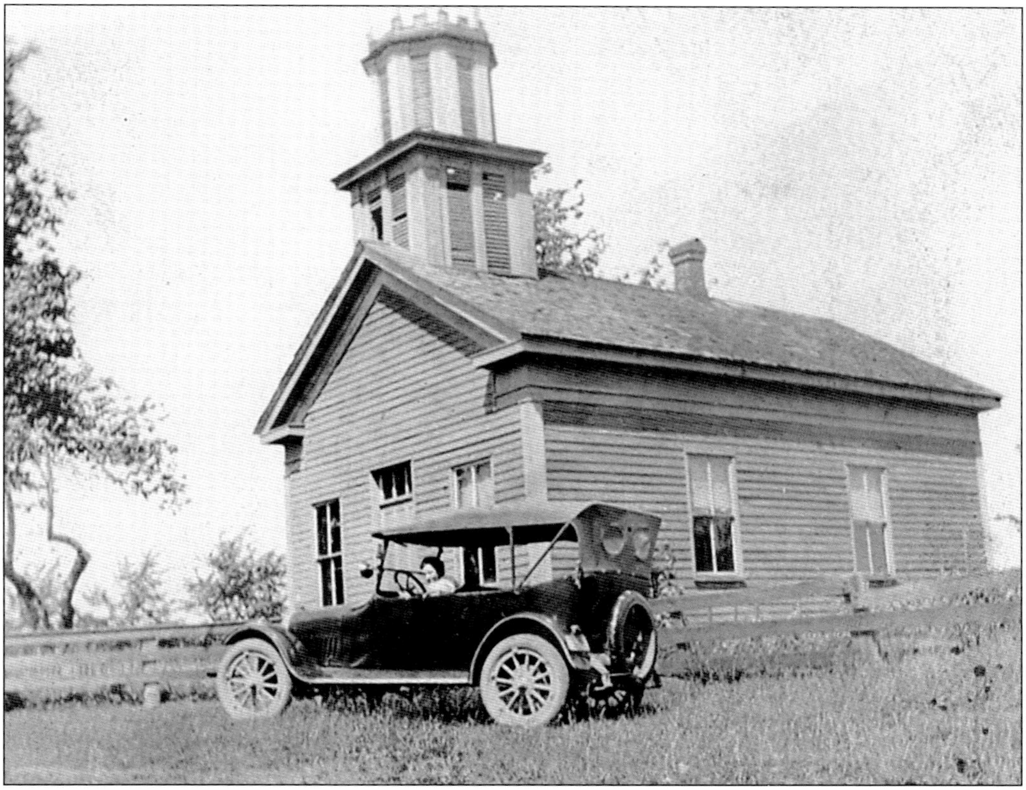

A woman in a 1915 car is seen outside the Claquato Church, which has fascinated people for years because of its frontier history. In 1929, the community raised money to repair the interior and install a new floor, using it for Sunday school and occasional church services in the 1930s. Eventually, it fell prey to vandalism and deterioration. The Chehalis American Legion restored the building, which was rededicated August 16, 1953, as a memorial to Lewis County's pioneers. The Lewis County Chapter of the Daughters of Pioneers of Washington provided a plaque at the church in observance of the building's centennial on August 10, 1958. The sign relates a brief history of the pioneer town of Claquato founded in 1853, which became a busy way station featuring two hotels, stables, a general store, blacksmith shops, and a carpenter's shop.

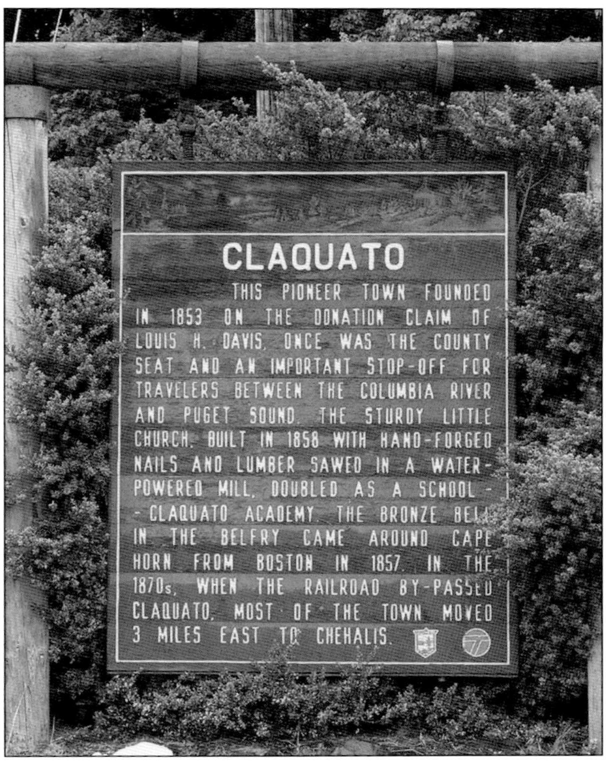

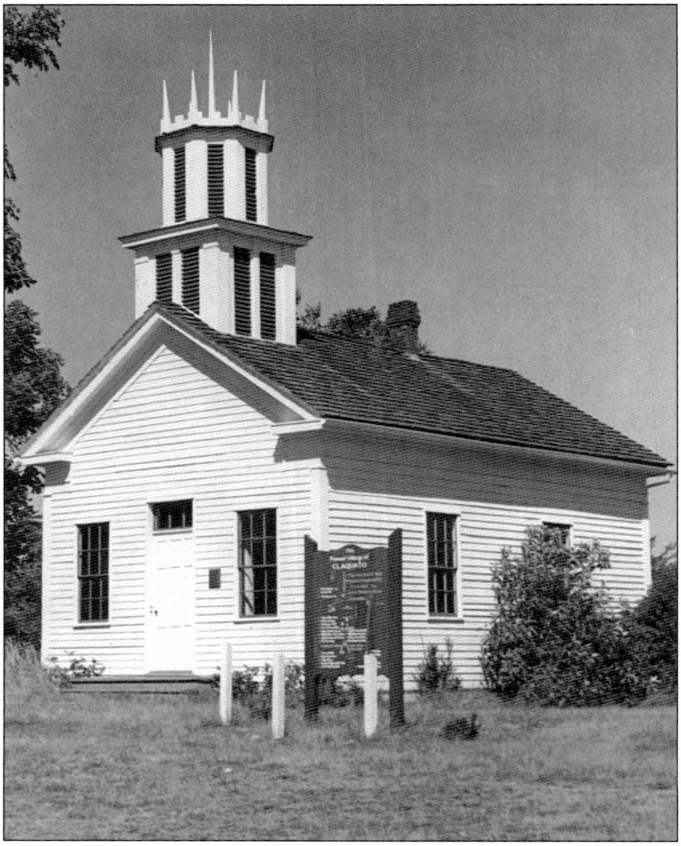

Today, the historic white church is the site of the annual Lewis County Historical Museum's Pioneer Pie Social each summer. The 1982 photograph below shows the interior of the church adorned with wallpaper. The building contains about a dozen white pews, a pulpit, and a small organ. Pioneer Lewis Davis donated land for the church to the Methodists, with the caveat that it would be open to people of all denominations. The church was a main preaching stop on the Chehalis River Methodist-Episcopal circuit, and Presbyterians also met in the building. Unlike many old buildings, the Claquato Church never suffered a major fire or gave way to business development, so the building remains standing in its original location.

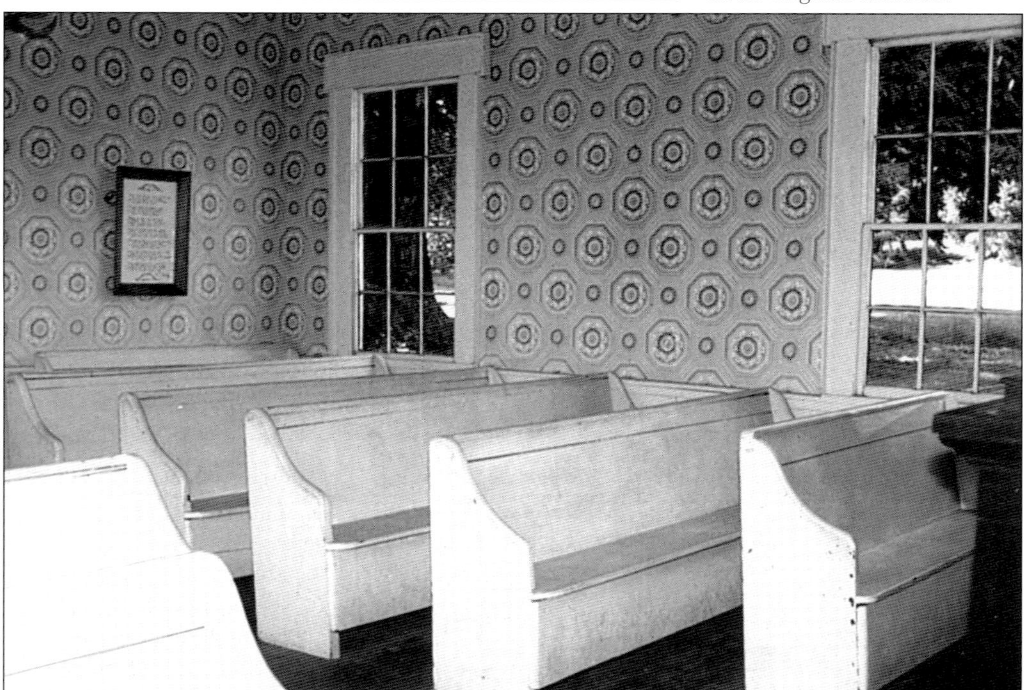

The wooden sign, dedicated May 8, 1966, at Westminster Presbyterian Church in Chehalis, tells how Rev. George Whitworth met with settlers on October 5, 1855, in the Davis schoolhouse, and they decided they needed a church. The reverend traveled by horse from Olympia twice a month, carrying a Bible, songbook, and rifle. He organized public schools, served as territorial university president, founded Whitworth College in Spokane, and organized 15 churches.

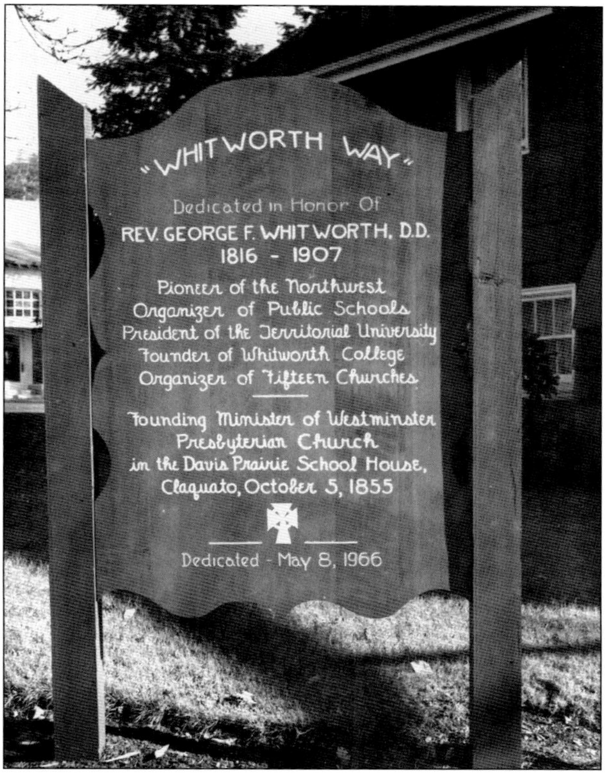

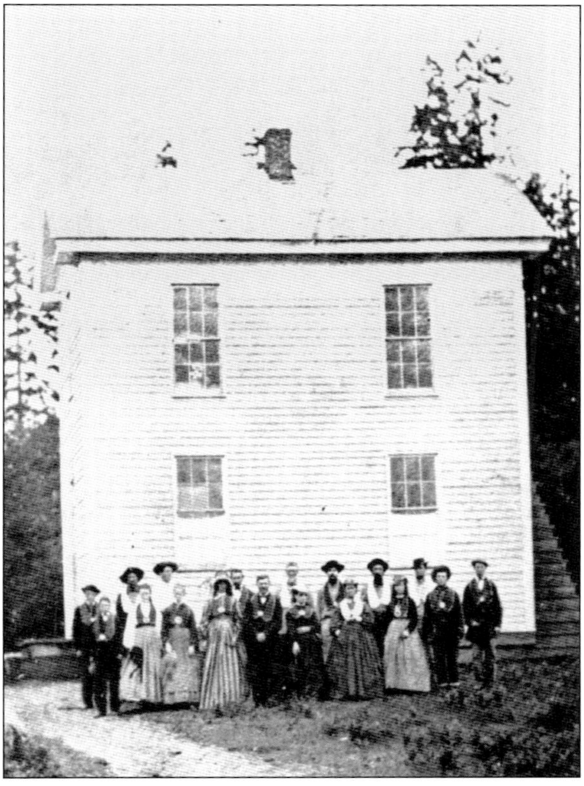

Claquato served as Lewis County's seat from 1862 until July 4, 1874, when it was moved to Chehalis. The 1862 legislature agreed to make Claquato the county seat if Lewis Davis donated land and supplied building materials. He provided a 161-by-250-foot lot and built a rectangular two-story courthouse with a 120-foot-high flagpole. The building served as a Grange hall and cheese factory before being demolished in 1888.

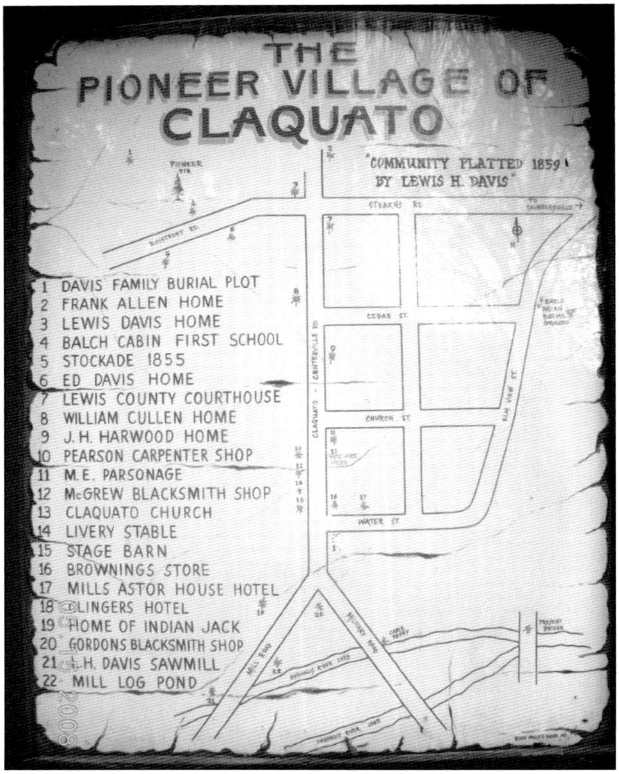

This Claquato Pioneer Village map shows the location of the Davis family burial plot; Frank Allen home; Lewis Davis home; first school; stockade; Ed Davis home; Lewis County Courthouse; William Cullen home; J.H. Harwood home; Thomas Pearson carpenter shop; M.E. Parsonage, McGrew blacksmith shop; Claquato Church; livery stable; stage barn; Browning's store; Mills Astor House Hotel; Clinger's Hotel; Indian Jack's home; Gordon's blacksmith shop; L.H. Davis sawmill; and mill log pond.

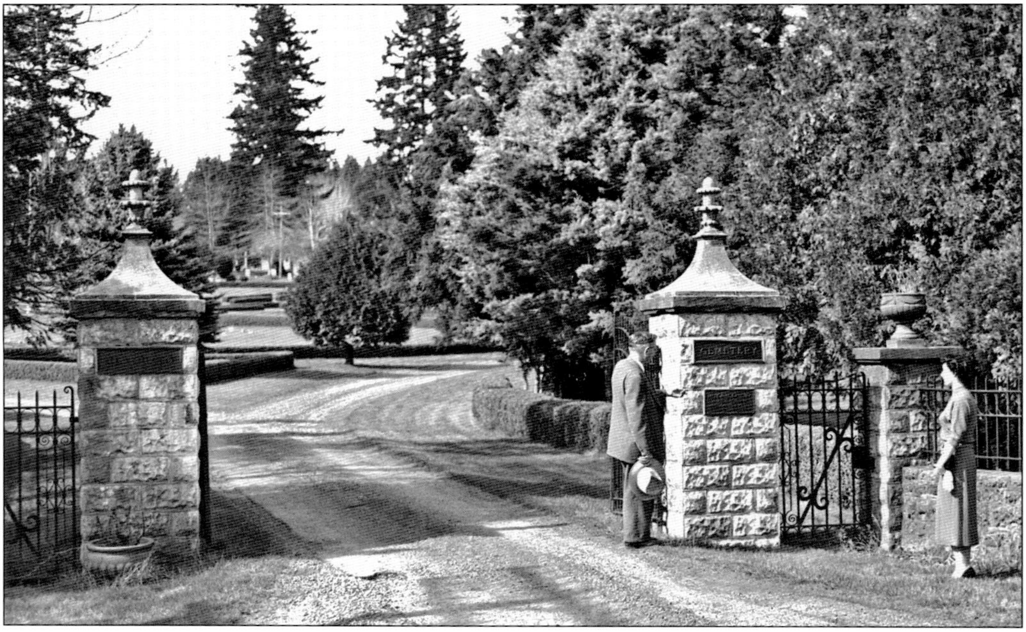

This mid-1950s photograph shows the main entrance to Claquato Cemetery, resting place of many Lewis County pioneers. The cemetery, started in 1856, features the large Pioneer Tree, where travelers often spent the night sheltered by its overhanging fir branches. Lewis Davis donated property for the cemetery. Since 1920, the nonprofit Claquato Cemetery Association, governed by volunteers, has maintained it.

Three

William West, Creating a City

William West, a man whose promotion of and devotion to the community earned him the nickname "the Father of Chehalis," arrived in the valley in 1864, and proved instrumental in bringing the railroad to town.

After Eliza (Tynan) Saunders refused to donate land for a Chehalis depot, Northern Pacific Railroad superintendent J.W. Sprague built one three miles south at Newaukum, forcing travelers to walk along train tracks and a high trestle. Although Sprague rejected settlers' petition for a Chehalis depot, after West and other men frequently waved a red flag to stop passing trains, he relented.

Soon warehouses, a packinghouse, and retail businesses opened, followed by churches and schools. Eliza platted the town's first three blocks, west of the railroad tracks on both sides of Main Street, on May 8, 1875, and more in the early 1880s when she established a saloon and Saunders Livery Stable.

In 1874, local business leaders persuaded the Territorial Legislature to shift the county seat from Claquato to Chehalis after they built a $3,000 courthouse dedicated July 4, 1874. Two years later, the newly formed Chehalis School District, under directors John Alexander, A. Burbee, and West, levied a tax to raise $600 for a new schoolhouse on North Street, west of the railroad tracks.

In the 1870s, the first bridge over the Chehalis River was constructed, eliminating the need for a ferry. In 1882, flooding created huge log jams that washed the new bridge downstream, along with rotting plank and corduroy roads. The bridge was later rebuilt.

The city incorporated and held its first council meeting on December 20, 1883. Also in that year, the *Lewis County Nugget* began publishing, with the *Lewis County Bee* appearing in 1884. In 1898, owner Dan Bush merged the two newspapers into the *Chehalis Bee-Nugget*. In the 1890s, two other newspapers began: the *People's Advocate* and *Chehalis Examiner*.

Banks, hardware stores, and grocers served workers at the sash-and-door factory, two brickyards, and flour, lumber, and shingle mills as the sleepy village became a bustling community. But in 1892, two suspicious fires swept through the Main Street business district, and merchants rebuilt on Market Street, effectively shifting the retail core away from Eliza's property.

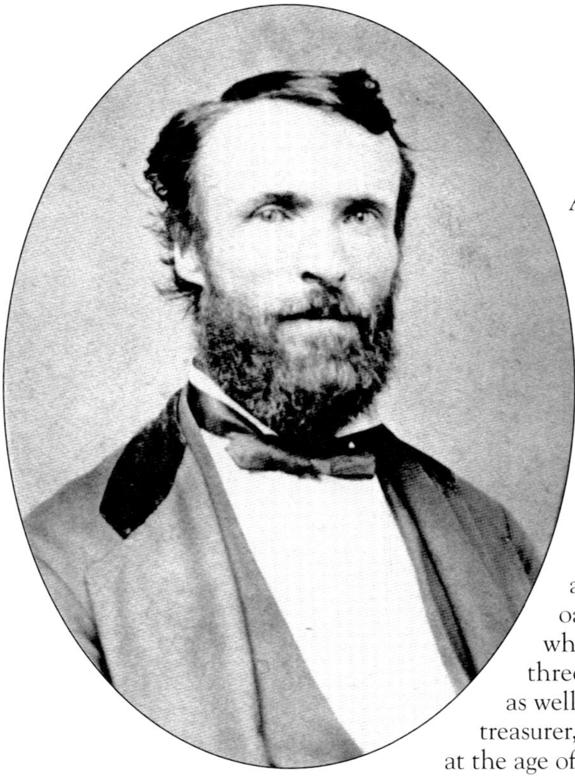

Among early Chehalis River Valley settlers was William West, a civic-minded community leader whose nickname was "the Father of Chehalis." West, a native of York, England, born in October 1838, farmed in Illinois before moving west in 1864 with his wife, Elizabeth; oldest son, Robert; and brother-in-law John Dobson. At Saundersville, he paid a homesteader $150 for 160 acres near where Alexander Park lies today. In his memoirs, he recalled clearing "giant forest trees, some of them four to eight feet in diameter." He cultivated a large vegetable garden and planted wheat, oats, peas, and potatoes. Later, he sold milk, which his son Bill delivered. West served three years as mayor and two on the council, as well as several years as county auditor, county treasurer, and deputy sheriff. He died May 8, 1915, at the age of 76.

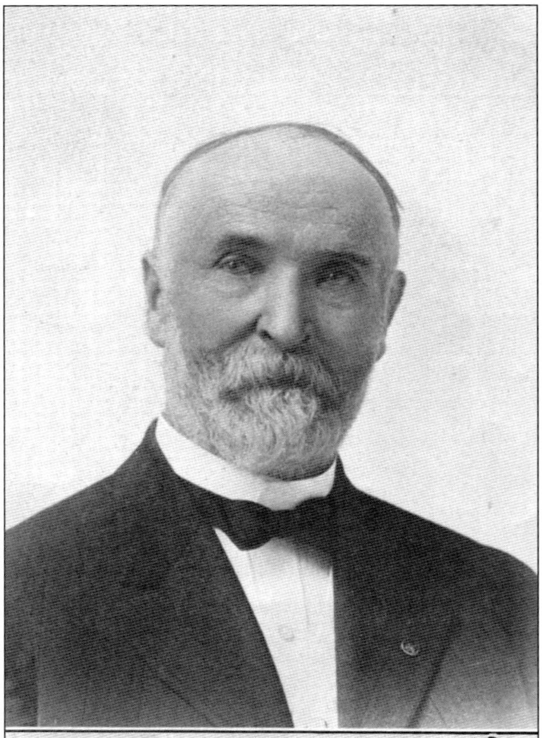

WILLIAM WEST —Dean, Photo

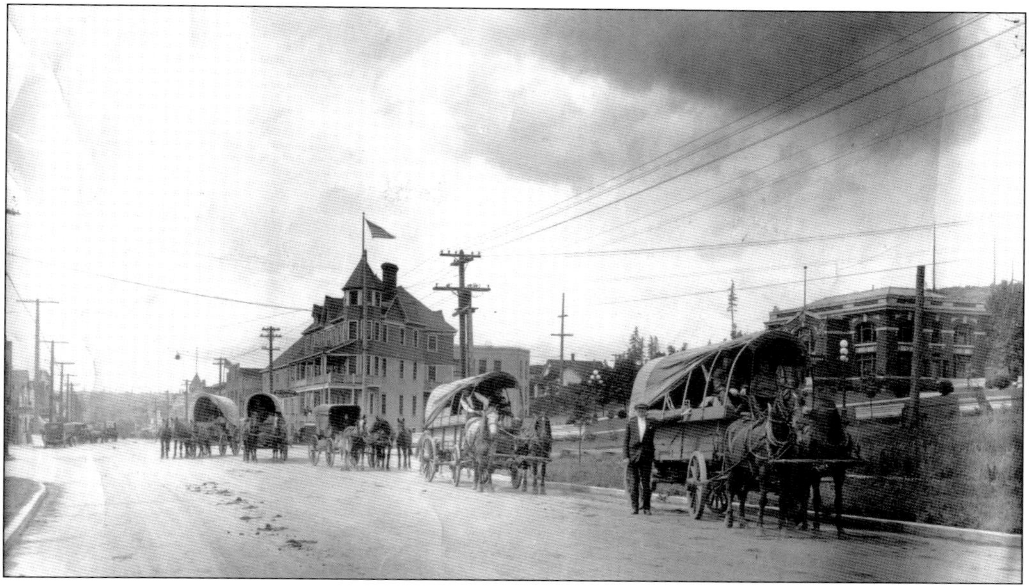

A wagon train bound for eastern Lewis County assembles in front of the St. Helens Hotel, one of the famous, early Chehalis landmarks. The hotel opened May 12, 1891, as part of a strategy to shift the city's center from Main Street to Market Street. Remodeled in 1914, the building was later moved to the corner of Washington Avenue and Division Street, becoming the Sticklin Apartments, which were destroyed in the late 1970s. At right is the Chehalis City Hall, built in 1910. The proprietor of the 70-room hotel in 1915 was 39-year-old William Francis West, the six-foot-two-inch-tall, 220-pound son of William West. He built a substantial brick addition in 1910, remodeled in 1914, and constructed the present St. Helens Hotel between 1917 and 1920. He later donated land for construction of the W.F. West High School.

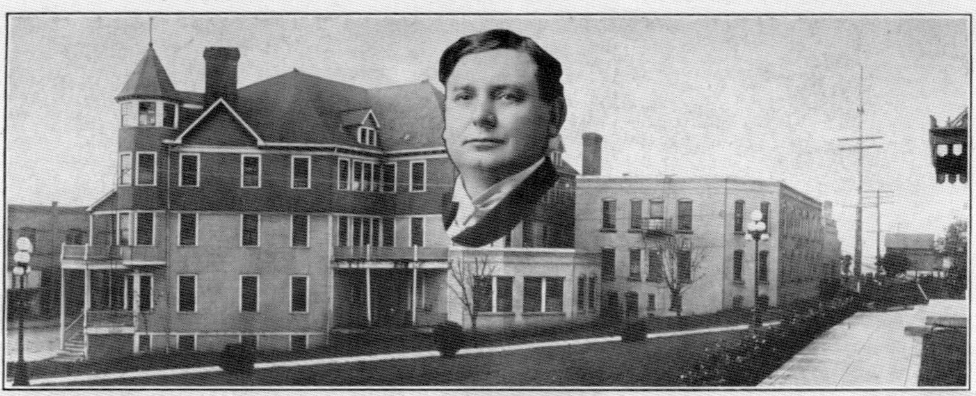

ST. HELENS HOTEL, W. F. WEST, PROPRIETOR —Dean, Photo

The Little Brother of Chehalis

Otherwise, W. F. ("Big Bill") West—Proprietor of Lewis County's Leading Hostelry—The St. Helens Hotel, Chehalis, Is

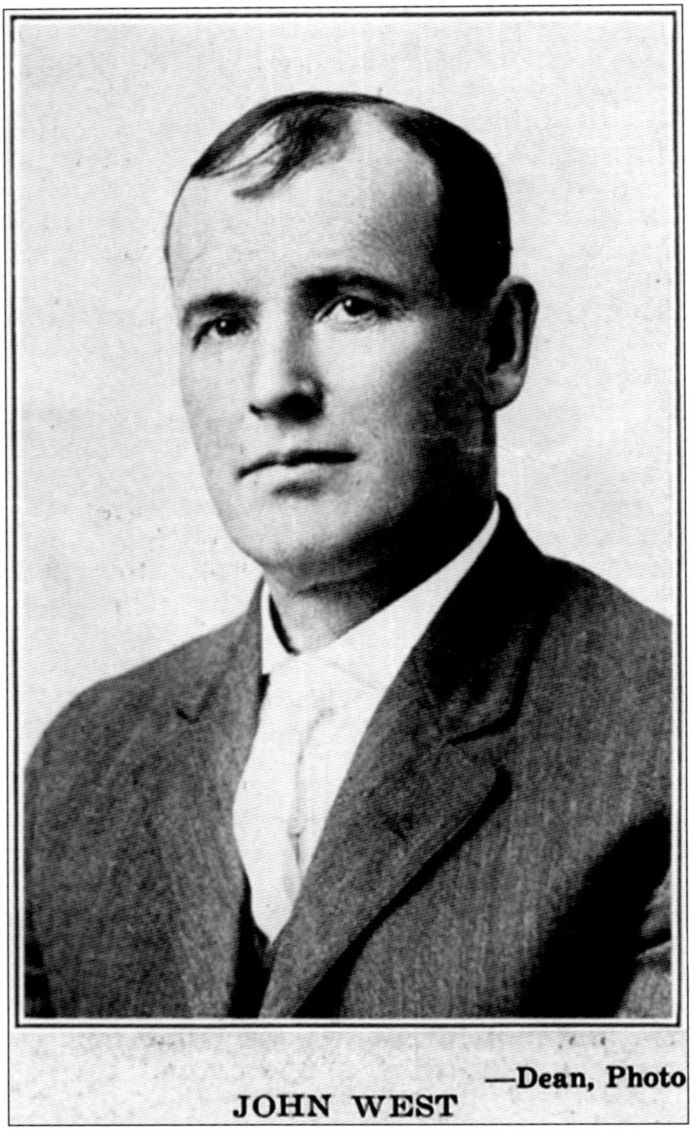

John West, another of William West's sons, was born in June 1868. The Chehalis merchant opened a small confectionery store on Chehalis Avenue in 1888 and began a large grocery store there in 1894, stating on his letterhead, "If from West, it's the best."

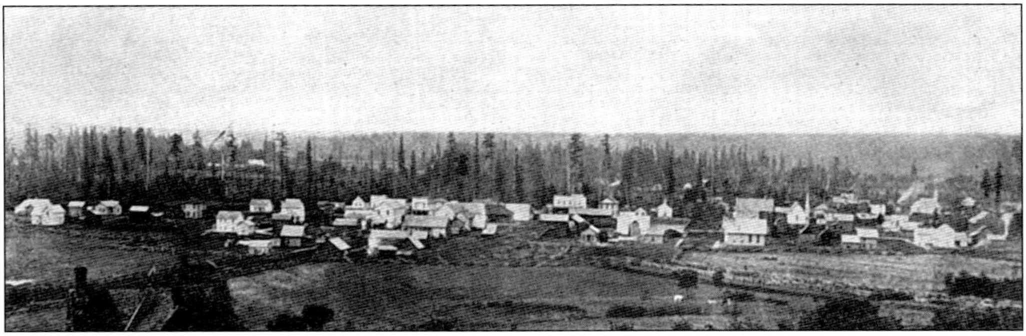

This bird's-eye view from 1885 offers a glimpse of early Chehalis buildings. By then, the town had several churches: the Westminster Presbyterian Church opened in 1882, the Baptist Church in 1884, and the Episcopal Church of the Epiphany in 1884.

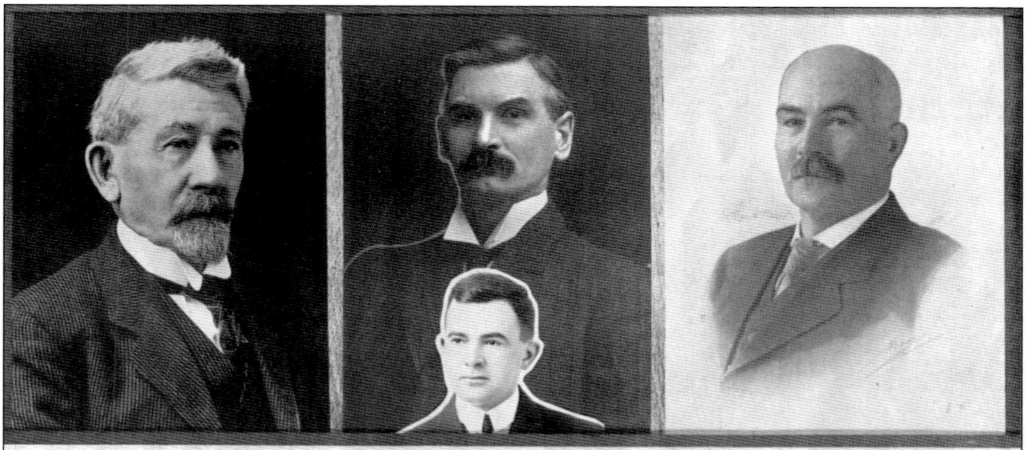

HON. FRANCIS DONAHOE—N. B. COFFMAN—WM. M. URQUHART
JAMES A. URQUHART —Dean, Photo

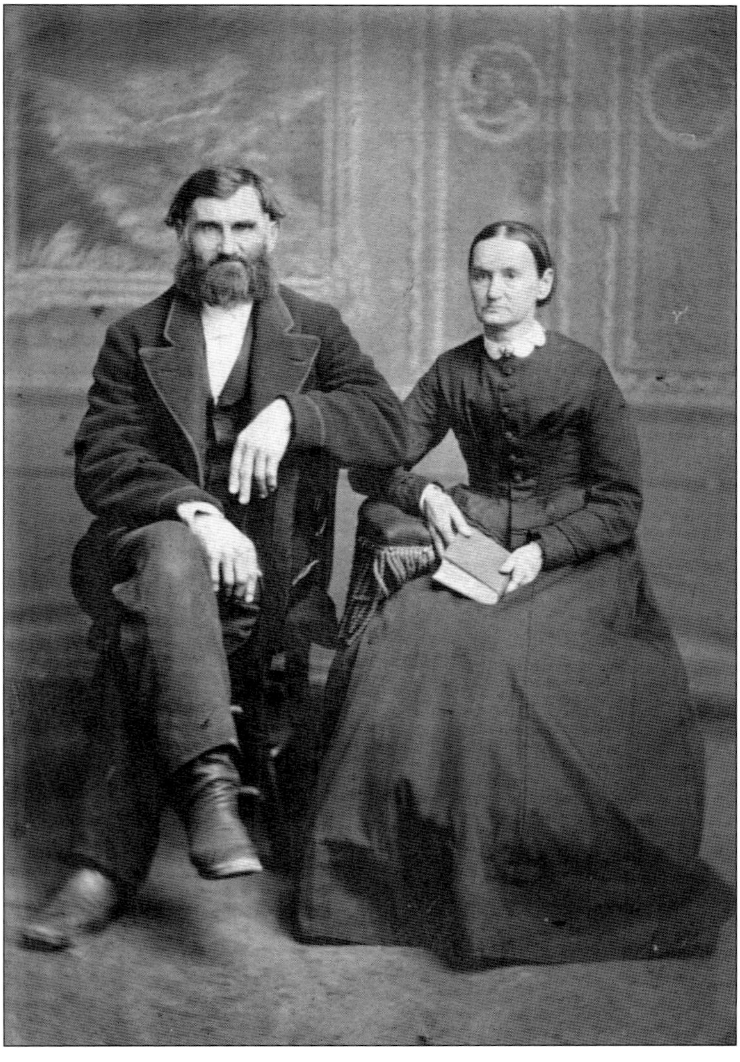

Francis Donahoe, Noah Berry Coffman, pioneer merchant William Muir Urquhart, John Dobson (not pictured), and Daniel C. Millett established a private bank in 1884 and incorporated it in 1890. William's son, James A. Urquhart, worked as a cashier at Coffman-Dobson Bank. Noah Berry Coffman Sr. is seen with his wife, Margaret (Wimp) Coffman, in the 1880s. Their son, also named N.B. Coffman, moved to Chehalis in 1884 in his mid-20s and quickly joined with C.H. Allen to form the Coffman & Allen Bank. He practiced law at the same time, and after his partner's death, served as sole proprietor until joining with Dobson, Donahoe, Urquhart, and Millett. He married Adelaine J. Tighe in 1883.

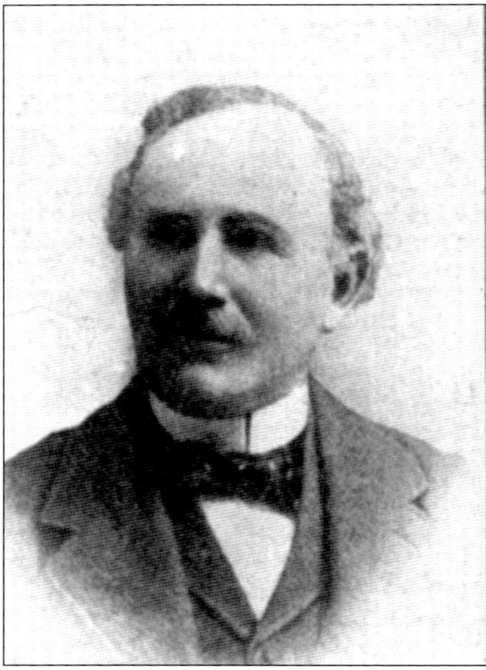
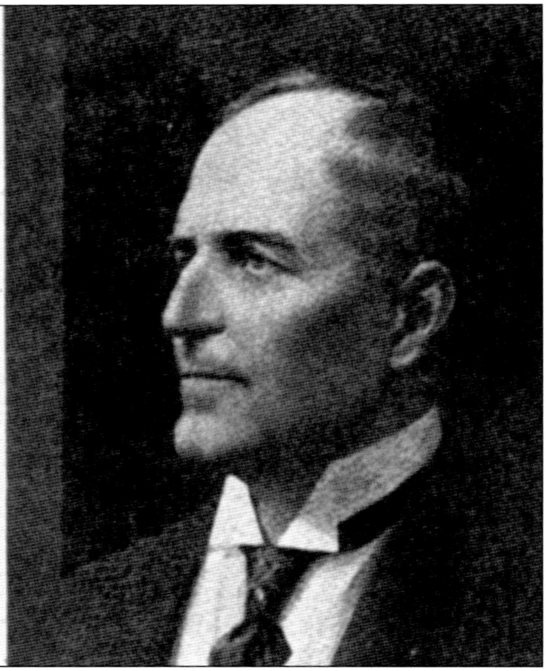

Attorney Daniel Caldwell Millett (right) and banker John Dobson were both prominent Chehalis citizens. Millett, who died in 1908 in his early 60s, had served as mayor of Chehalis in 1891, city attorney for five years until 1902, and school board member. He donated land used as an athletic field, Millett Field. John Dobson, brother-in-law to William West, served eight years on the Chehalis City Council, one term as mayor, and many years as city treasurer. He suffered a tragic loss December 8, 1881, only a year after his marriage to Hannah West, when his wife and infant daughter, Kathleen, drowned after their wagon overturned while fording the Chehalis River near Lincoln Creek. Below, a ferry carries a flatbed wagon across the creek in 1896. After Dobson died in 1907, the Chehalis Land and Timber Company donated 18 acres for the John Dobson Park.

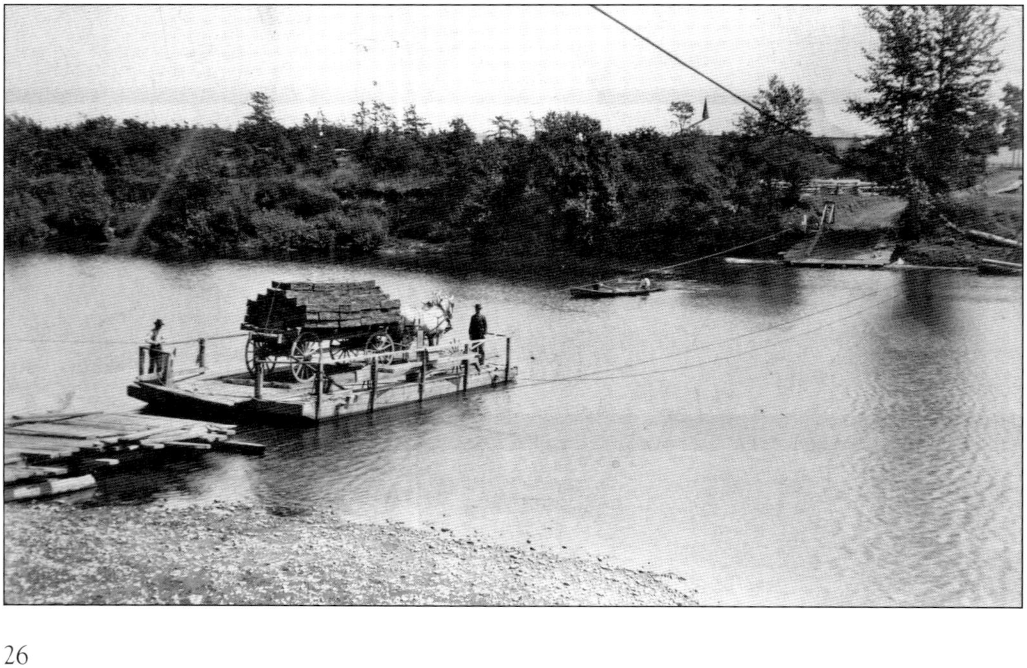

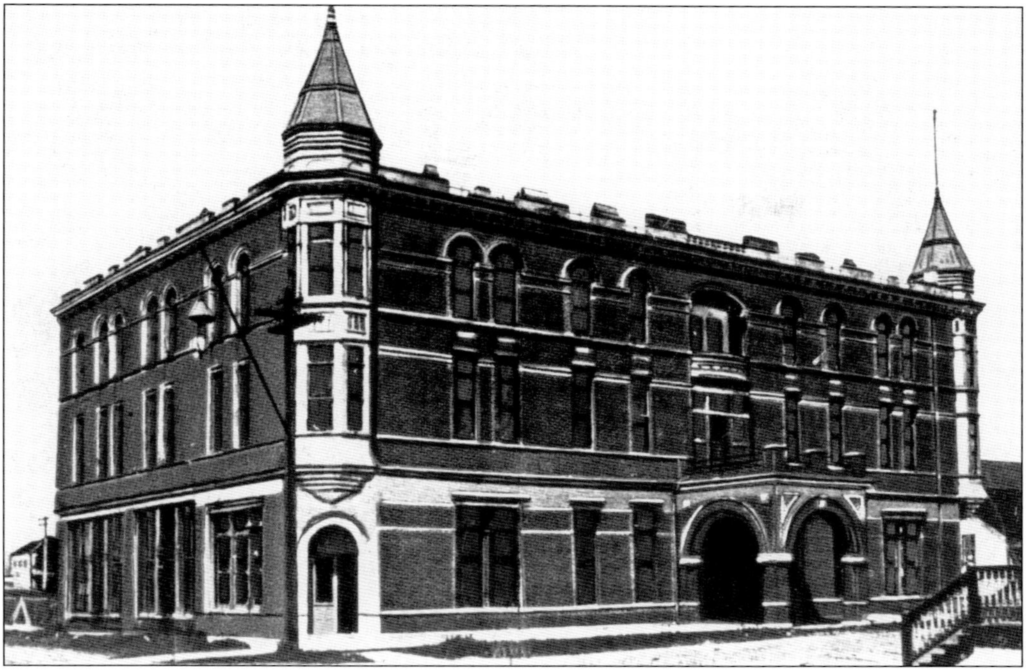

Eliza (Tynan) Saunders Barrett, a lifelong Catholic, built St. John the Evangelist Catholic Church in 1889 on St. Helens Avenue near Prindle Street, as well as the Holy Rosary Academy (below), a Catholic girls' boarding and day school operated by the Dominican Sisters, in 1895. The school remained open until June 1918, when the nuns closed it over safety concerns. The church was relocated to Pacific Avenue in 1922, and when the church, school, rectory, and convent were completed in 1923, the name was changed to St. Joseph Church and School. In 1889, Barrett constructed the Tynan Opera House at the southeast corner of Chehalis Avenue and Main Street, and in 1891, built the three-story, $40,000 Grand Central Hotel, also known as the Barrett Hotel, kitty-corner from the opera house. The hotel building above later served as the county courthouse until 1927.

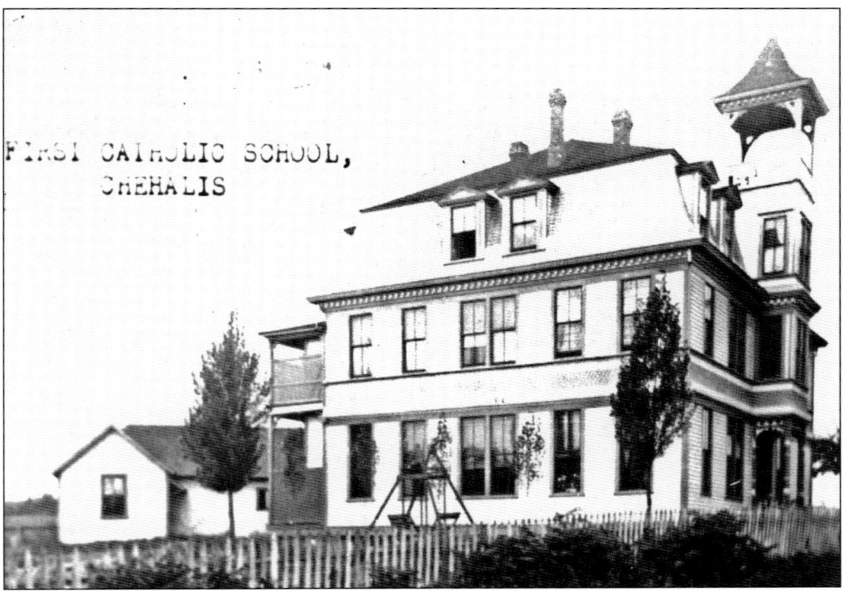

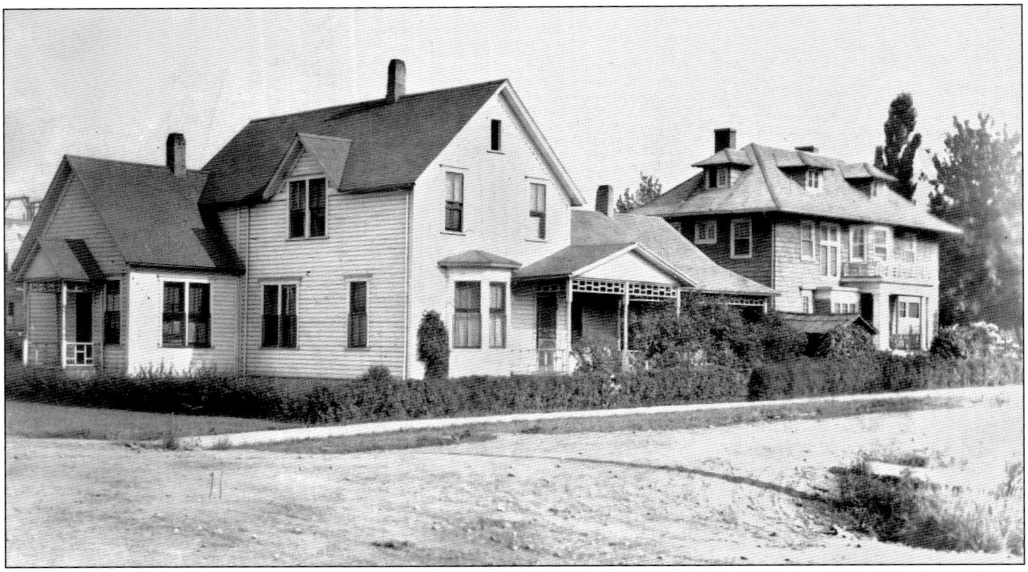

Dr. Guy W. Kennicott, a Chicago native who practiced medicine in Chehalis from 1895 until the mid-1930s, built Lewis County's first hospital on State Street at Prindle Street in 1899. He lived at 1030 State Street in a house next to the Chehalis General Hospital (his home is at right in the photograph). The house remained standing but across the street from its original location. Below, Dr. Kennicott is seen in a horse-drawn buggy at the intersection of Market and Boistfort Streets in Chehalis. Although small in stature, whenever his horse, Tanglefoot, grew unruly, the physician and surgeon would reportedly grab its legs and flip it over. The doctor died March 13, 1944.

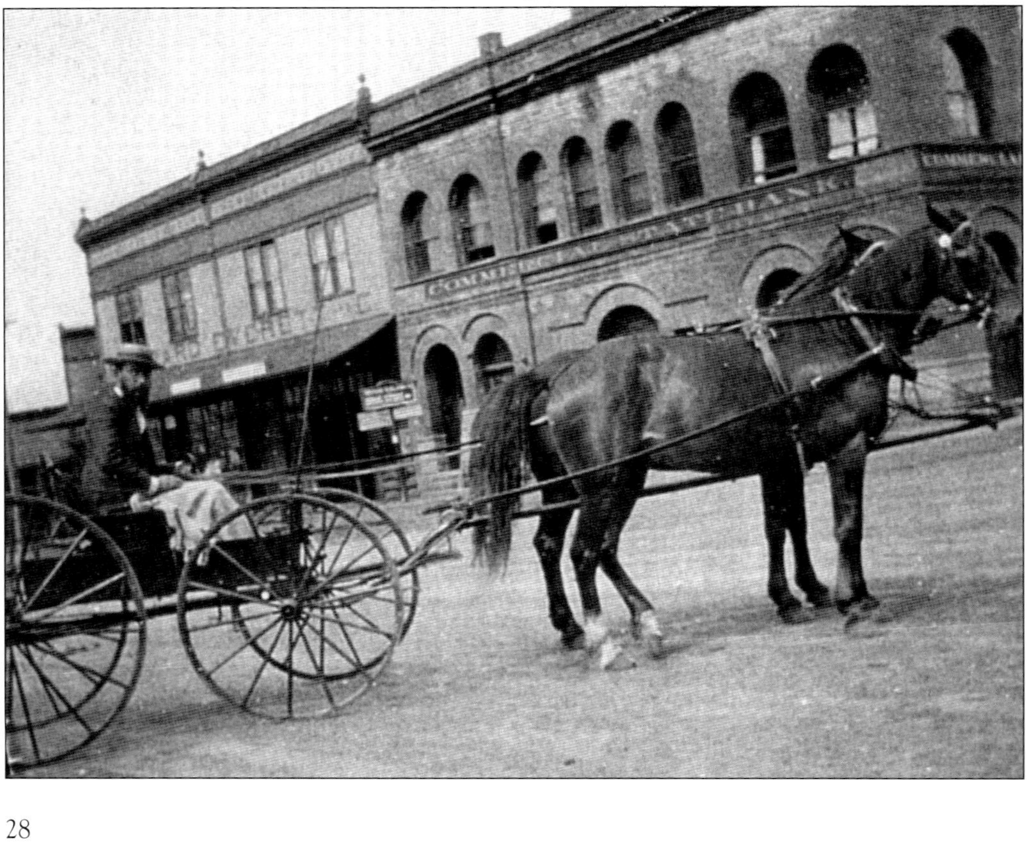

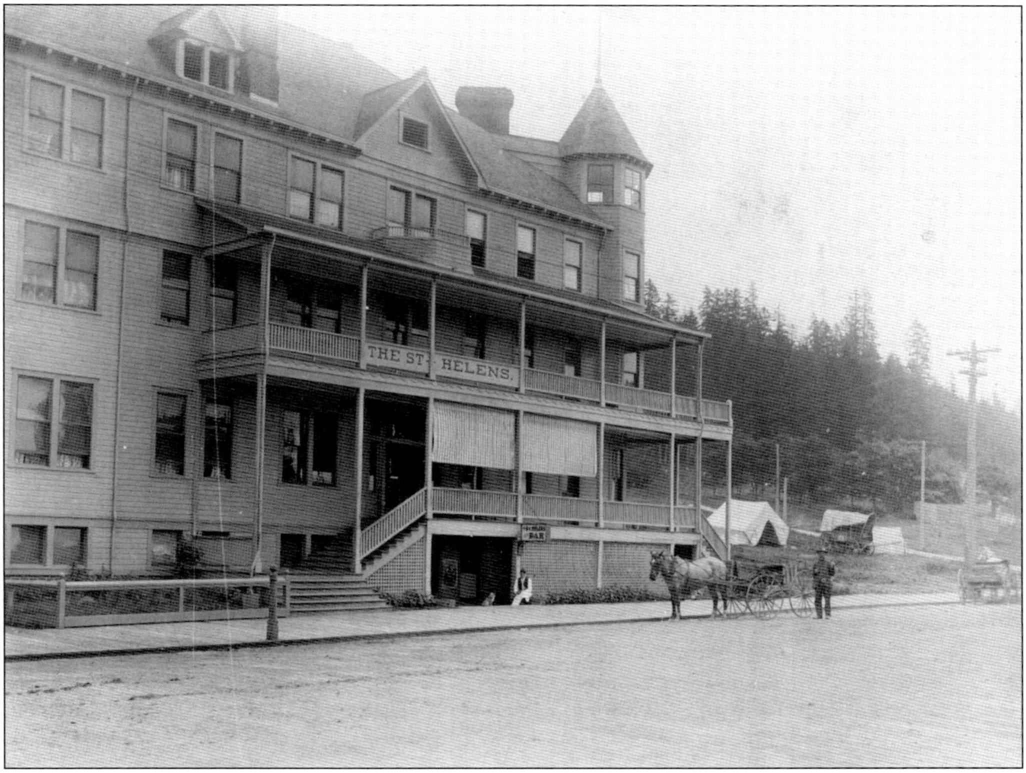

This photograph shows bartender Jim Rush sitting outside the St. Helens Tavern at the St. Helens Hotel, which opened May 12, 1891, on Market Street. At right in the 1906 image is pioneer Ezra Meeker's camp on what later became the Civic Center. Meeker, who traveled west in 1852 along the Oregon Trail with his wife and infant son, retraced his route in 1906, encouraging communities to erect monuments marking the historic trail where up to 1,600 wagons a day rumbled west. Two of the three communities that failed to erect markers were in Lewis County—at Claquato and Chehalis. That oversight was rectified a century later.

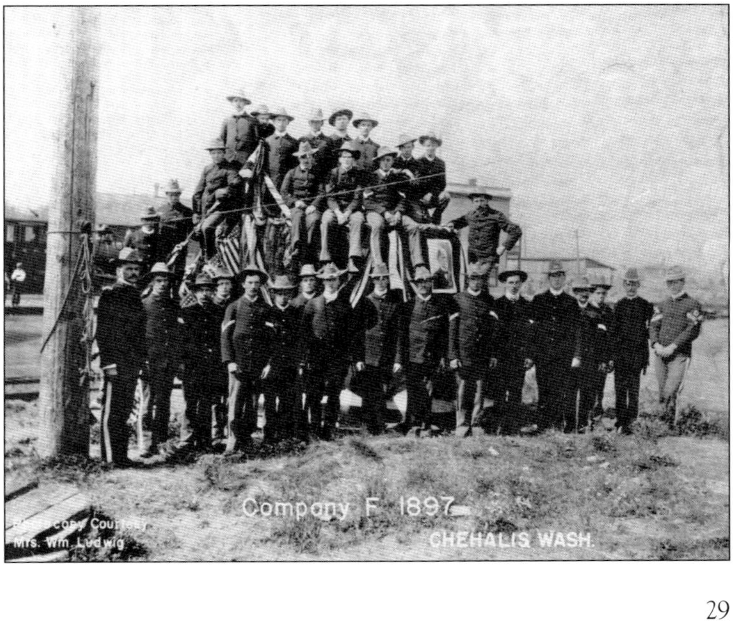

Chehalis men mustered for service in the Spanish-American War, as seen in this 1897 image of Company F. No identification is available of the men in the photograph, which was taken near the railroad tracks. Congress declared war on Spain in April 1898, hostilities ended in August of that year, and the Treaty of Paris was signed in December and ratified by the US Senate in February 1899.

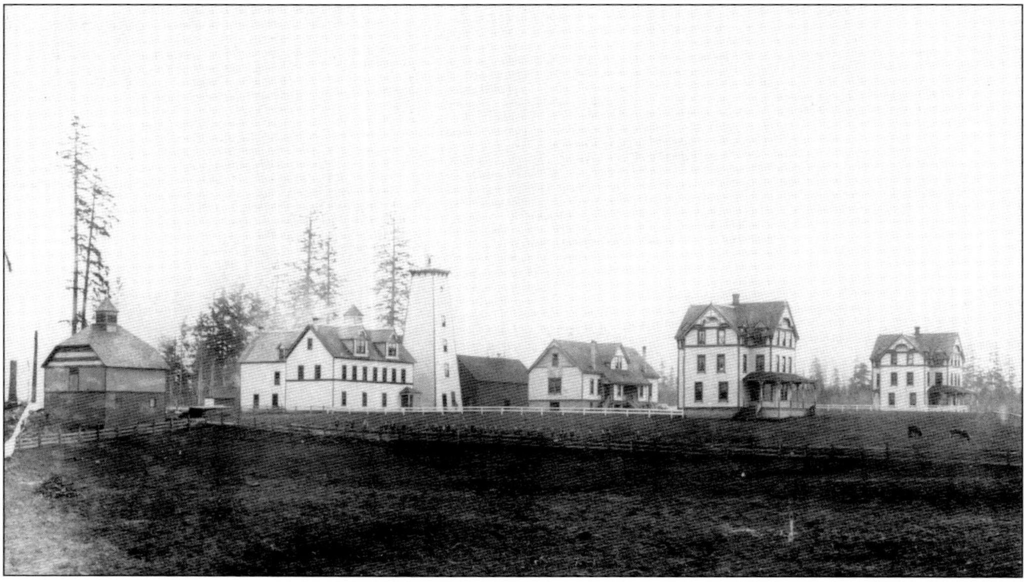

In 1891, Chehalis became home to the Washington State Reform School, later known as Green Hill School. The school opened June 10, 1891, as a reform school for boys and girls between the ages of 8 and 18. The legislature mandated they be taught and trained in "morality, temperance and frugality" and instructed in trades and callings appropriate to their sex. It was designed to punish juvenile offenders and help abandoned children. In addition to living quarters and classrooms, the property contained a farm where students could learn to raise crops and animals and workshops to teach tailoring, shoemaking, carpentry, machine work, and laundering. These photographs, one of the campus and another of boys conducting drill exercises, were taken in 1899. Tragedy occurred in 1956 when an arsonous fire killed a 16-year-old boy trapped inside a concrete building.

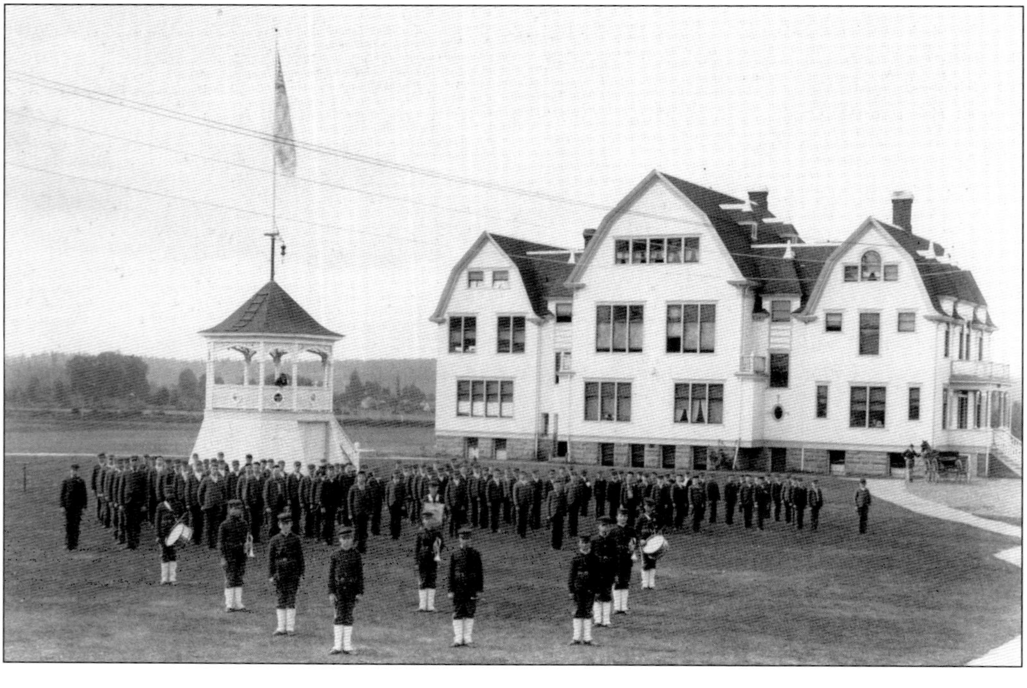

Four

Dawn of a Century

By the turn of the 20th century, the town had grown into a thriving agricultural, lumbering, and coal-mining community with 2,300 residents.

Each day, workers at Superior Coal, Sheldon Coal, and the Chehalis Coal companies combined mined 400 tons of black gold from beneath the ground.

Dairy farmers found a local market for their milk at Pacific Coast Milk Company or the farmer-owned Lewis County Cooperative Creamery. Farmers producing fruits and vegetables in the fertile valley found local markets at the Lewis County Cannery Association and Lewis County Berry Growers cannery, which was purchased in 1928 by the National Fruit Canning Company.

Local forests provided a living for loggers, lumbermen, and woodworkers employed at Palmer Lumber and Manufacturing, Coal Creek Lumber, Chehalis Furniture and Manufacturing, Chehalis Fir Door, Dornbecker Furniture Factory, Chehalis Shingle Mill, Chehalis Fir Gutter Company, and Chehalis Milling and Manufacturing Company. Altogether, in 1913, mills and manufacturers brought the town's production to 350,000 board feet of lumber and 200,000 shingles daily.

Other manufacturers included Chehalis Brick and Tile, Pacific Tank and Silo, Imperial Powder, Chehalis Bottling Works, the Chehalis Mattress Factory, Chehalis Ice, Simmons Glove Factory, Chehalis Produce, Chehalis City Laundry, Chehalis Foundry and Machine, P. Gustavson Foundry and Machine Shop, and two marble works.

I.P. Callison and Sons, which began in 1903 to process cascara bark and digitalis into pharmaceuticals, later extracted peppermint and spearmint oils, giving Chehalis its nickname, the Mint City.

The first decade also saw Washington Electric Company provide electricity locally, as well as the opening of First National Bank, and, in 1903, Security State Bank.

A tragedy occurred on November 1, 1911, when a major industrial flash fire killed eight Chehalis girls between 14 and 18 years old who were working at the Imperial Powder Company, an explosive materials plant off Coal Creek Road. Most were buried in one unmarked grave.

By 1913, Chehalis had dozens of businesses, including 5 hotels, 4 billiard and poolrooms, 11 saloons, 8 restaurants, 3 bakeries, 4 drugstores, 10 large grocery stores, 4 meat markets, 3 dry goods stores, 2 jewelers, 2 department stores, 3 hardware shops, 2 bookstores, 5 blacksmiths, 5 livery stables, 3 harness and saddlery businesses, 3 garages, and 2 bicycle and automobile repair shops.

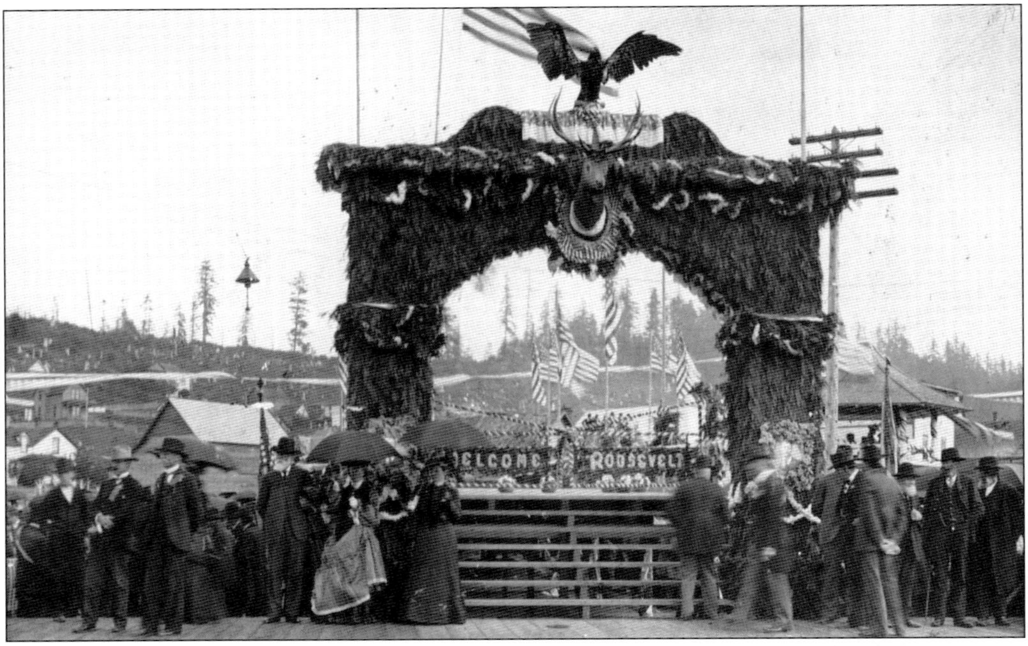

In 1901, Pres. William McKinley had scheduled a stop in Chehalis, so citizens hauled in a stump from a 360-year-old giant fir tree cut in May near Pe Ell and placed it at the train depot. However, McKinley never arrived because his wife fell ill in San Francisco, and then he was assassinated in September 1901. Two years later, the city again prepared for a presidential visit. Below, Pres. Theodore Roosevelt spoke May 22, 1903, from the McKinley Stump at the Chehalis train depot. Citizens turned out en masse. Roosevelt's vice president, former Indiana senator Charles W. Fairbanks, and Secretary of War William Howard Taft, both Republicans, campaigned from the stump during the 1908 presidential election, and Socialist presidential nominee Eugene Debs gave a speech there in 1908. So did Franklin D. Roosevelt in 1920 as a vice presidential candidate.

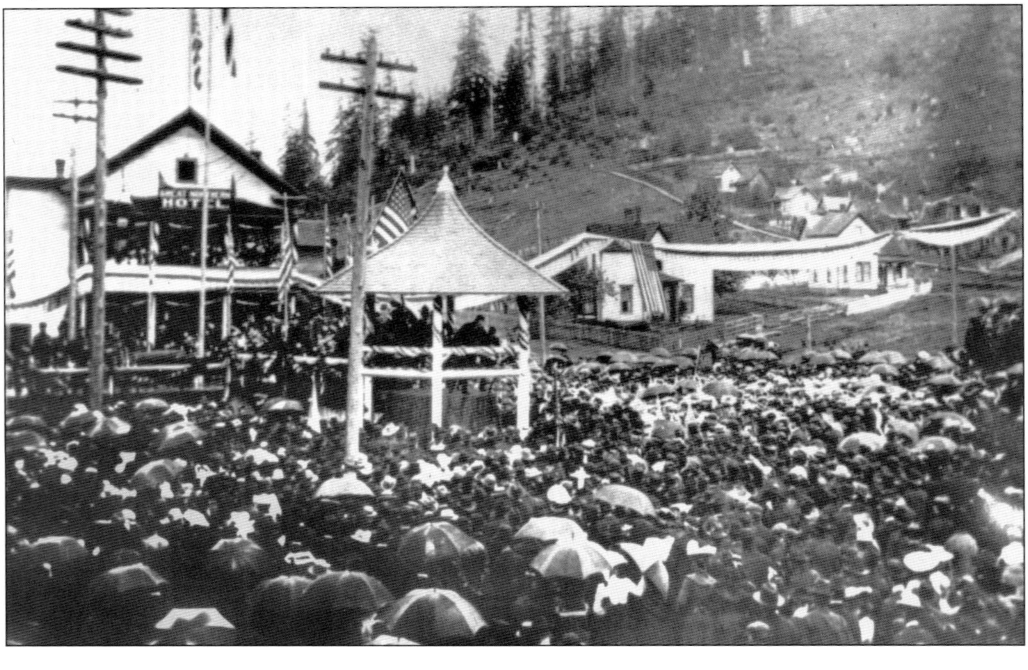

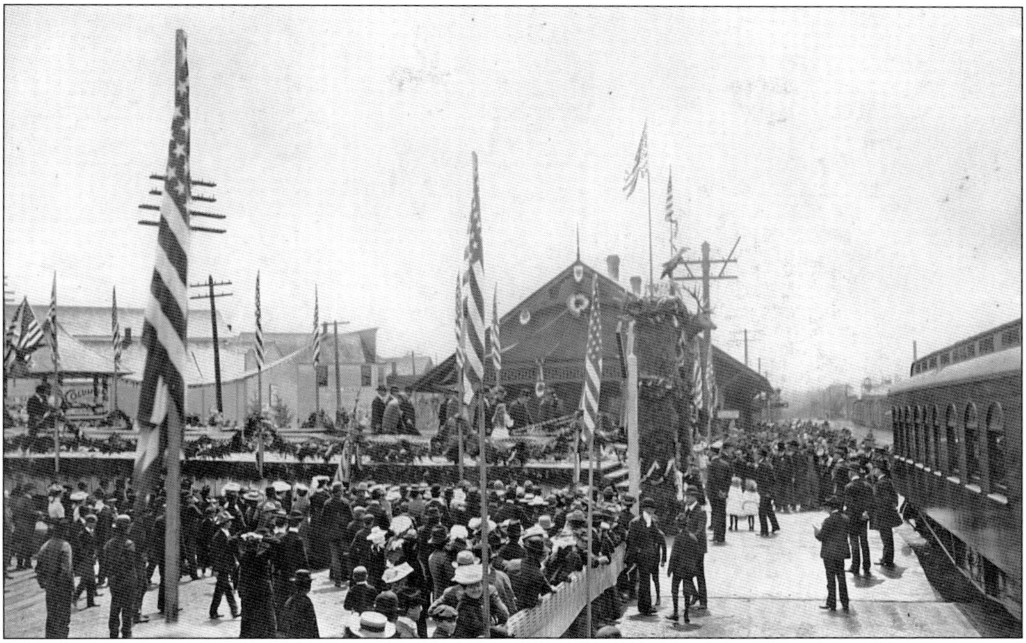

US flags lined the Chehalis train depot and the walkway to the McKinley Stump in preparation for the visit from Pres. Theodore Roosevelt on May 22, 1903. He spoke from the stump, seen on the left. The Washington Training School Band paraded along Market Street near Boistfort Street before the president's speech. Their route took them past the Gem Drug Store, which was built in the Chehalis Improvement Block constructed in 1891. To create a solid appearance for the town, prominent business leaders—including the Wests, Coffmans, Dobsons, and Milletts—organized the Chehalis Improvement Company to build business blocks in the Market Street area.

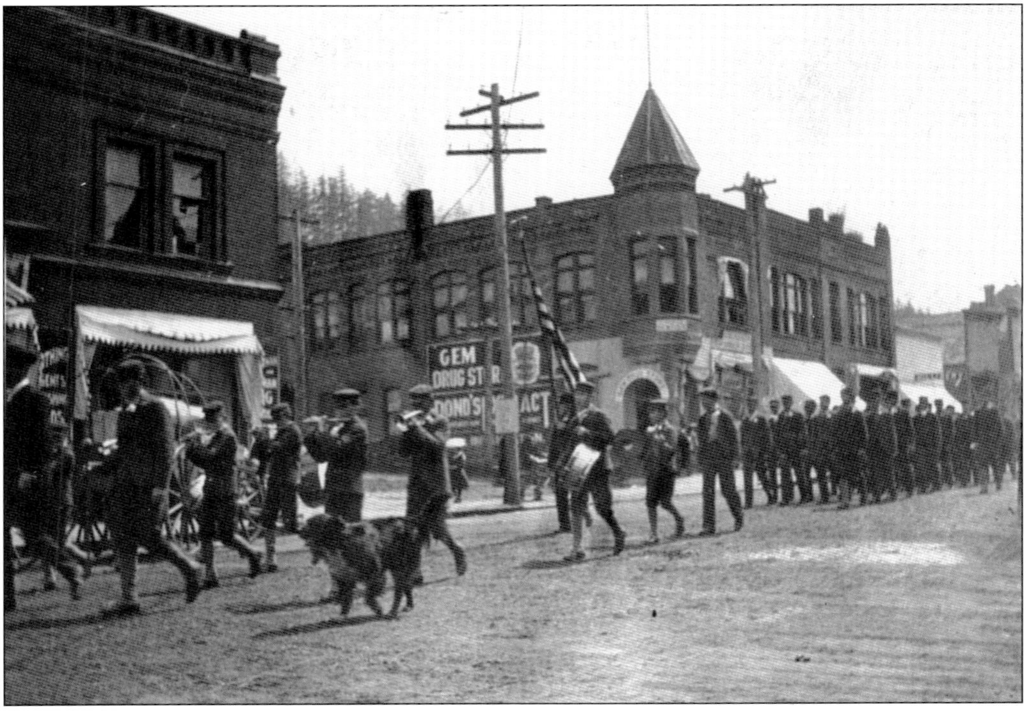

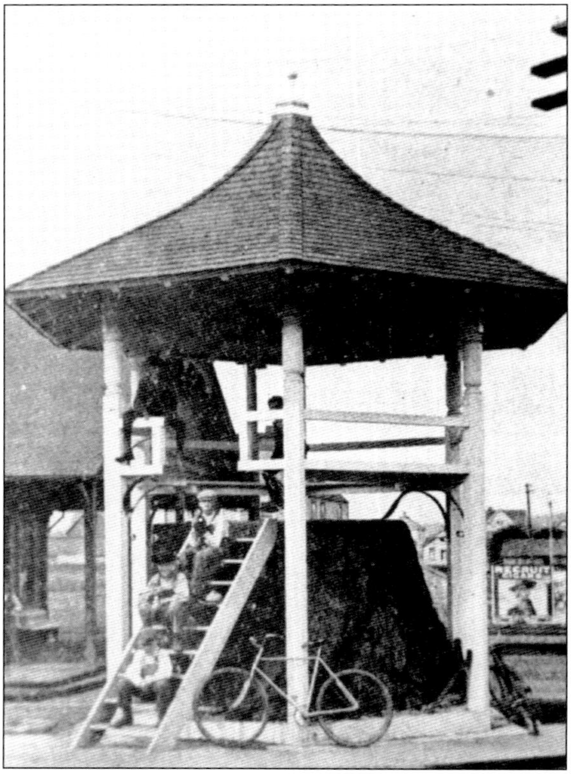

This close-up view from the early 1900s shows three boys sitting on the steps of the gazebo covering the McKinley Stump, while two other boys are at the railing above the stump. They leaned their bike against the gazebo. Part of the Chehalis train depot is visible.

The Episcopal Church of the Epiphany on St. Helens Avenue is seen around 1907, flanked by two houses and dirt roads. The parish was established December 22, 1883, under leadership of a missionary from Tacoma, Rev. Reuben D. Nevius. The church, built in 1884, was comprised of 800 people in its congregation. The Jane A. Tighe Parish House was built in 1904.

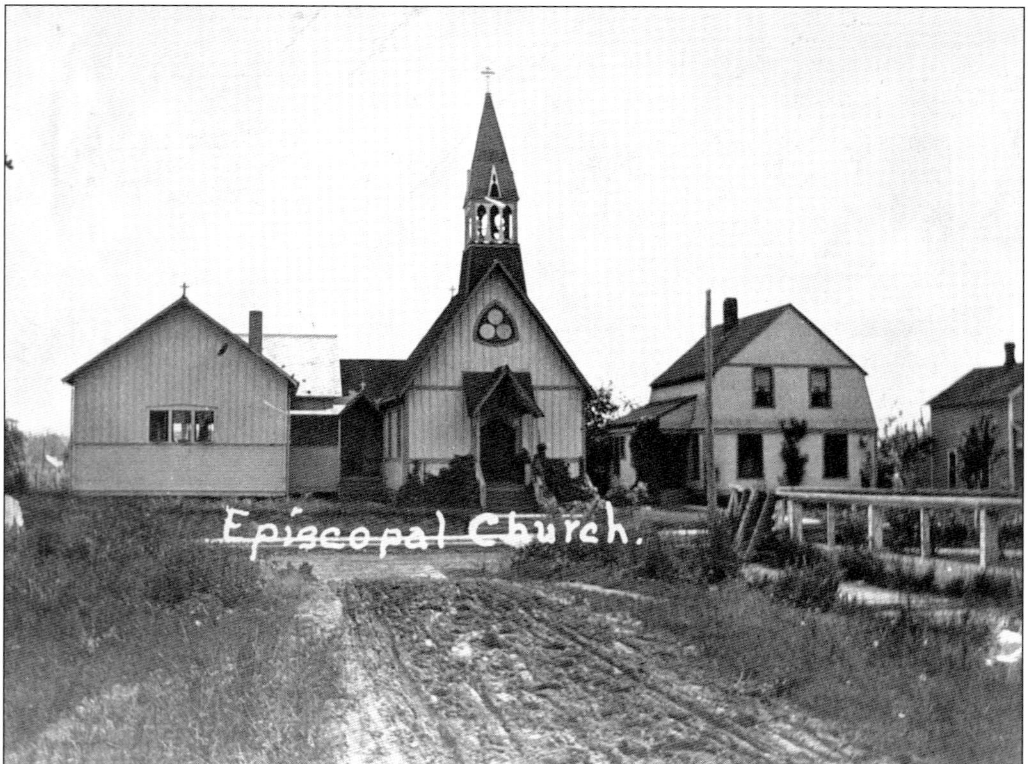

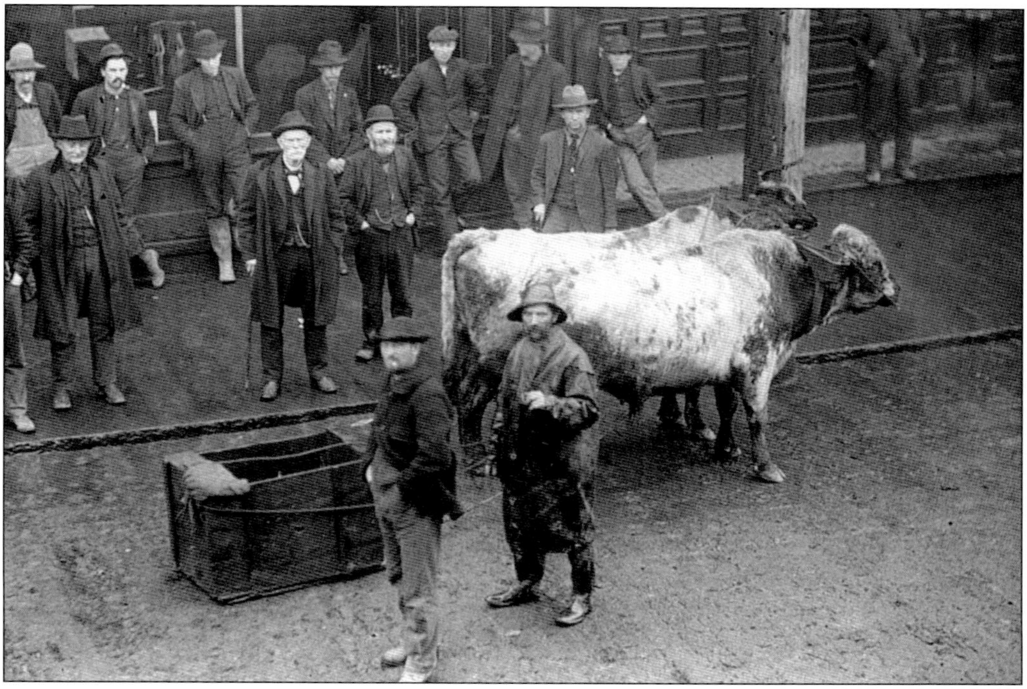

Men line a planked road to watch an ox-pulling contest in the early 1900s. In 1863, Judge Obadiah McFadden raised $1,000 in Olympia to pay for a corduroy road through Saunders Bottom so that wagons could travel without sinking axle-deep in mud. The community preferred plank roads to corduroy, but after installing miles of them, they learned that the undersides rotted and traffic wore away the topsides.

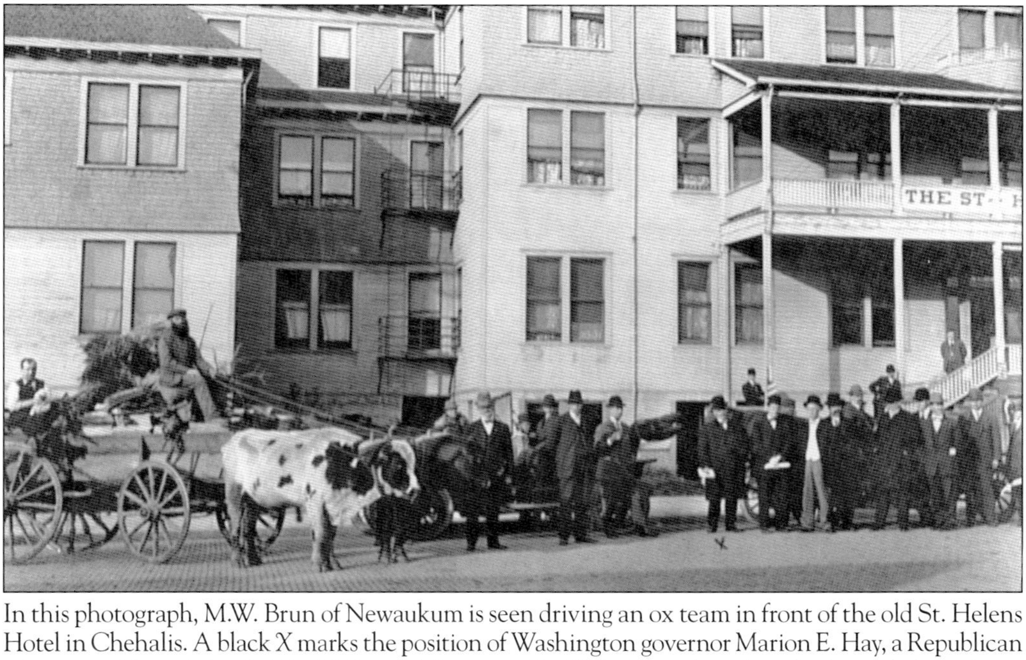

In this photograph, M.W. Brun of Newaukum is seen driving an ox team in front of the old St. Helens Hotel in Chehalis. A black X marks the position of Washington governor Marion E. Hay, a Republican who served from March 28, 1909, until January 11, 1913. Note that the plank roads have been replaced by brick streets. The hotel was moved in 1918 and became the Sticklin Apartments.

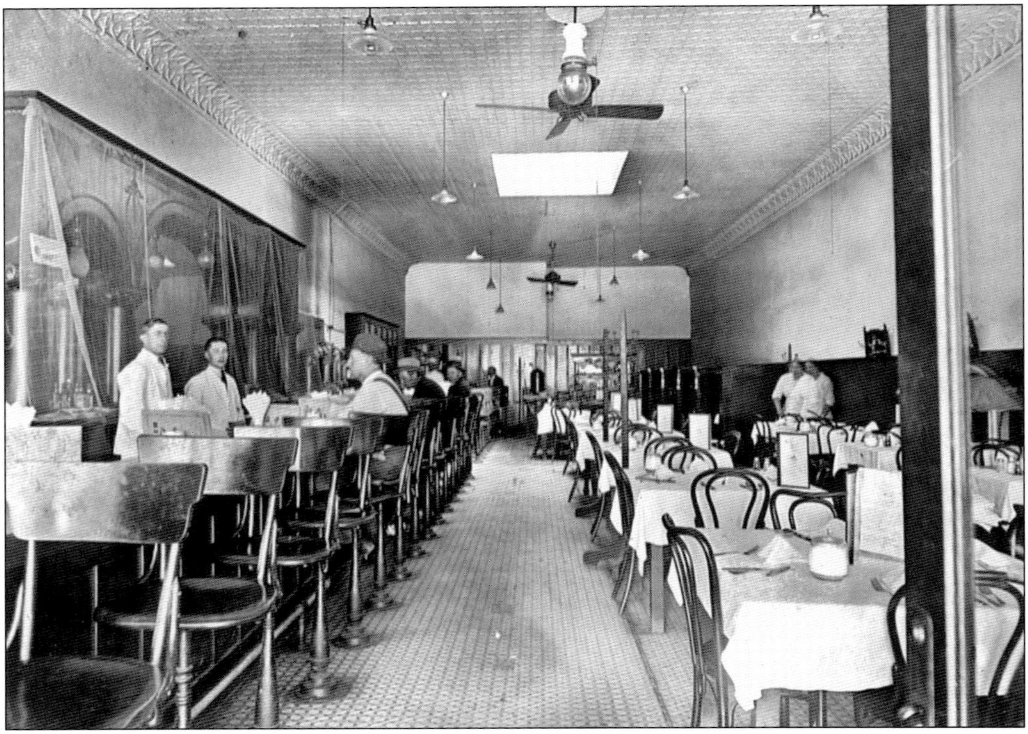

Although still a relatively small community, Chehalis had plenty of business establishments at the turn of the 20th century, such as the San Francisco Chop House on Market Street. By 1913, the town featured eight restaurants with meals at 25¢ and up, four billiard and poolrooms, and 11 saloons where people could wet their whistles.

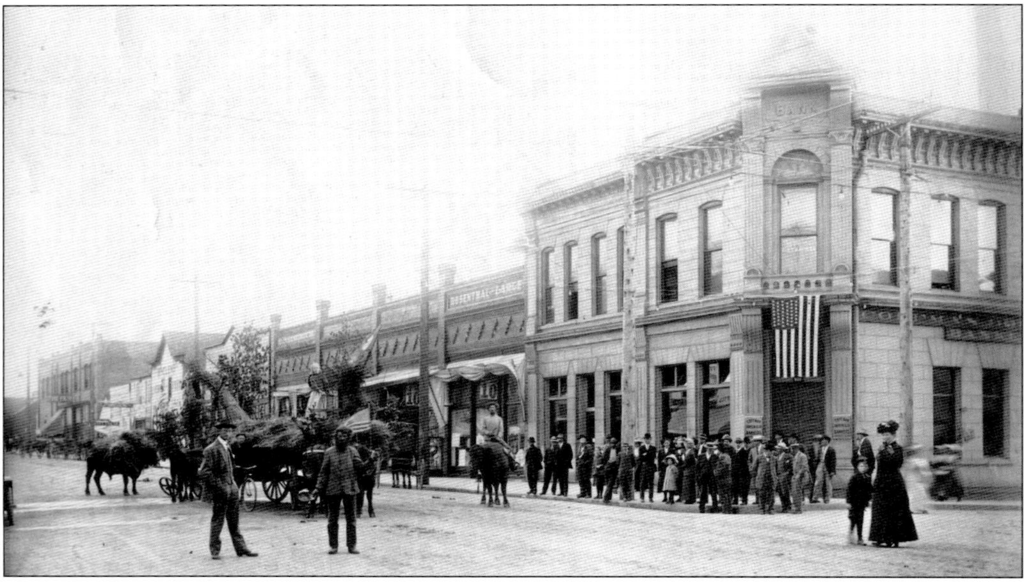

This photograph shows the main part of Market Street at the corner of Boistfort Avenue, where the Coffman-Dobson Bank was located. A crowd has gathered to watch a parade. The man with his hands in his pockets was identified as Joe S. The C.O. Gingrich store and the St. Helens Livery and Feed are down the street.

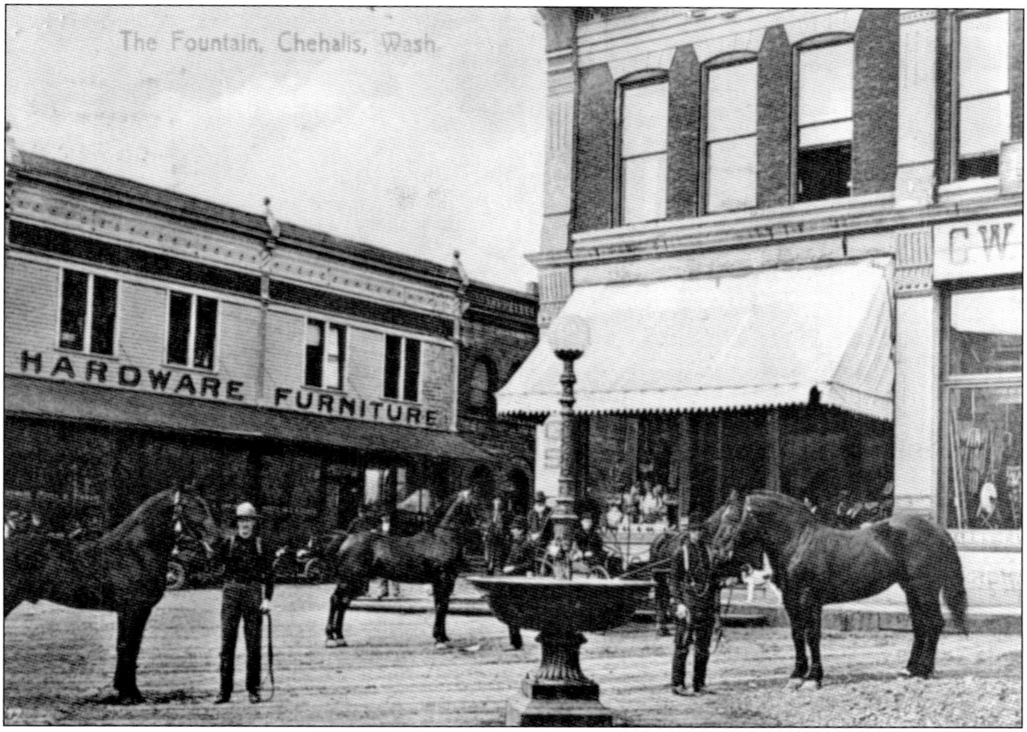

The elaborate Chehalis Fountain, pictured here around 1910 with horses and a trainer nearby, once graced a main downtown intersection at the head of Northwest Chehalis Avenue where it intersects with Northeast Boistfort Street. It featured a lighted ball at the top. None of the people have been identified. The original Coffman-Dobson Bank is at the right, with its main entrance on Market Street. The drugstore with an awning is Pheasant Pharmacy.

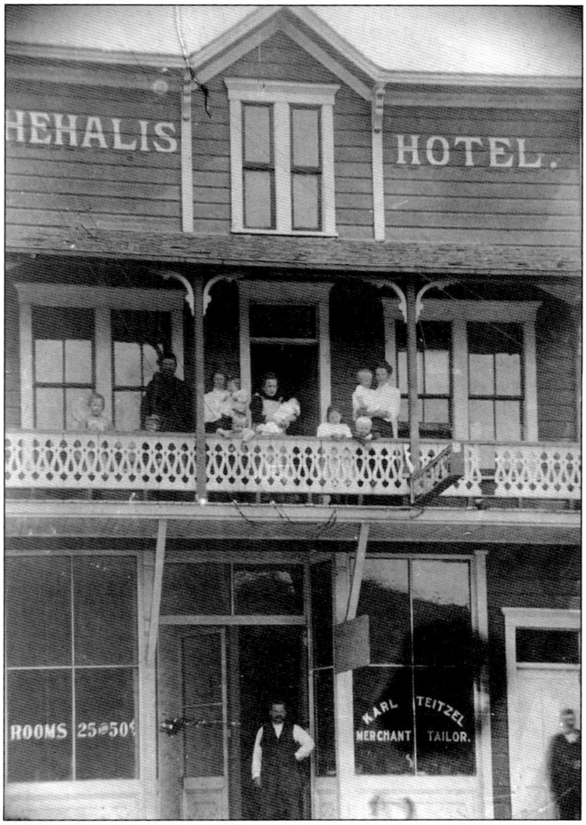

The Chehalis Hotel, seen about 1900, provided an upstairs balcony where hotel guests could watch the goings-on in the main part of Chehalis. Rooms cost 25¢ and 50¢ each. Note the mothers holding infants on the balcony while their children lean on the railing for a closer look. The lettering below advertises the business of Karl Teitzel, merchant tailor.

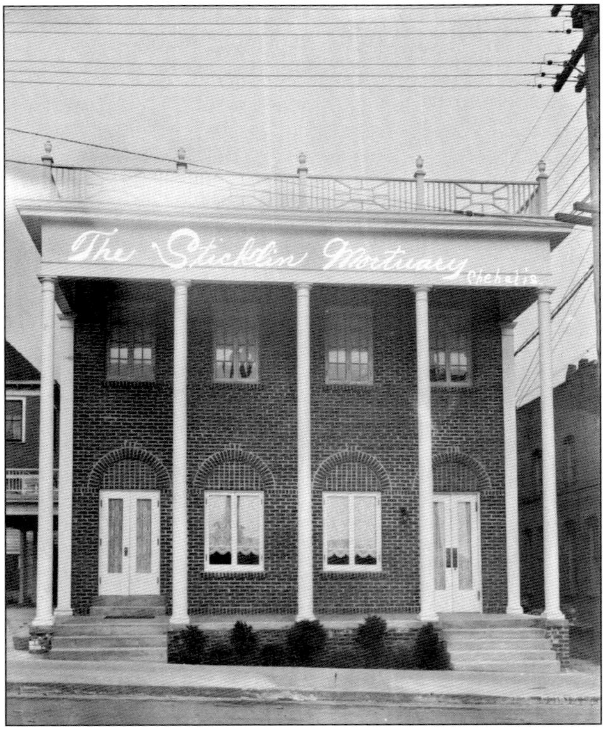

The Sticklin Mortuary, owned and managed by Louis J. Sticklin, son of a pioneer, was built at 111 Division Street in Chehalis about 1907 or before. The Sticklin family came to Lewis County in the 1880s from Pennsylvania, where L.J. Sticklin's father had been an undertaker. In 1972, the building was sold to William Kershaw, photographer, and later became the Colony House, which catered to special gatherings, such as weddings and receptions.

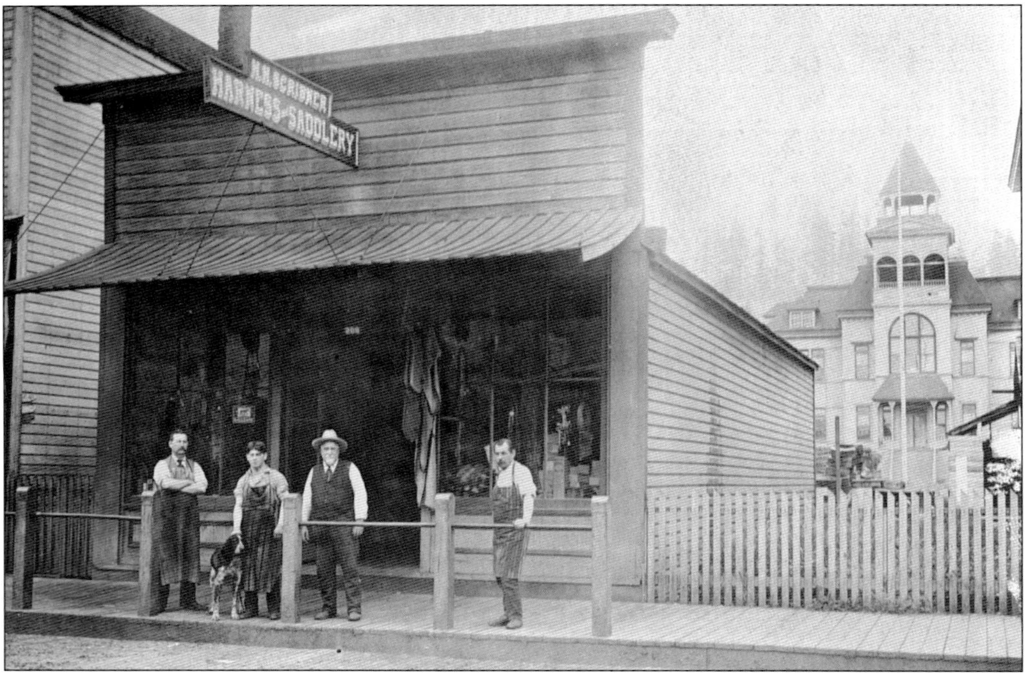

Henry Scribner is on the far left outside the H.H. Scribner Harness and Saddlery at 208 Chehalis Avenue around 1905. At right is the Chehalis all-grade school, built in 1889 at a cost of $10,000, with money raised by selling eight lots. In 1909, the school was moved to Cascade Avenue, between Second and Third Streets, and in September 1922, became known as the South Ward School. The building was demolished in 1926.

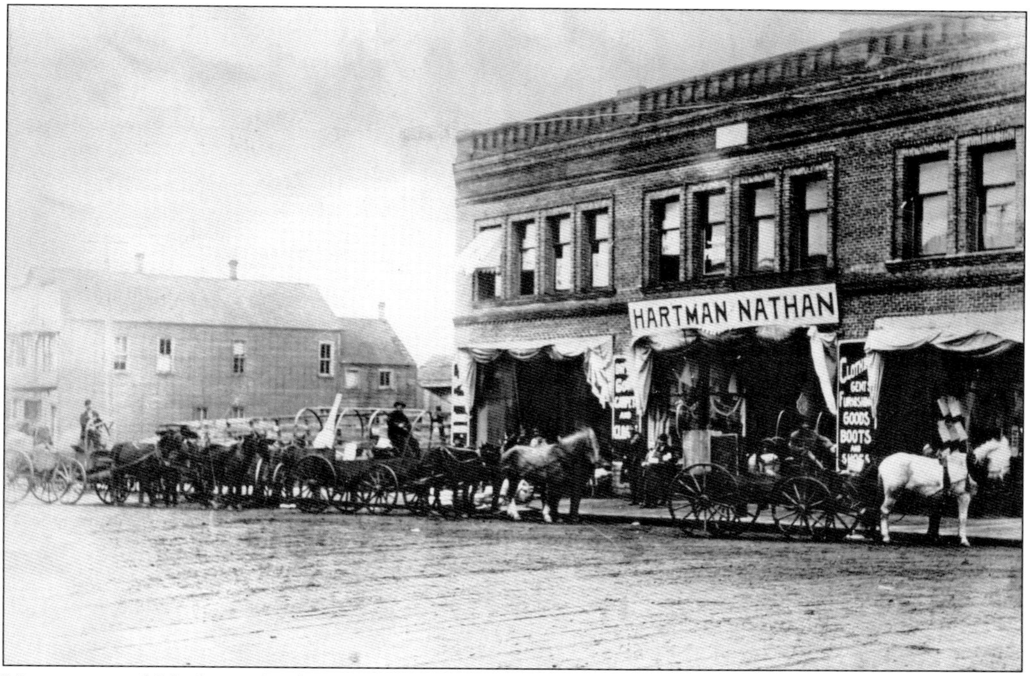

Hartman and Nathan, the largest mercantile house between Tacoma and Portland, was owned by Samuel Hartman and Nuce Nathan. The clothing store is seen around 1905 with a banner, and two years later with painted lettering advertising the Big Department Store. Market Street is a plank road in both photographs. Owners of the buggies and horses were West Virginians on their way to settle in eastern Lewis County.

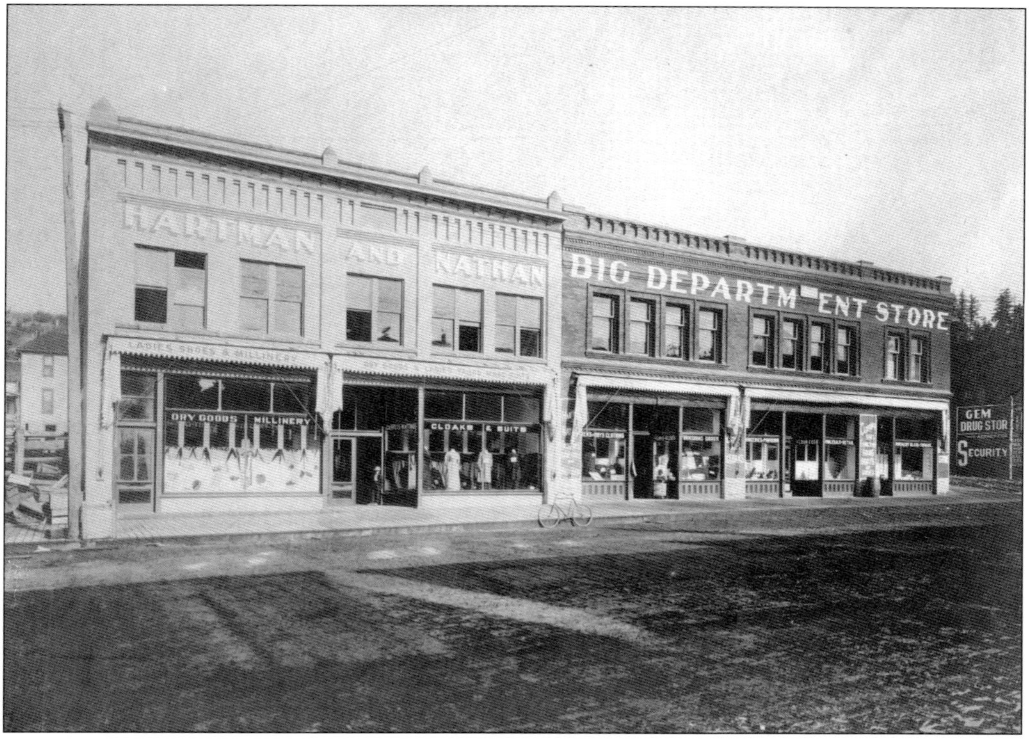

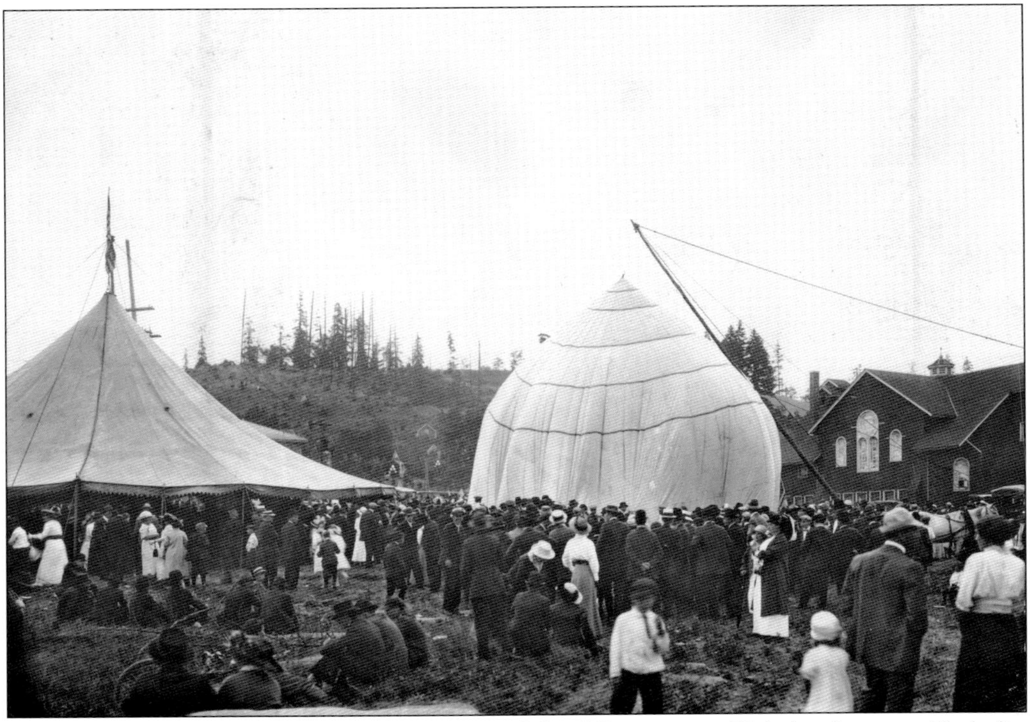

A crowd of people gathered for a Chautauqua on School Street, just off Market Street in Chehalis, between 1909 and 1913. A Chautauqua, popular in the early 20th century, was a traveling show providing education and entertainment. The large tent was used for lectures and entertainment, such as concerts or plays, patterned after the Chautauqua Institution in New York. A balloon was used for exhibitions and rides. On the right is the Westminster Presbyterian Church.

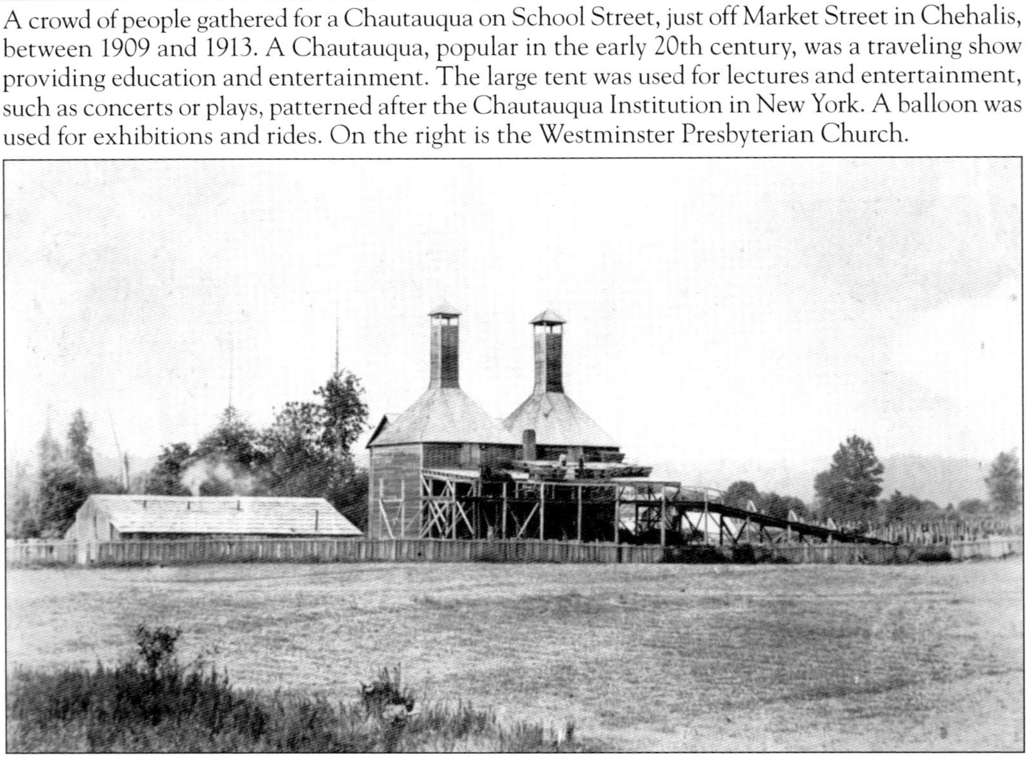

Farmers in the 1880s received a good price for hops, especially in the European market. Pictured are hops kilns near the end of Prindle Street in Chehalis around 1910 to 1912, possibly on the Dobson property. Lewis County earned a reputation in the 19th century as a strong agricultural center.

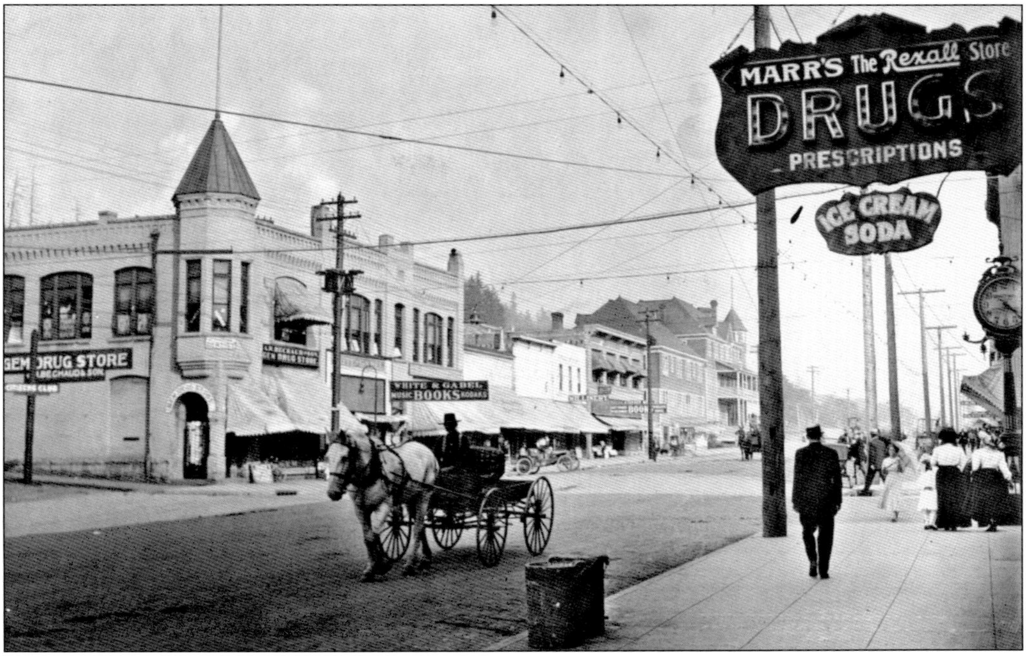

This c. 1908–1910 scene shows Market Street with businesses lining both sides. On the left are Bechaud's Drug Store (with Dr. Parrish's dentist office upstairs), White & Gabel Books, Daugherty's Millinery, Staeger's Book & Stationery, and the St. Helens Hotel. On the right are Marr's Drugs, Burnett's Jewelers, a clock on the sidewalk, Coffman-Dobson Bank, and Merchant's Tailor Shop. Horses and buggies shared the streets with motorcars.

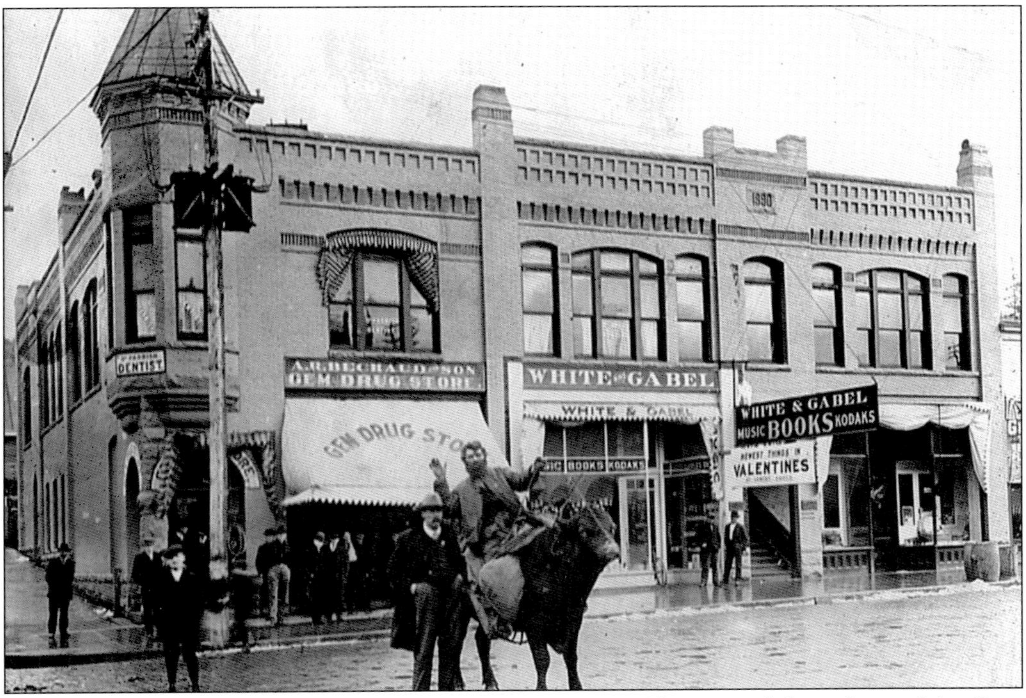

This 1909 image shows M.W. Brun on an ox next to Grant Gleason, at left, in front of the Gem Drug Store and White & Gabel Books on Market Street.

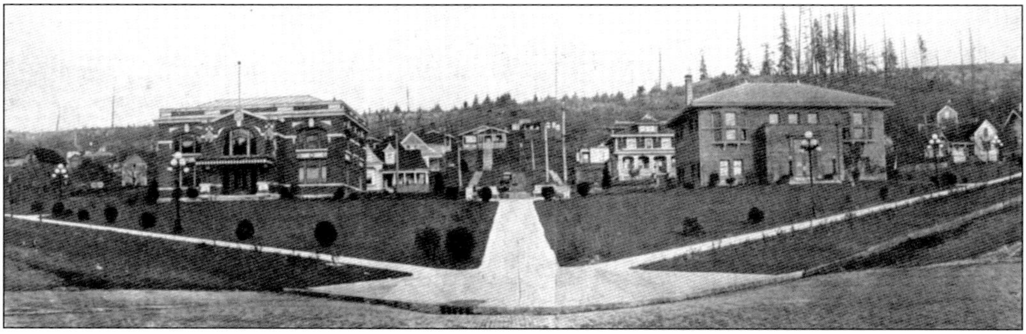

The Chehalis City Hall and Chehalis Free Public Library, known as the Civic Center, both opened in 1910, erected on a slight hill overlooking the city. The library, which opened May 11, 1910, was built with a $10,000 grant from Andrew Carnegie. Harry C. Coffman, former librarian at the University of Washington, spurred the movement to build a library. From 1910 to 1933, N.B. Coffman gave $100 each year to purchase books. The image above shows the City Hall and library in 1915, with newly planted shrubs and trees, but the later photograph with the car in front shows the buildings with a beautiful lawn and landscaping. Damaged by the 1949 earthquake, the buildings were remodeled and, in 1970, Chehalis joined the five-county Timberland Regional Library system.

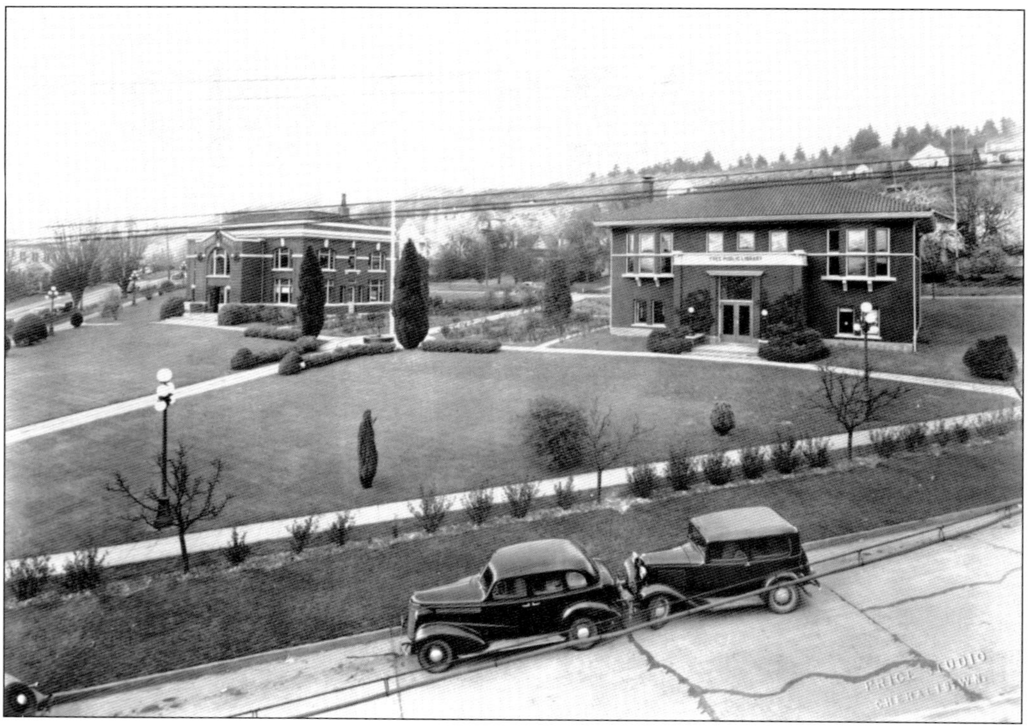

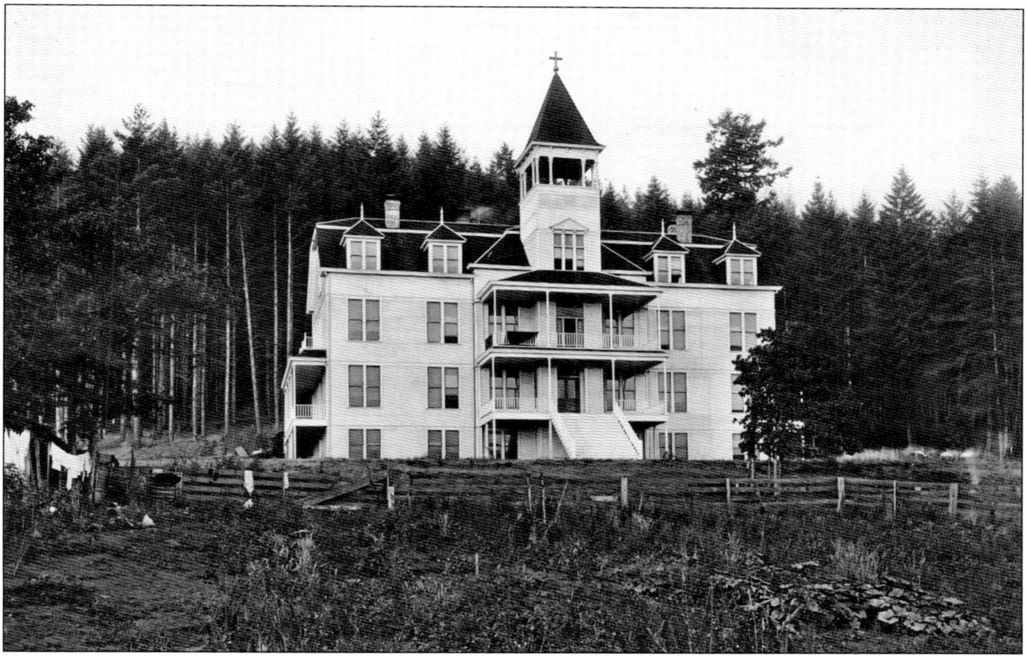

This photograph of the St. Helen Hospital constructed in 1907 shows a rail fence in the foreground and laundry hanging on the line at the left. The Dominican Sisters opened the St. Helen Hospital at 1332 Washington Avenue in Chehalis in the early 1900s, while Dr. Kennicott's hospital continued serving patients. When the Sisters of Providence bought the hospital in 1988, it became the Chehalis campus of Providence Centralia Hospital.

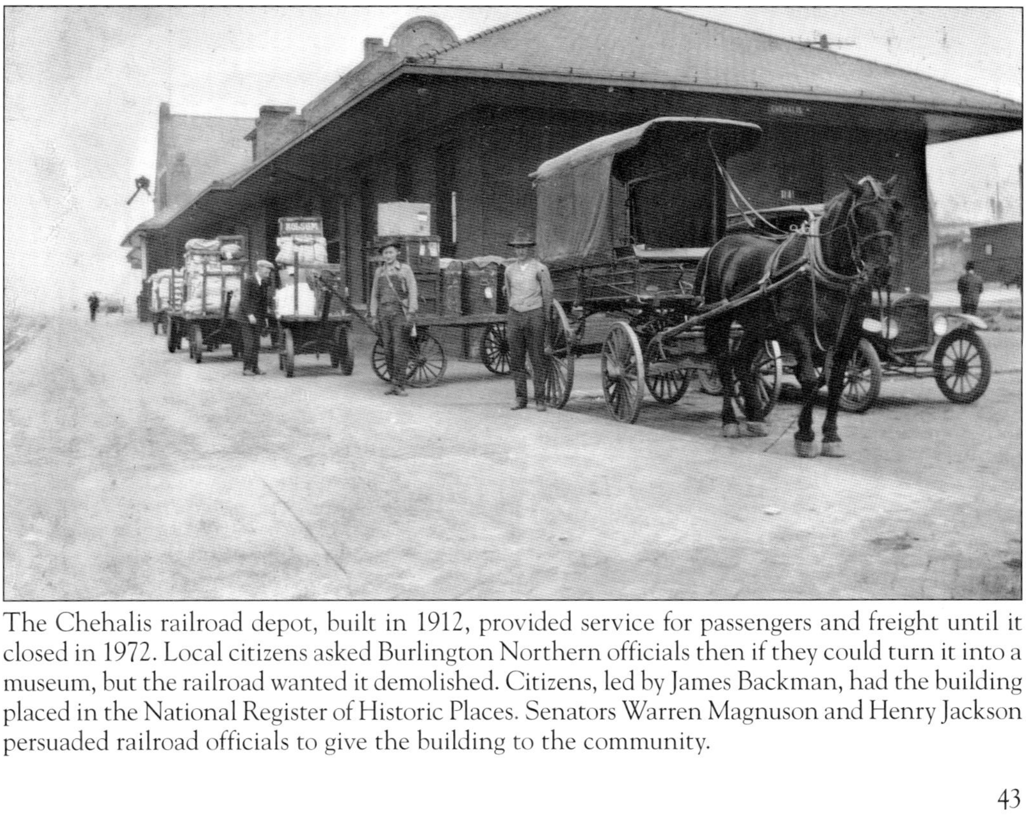

The Chehalis railroad depot, built in 1912, provided service for passengers and freight until it closed in 1972. Local citizens asked Burlington Northern officials then if they could turn it into a museum, but the railroad wanted it demolished. Citizens, led by James Backman, had the building placed in the National Register of Historic Places. Senators Warren Magnuson and Henry Jackson persuaded railroad officials to give the building to the community.

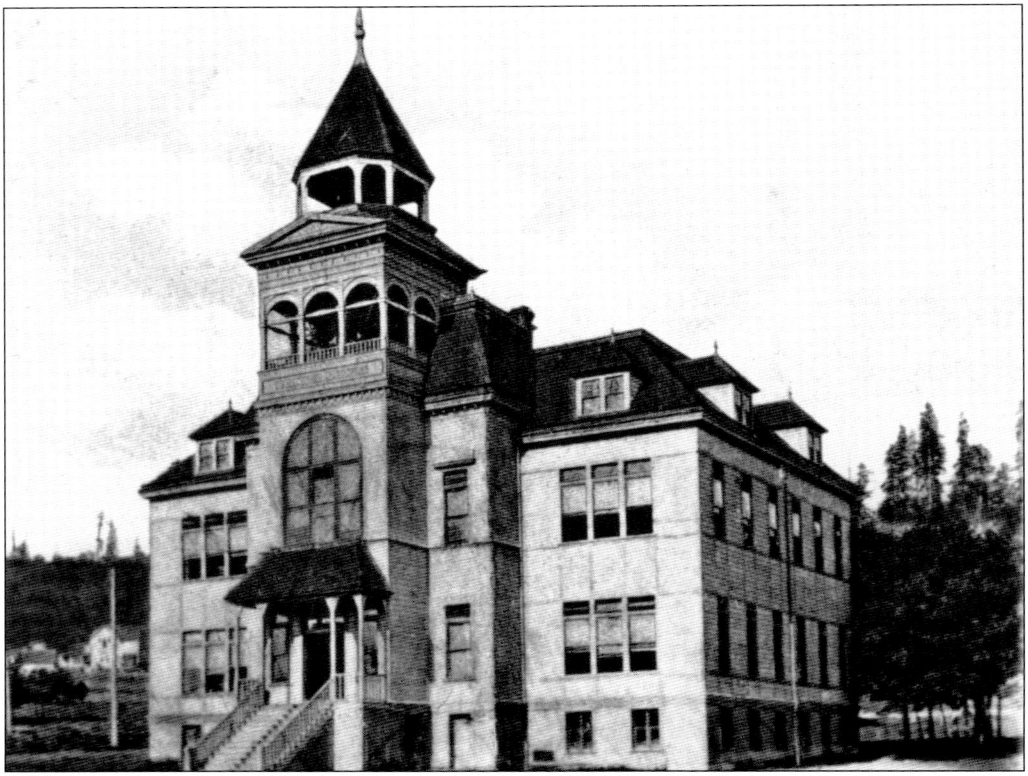

The wooden East Side School in Chehalis is pictured around 1905, four years before construction of the $40,000 Chehalis High School below at the head of Main Street at Market Street. The high school was extensively damaged by the 1949 earthquake and replaced by W.F. West High School in the early 1950s. In 1913, the district employed 38 teachers who educated 1,200 students at the community's high school and two grade schools. An early-morning fire on February 9, 1910, destroyed the West Side School, which was replaced that same year by an eight-room school costing $26,838. The district bought the park across the street and, in 1925, added a play shed.

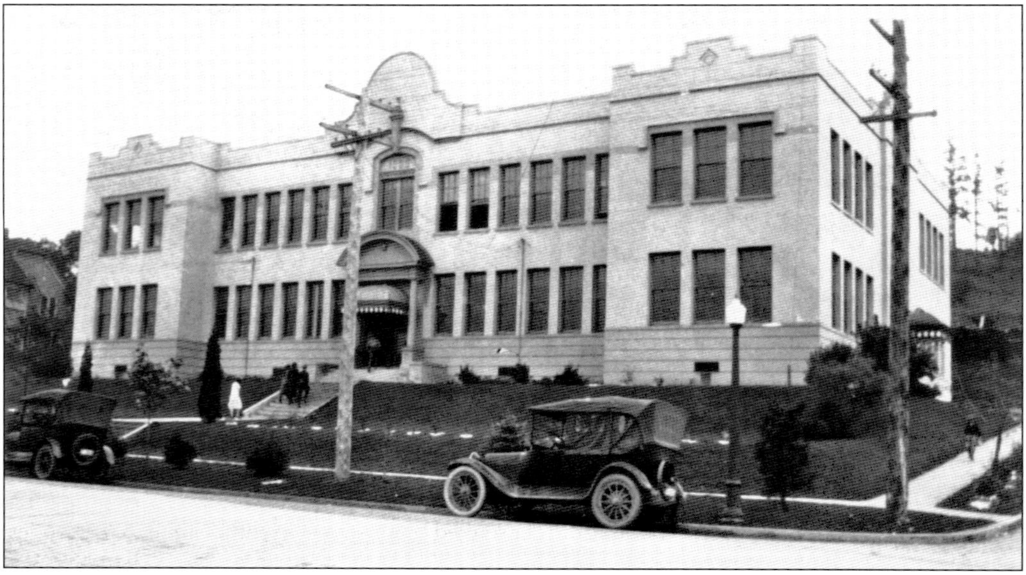

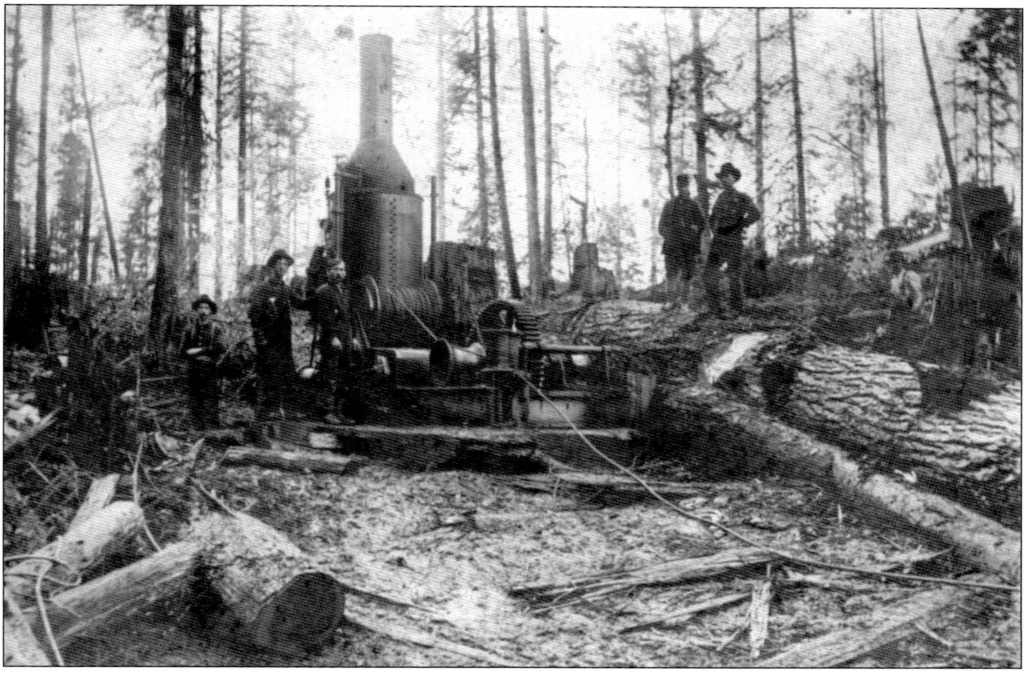

Logging provided jobs for many Lewis County residents for decades. This 1902 photograph shows a logging crew beside a steam donkey in the Salzer Valley area east of what later became the Southwest Washington Fairgrounds.

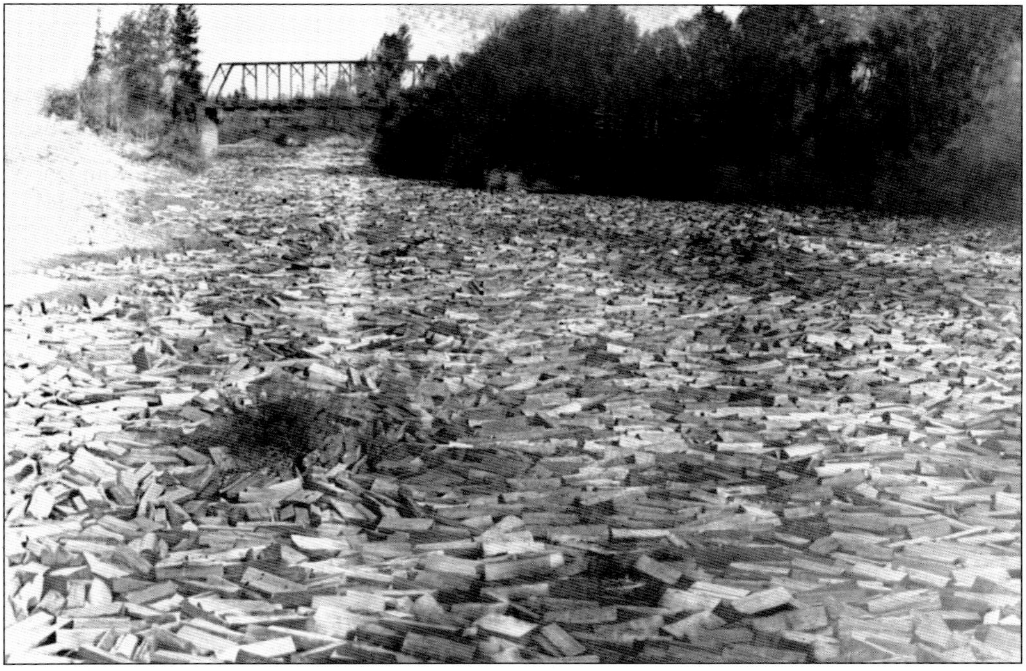

Shingle bolts float in the Chehalis River just below Alexander Park around 1900. Chehalis was home to several shingle mills. High water often flooded the community. In the winter of 1865 and 1866, William West recalled that high water soaked crops stored in his barn near Alexander Park, "which taught me to in future keep my crops above high water."

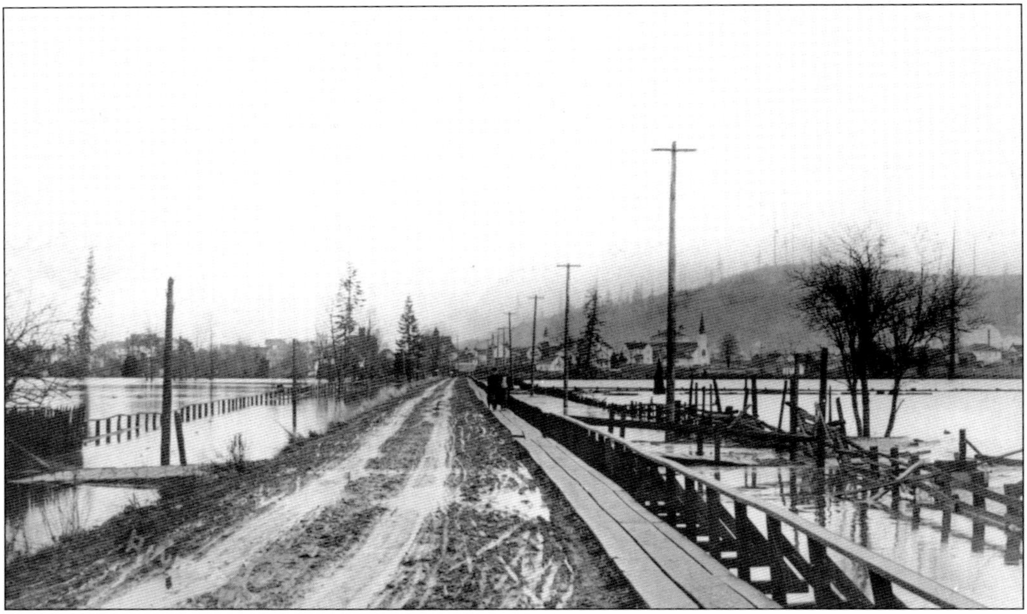

This 1910 photograph shows the road to the Riverside District, today known as State Highway 6, leading from Chehalis west toward Pe Ell and the Pacific coast. During the rainy season, floodwaters encroached on the roadway, and mud covered the hubs of cars. The image, looking toward Chehalis, shows the dirt road and plank sidewalk along Southwest Riverside Drive near Alexander Bridge.

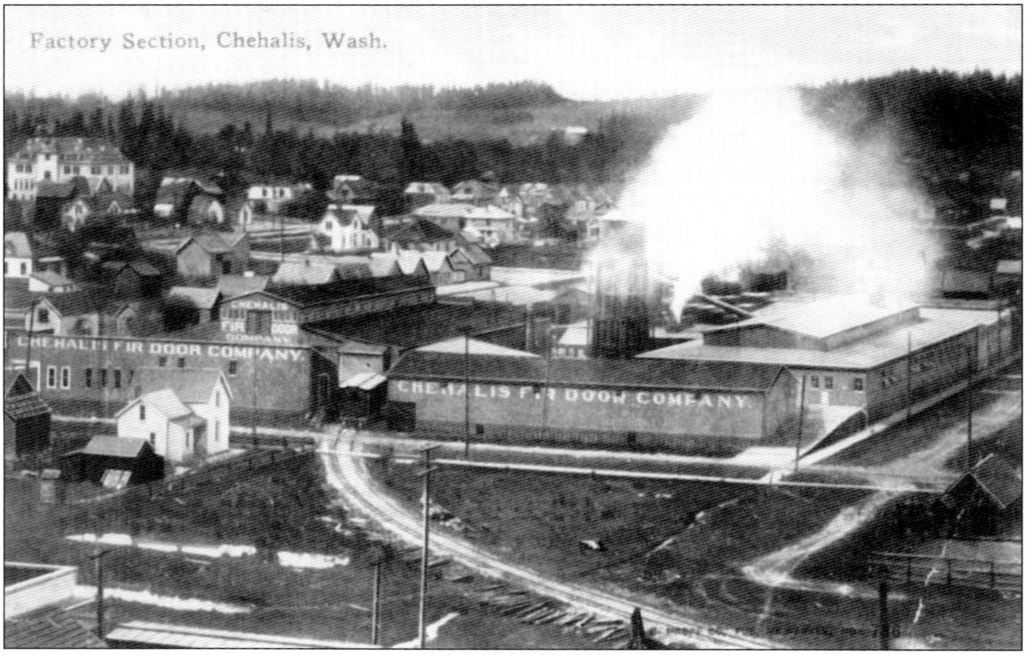

The Chehalis Fir Door Factory at First Street and Northwest Lafayette Street operated in the early 1900s and provided a $7,000 monthly payroll. After First Street was removed to provide room for the South Bend railroad line, State Street was built in front of the factory. In the background is the first West Side School and a view of hills west of Chehalis.

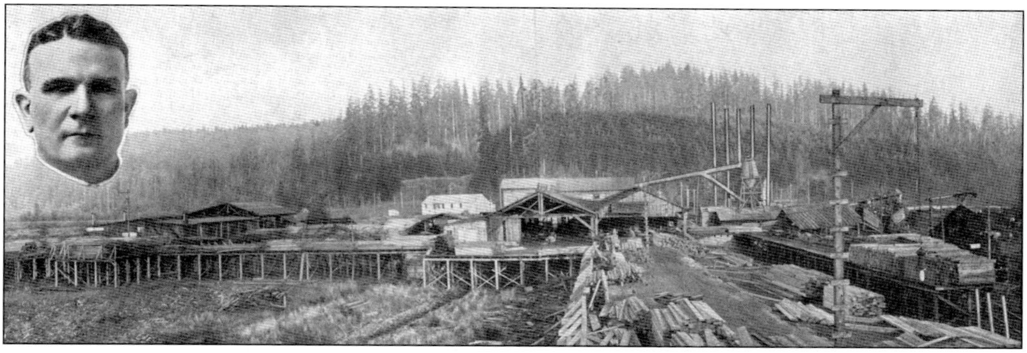

C.L. Brown's Coal Creek Lumber Company, established in 1905 and pictured in 1915, employed 135 to 150 people with a monthly payroll of about $10,000. It operated until about 1930, when Winston Lumber and Timber Company took over until about 1934. At that time, it became Woodproducts Corporation under the management of Lloyd Owen and Sons. In May 1954, Hemphill-O'Neill Company bought shares and later purchased the plant, which it ran until 1985. Columbia Harbor purchased the mill in 1989.

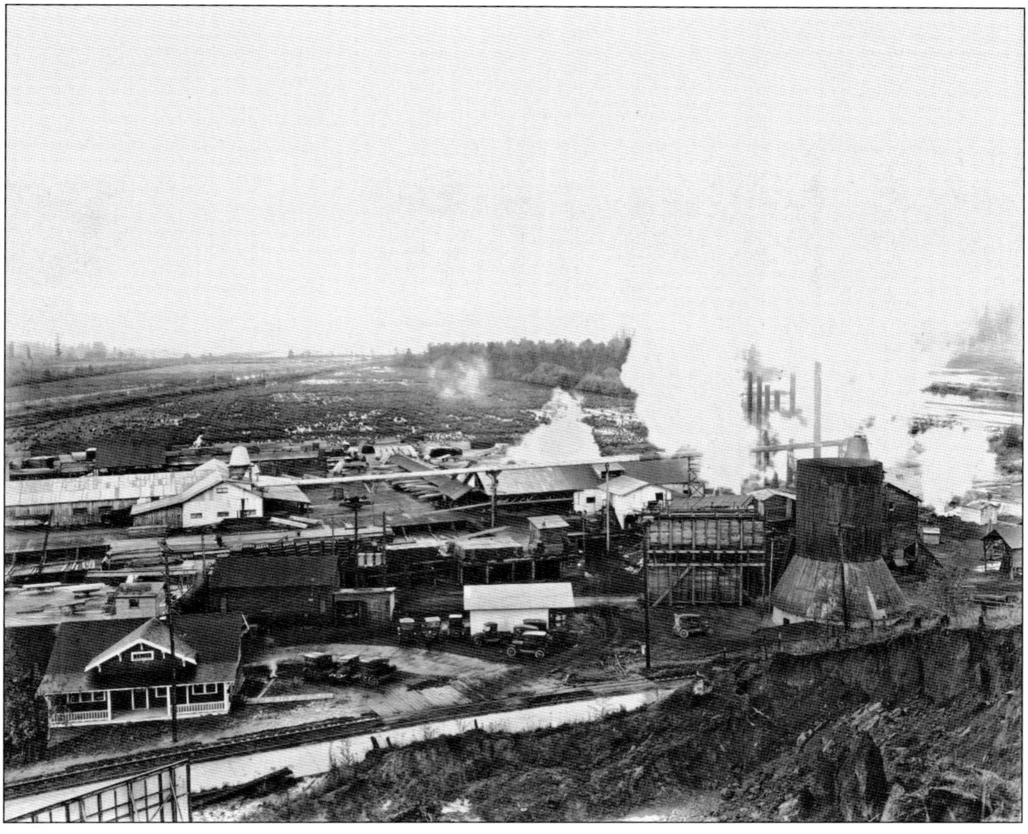

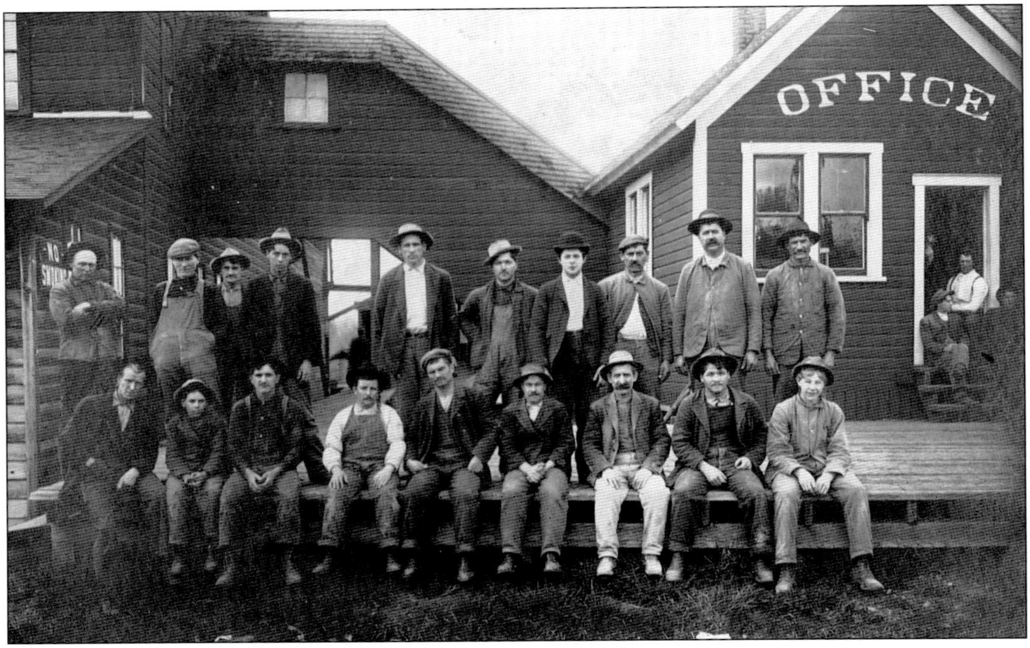

The Chehalis Furniture and Manufacturing Company employed 70 to 125 men with a monthly payroll of at least $4,500. The crew is seen outside the office in 1908, with a "No Smoking" sign painted on the wall at left. Standing in back wearing a derby hat, seventh from the left, is Robert Warmuth. The company made high-grade furniture sold in Washington, Oregon, and California. In the photograph below, from around 1918, crew members identified include a man named Aust (second row, second from the right), and company president Christian O. Gingrich (near the center of the first row, wearing a white cap). The back of the photograph states that it is the finishing department. William Van Woert was manager.

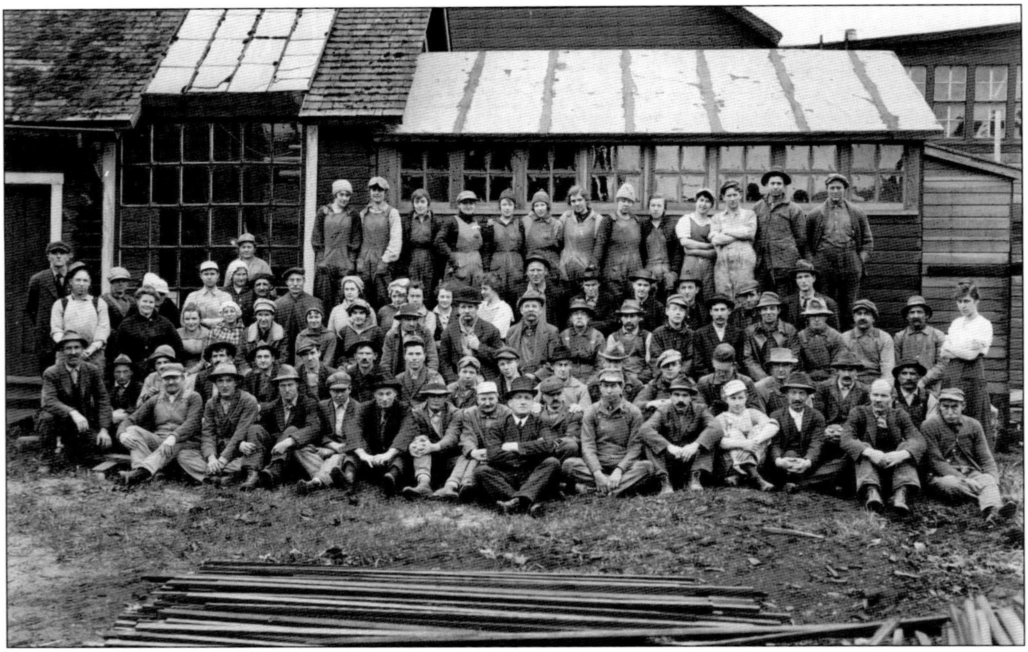

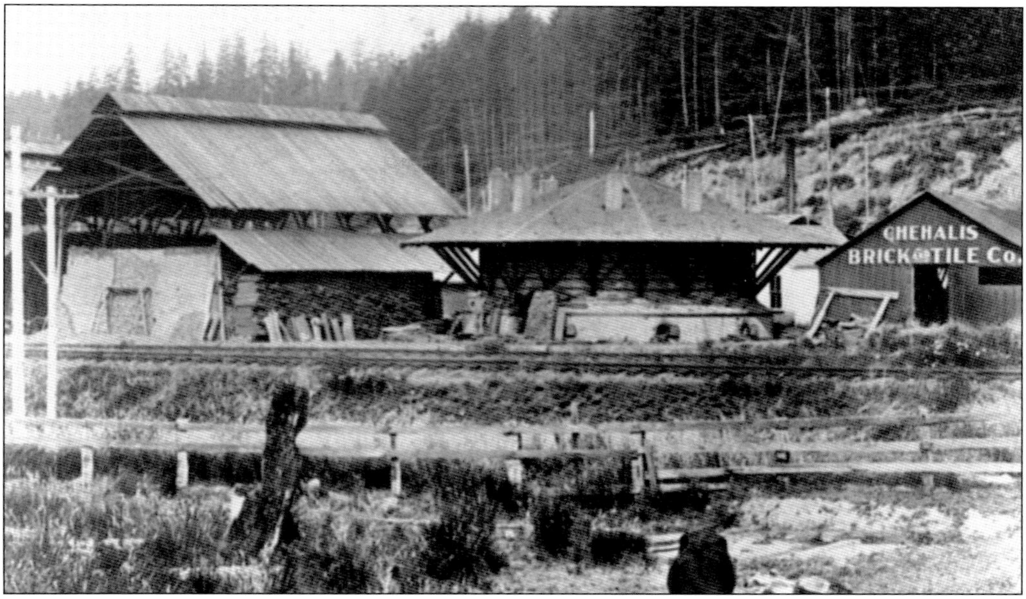

The Chehalis Brick and Tile Company was established in 1902 by A.F. Bickford and George H. Burrows, who began small-scale manufacturing of bricks by hand at the northern outskirts of Chehalis, half a mile north of the Chehalis depot on the main railroad lines. Initially, the plant produced up to 5,000 bricks a day, but by 1915, it was among the largest in the Pacific Northwest, producing 25,000 bricks or 15,000 feet of drain tiling each day. S.J. Saindon was the company's secretary and treasurer. It employed 14 men with a monthly payroll of about $1,000 and provided 300,000 bricks for the construction of the Girls' Training School at Grand Mound (most recently known as Maple Lane School).

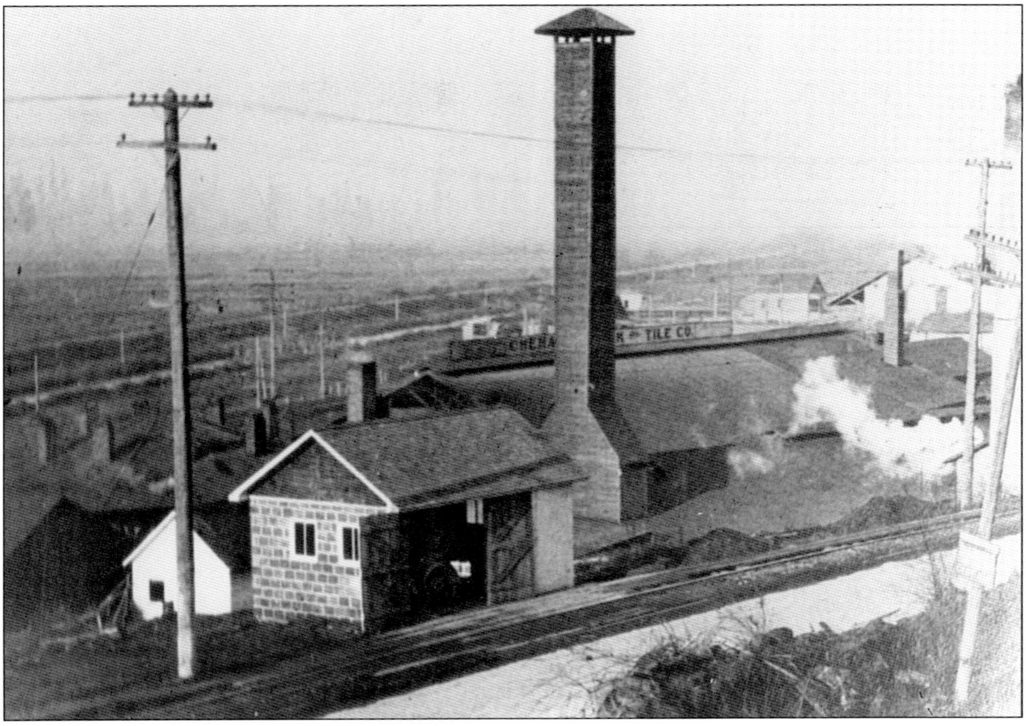

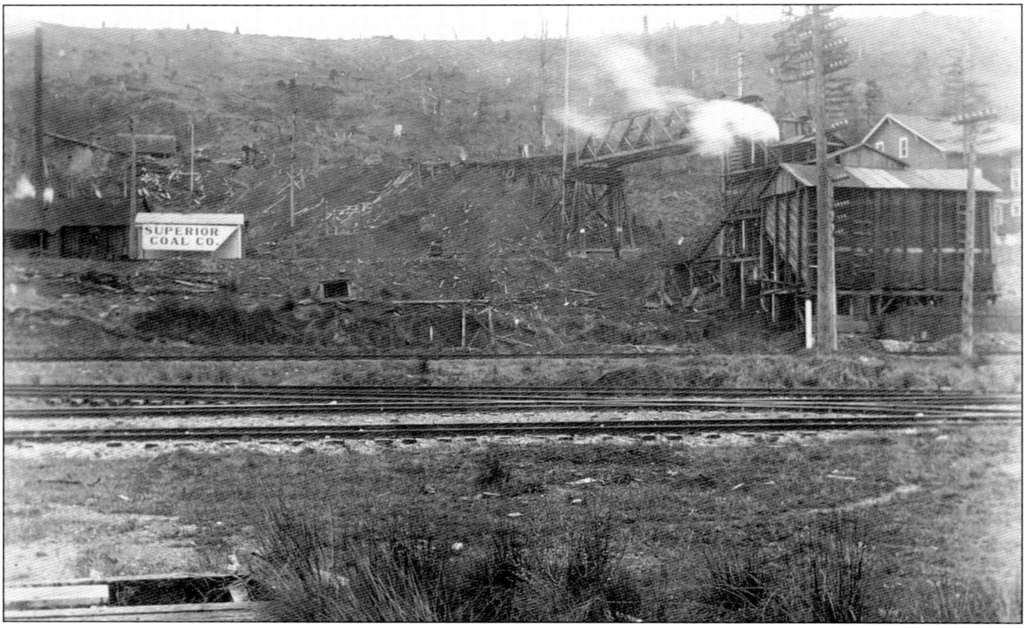

The offices of the Superior Coal Company at the end of National Avenue are seen between 1910 and 1925 in an area where Kostick Brothers Steel Company later operated. During the first decade of the 20th century, several coal-mining companies began operating in Chehalis. By 1913, the Superior Coal Company mined more than 200 tons of lignite coal daily from beneath the hill at the end of today's Chamber Way. The Chehalis Coal Company and Sheldon Coal Company each mined another 100 tons each day. Coal found in the mines ranged from low-grade lignite to the highest grade of anthracite and included veins of bituminous coal. The other image shows the men working in the dark shafts inside the mines. From left to right are Tom Campbell, Joe Graham, W.M. Garbe, and Walter B. Graham Sr.

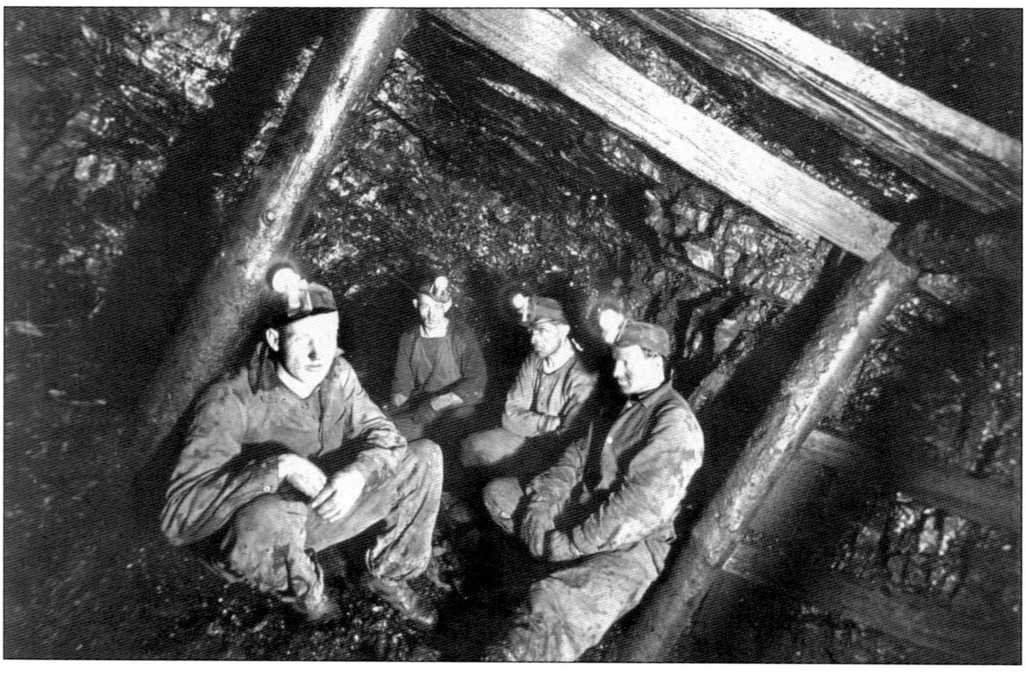

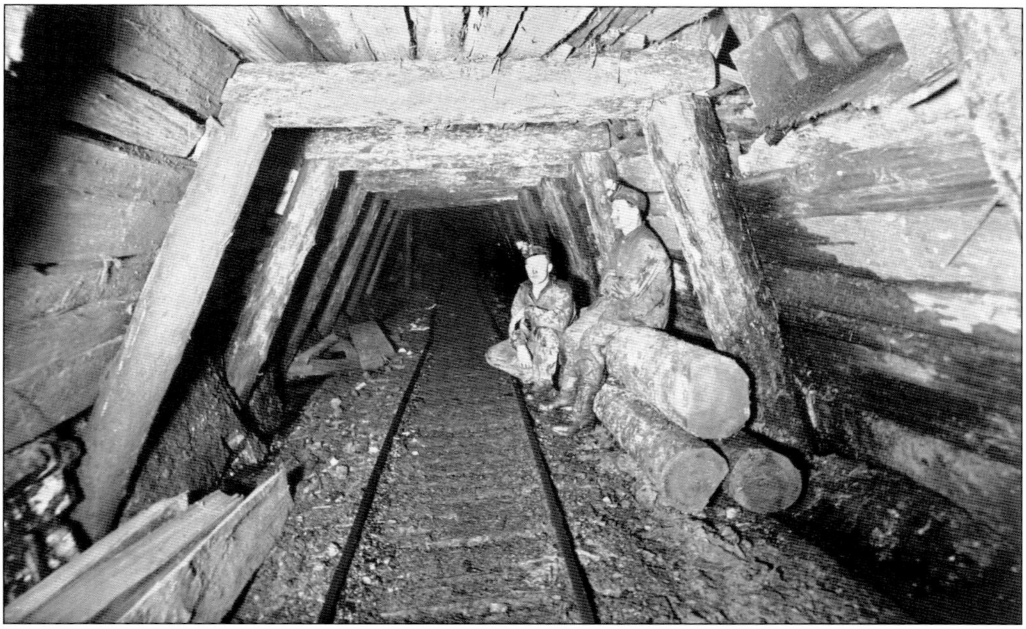

These photographs show workers inside the Superior Coal Company's mine beneath the hill at the end of today's Chamber Way. The image of the gangway, second level east, shows Tom Campbell and Walter Graham. In the other image, from left to right are Fred Richards, Walter Graham (later, mayor of Chehalis), Anton Busek, Mike Oppe, Jack the Mule, Sanford Loomis, Horace Giesey, John Vice, and owner Tom Campbell.

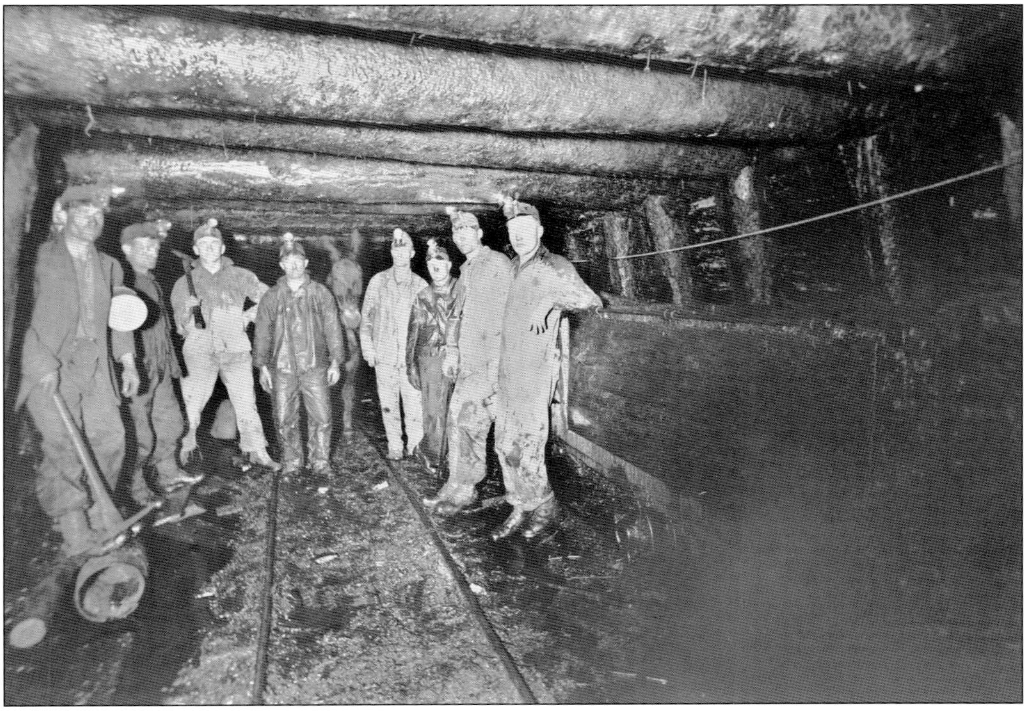

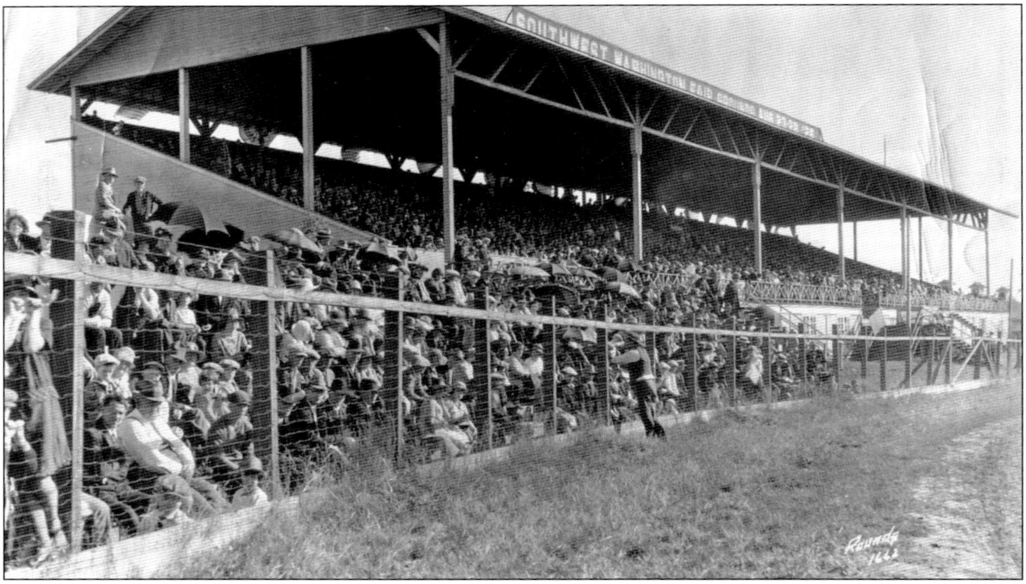

Farmers in Lewis County, a mecca for agriculture, showcased their produce at the first Lewis County Agricultural Association Exhibition, a three-day event in September 1877 held in a schoolhouse in the southern part of Chehalis. The 1882 event took place at the county courthouse with blue and red ribbons awarded as prizes. The association incorporated November 21, 1882. Two decades later, the 1909 state legislature created the Southwest Washington Fair, a regional event, and appropriated $15,000 to construct buildings and run the event for two years. One image shows a packed grandstand in August 1926 as spectators probably watched the ever-popular harness racing. The other photograph gives an overview of the fairgrounds, possibly taken from the grandstand roof, looking southeast toward Kresky Boulevard in the mid-1930s.

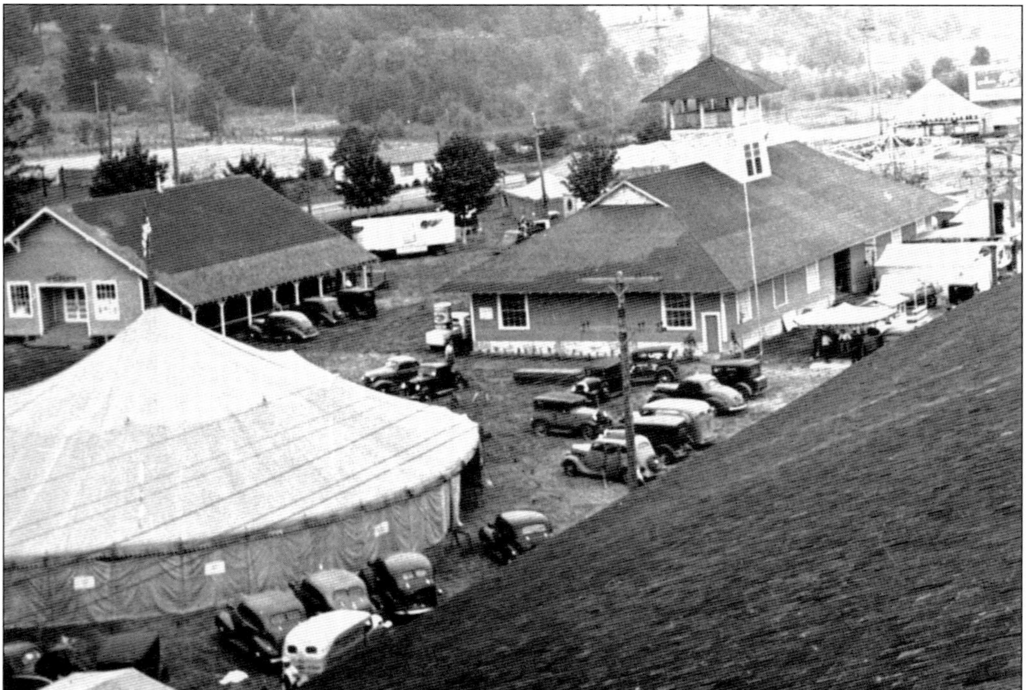

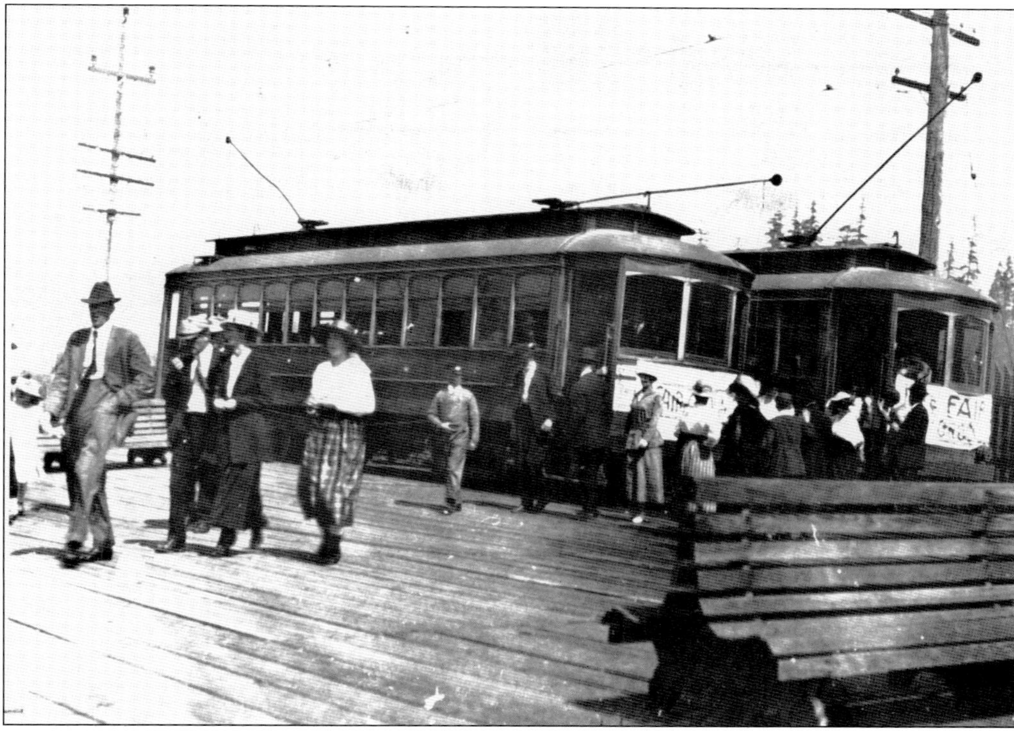

The postcard below shows a streetcar traveling through the Chehalis business district, past C.O. Gingrich's store and Rosenthal & Large Clothing and Dry Goods. The first decade of the 20th century proved a transition time for transportation, as people traveled by horse and buggy, automobile, bicycle, and streetcar. It was also when the city started replacing the deteriorating plank roads to improve travel.

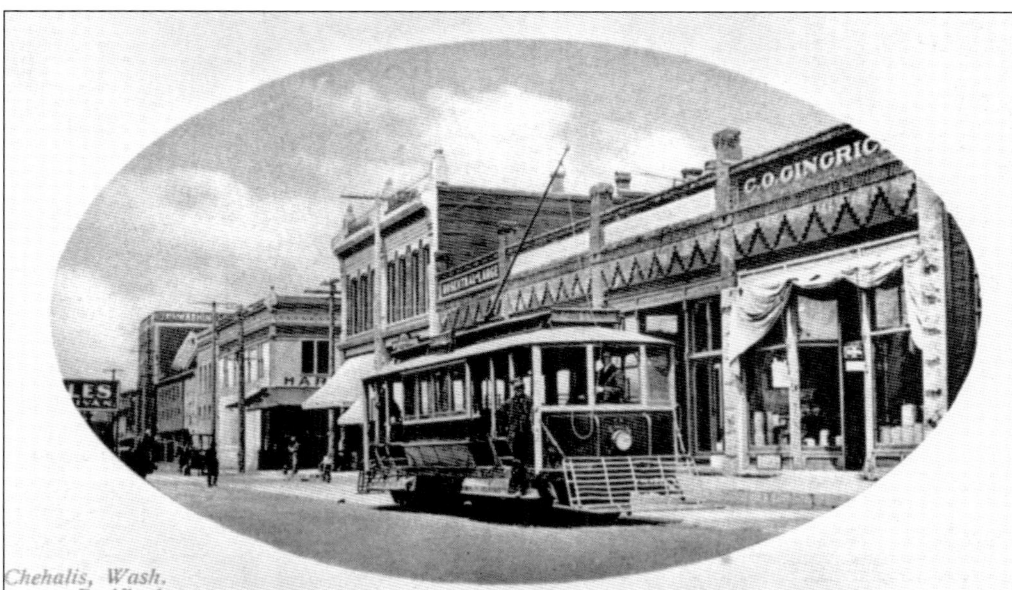

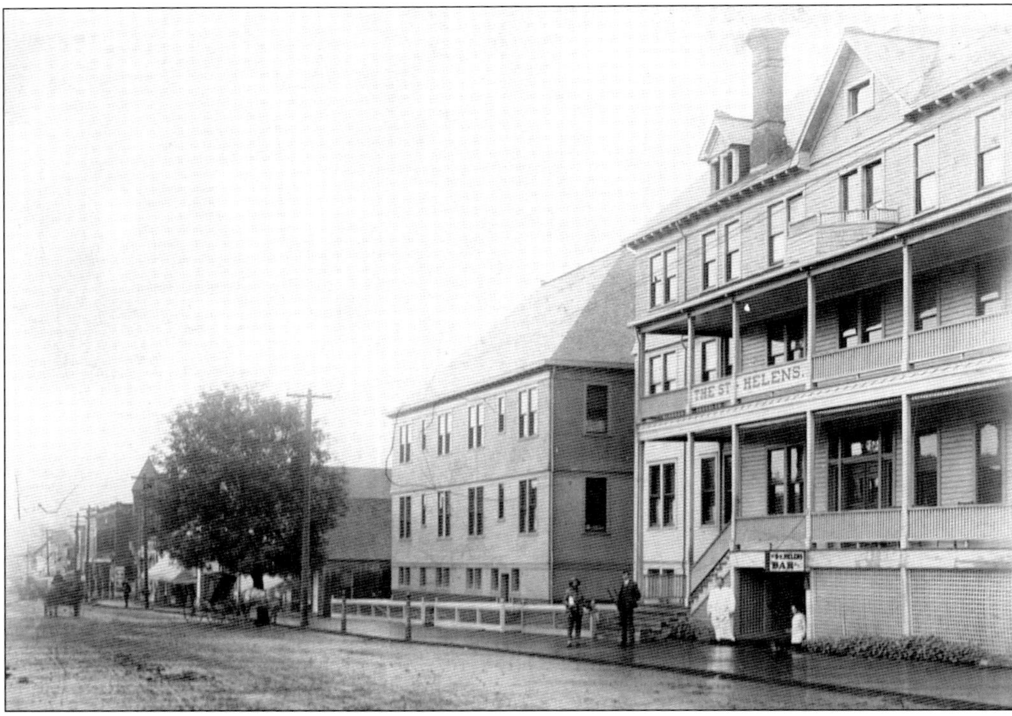

This 1906 photograph shows the exterior of the St. Helens Hotel with Bill West in a business suit on the street with Jim Rush. West borrowed money from his banker uncle, John Dobson of the Coffman-Dobson Bank, to buy the hotel, which he owned by 1915. Market Street was dirt with wagon tracks on it. The photograph also shows the hotel's bar and the cooks outside taking a break.

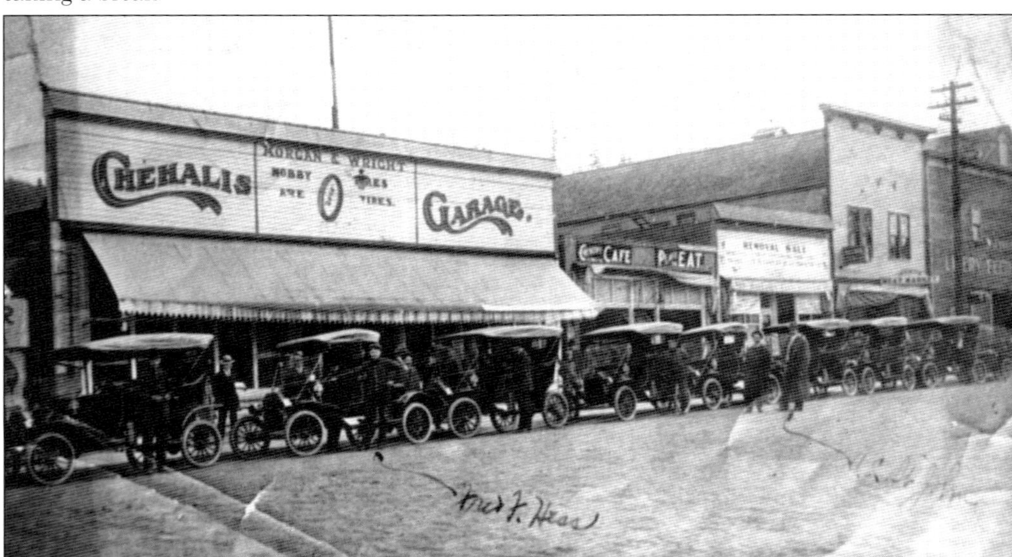

From buggies to horseless carriages, the street in this photograph is lined with vehicles. The Chehalis Garage, run by Morgan & Wright, states that "Hobby Tires Are Good Tires." Fred Hess is marked on the picture, standing beside a car in front of the garage. Down the street are the Crescent Café, the Meat Market, and W.J. Vaughn Livery and Feed.

Five

Growth in the Teens

Anchored by its impressive Carnegie Library and city hall, Chehalis and its 6,500 residents experienced tremendous changes during the 20th century's second decade.

Many people left horses in the fields and traveled by automobiles often purchased from Arthur St. John at the Twin City Automobile Company and repaired at his garages on Market Street in Chehalis or West Main Street in Centralia.

In 1912, the Cowlitz, Chehalis, and Cascade Railway laid track linking resources in the Big Bottom region of eastern Lewis County to Centralia and Chehalis.

In 1914, the school district faced a financial crisis. Under threats by the state to close Chehalis schools, local leaders cut wages, reduced the number of employees, and closely guarded spending until 1925, when the district was nearly debt-free.

Changes also took place at the state reform school, renamed the Washington State Training School in 1907. In 1913, girls were moved to Maple Lane, a school constructed at Grand Mound, north of Centralia. Most of the 190 boys at the Chehalis school had been convicted of the crime of "incorrigibility," and sometimes they just walked away, since the school had no fences.

In 1912, the city switched from the old council-mayor form of government after voting to adopt a commission form. The city has had a council-manager form of government since November 1975.

Dairy farming grew during the decade, and cooperatives formed, producing Carnation and Darigold milk products.

Flooding continued to swamp Chehalis periodically. In late November 1909, landslides washed out roads and train tracks, and flooding left the Southwest Washington Fairgrounds, which opened in 1909, resembling "a small-sized ocean," according to the *Chehalis Bee-Nugget*. Five years later, a December downpour closed sawmills and, according to the *Chronicle-Examiner* in Centralia, "plank and puncheon roads and small bridges have floated away." In mid-January 1919, floodwater again closed schools and mills and knocked out electricity.

The *People's Advocate* became the *Lewis County Advocate* in 1903, and Dan Bush sold the *Bee-Nugget* in 1916 to Clarence Ellington. Chapin Foster bought it in 1925, and in 1937, Advocate Publishing bought the *Bee-Nugget* and combined the two newspapers as the *Chehalis Advocate*, which ceased publication in 1962.

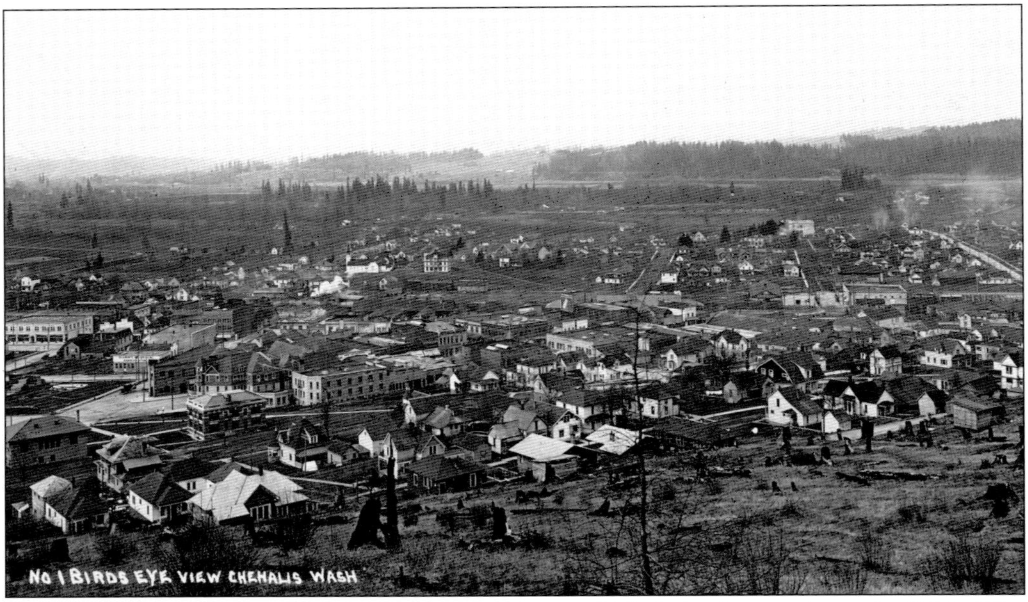

This bird's-eye view shows the growing community of Chehalis during the early 1900s. The photograph was taken from the hillside looking west toward the Chehalis River. The new library is visible at right, near the empty lot where Westminster Presbyterian Church was built in 1923 and across the street from the old St. Helens Hotel, which was moved in 1918. The postcard was postmarked August 3, 1914.

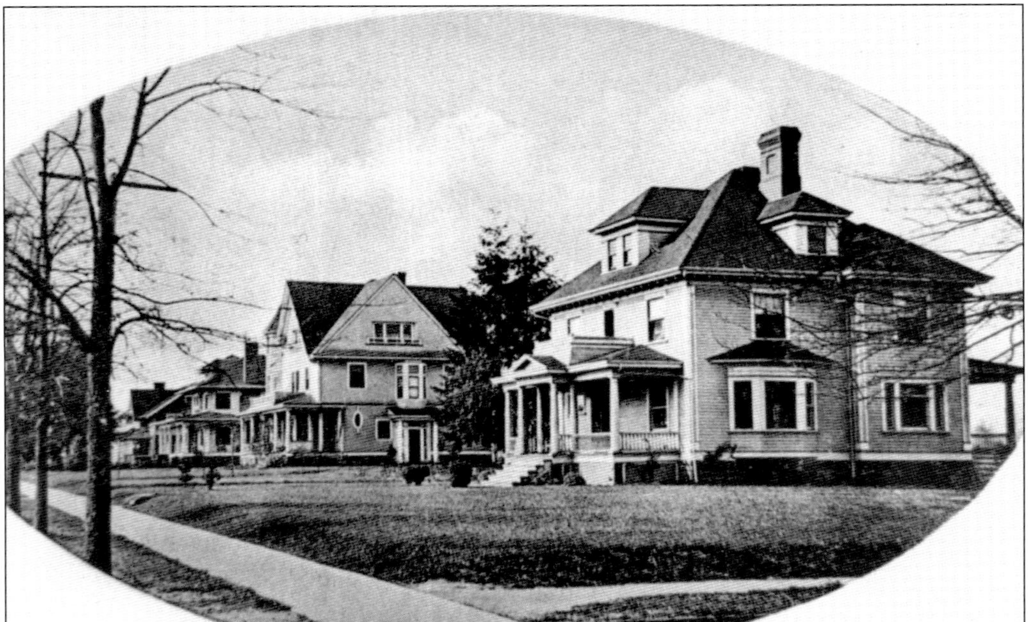

This 1909 photograph shows Pennsylvania Avenue in Chehalis. The homes visible, from left to right, belonged to James Urquhart, A.L. Coffman, and William Urquhart (father of James). In the distance, not clearly visible, are the homes of Daniel C. Millett and Edgar Frost. The historic West Side neighborhood, known for its beautiful turn-of-the-century homes and antique streetlamps, is listed in the National Registry of Historic Places.

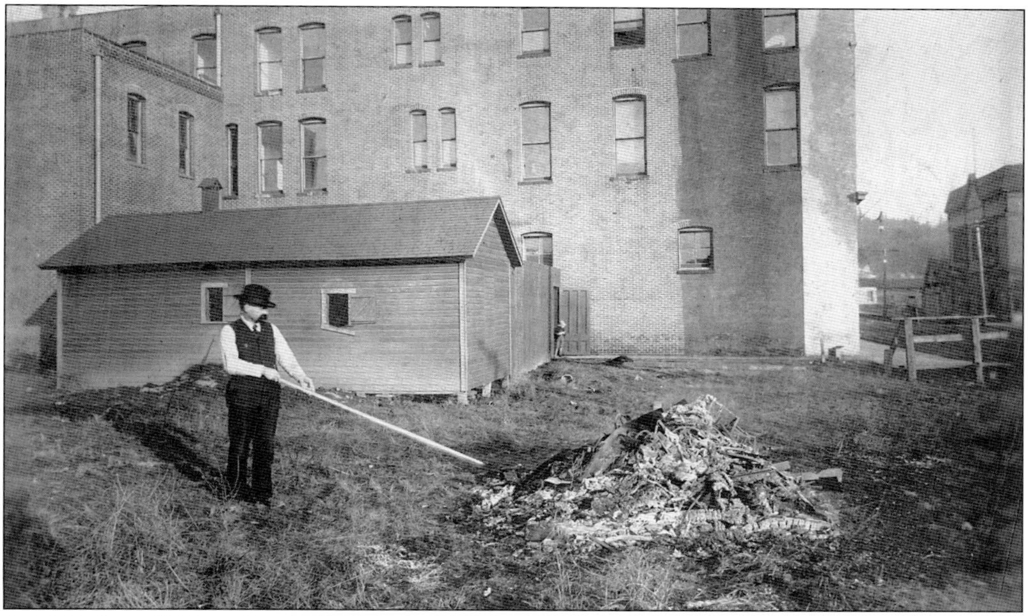

In 1908, Sheriff Edward Deggeller burns 9 slot machines and 12 gambling tables in the yard behind Eliza (Tynan) Saunders Barrett's old Grand Hotel, which by then served as the county courthouse. The Methodist Church at right became the site of the new courthouse in 1927. Deggeller, who was born in Ontario, Canada, to Swiss parents, arrived in Lewis County from Minnesota with his parents and five siblings in October 1875. He worked as a lumberman and farmer before being elected sheriff in 1898. After two consecutive two-year terms—the maximum allowed by state law—he was elected again in 1906. He had served two terms on the Chehalis City Council and, in 1911, was elected to the city commission and reelected in 1914. Below, Deggeller is seen on the right after an early-1900s raccoon hunt with George King, a deputy sheriff.

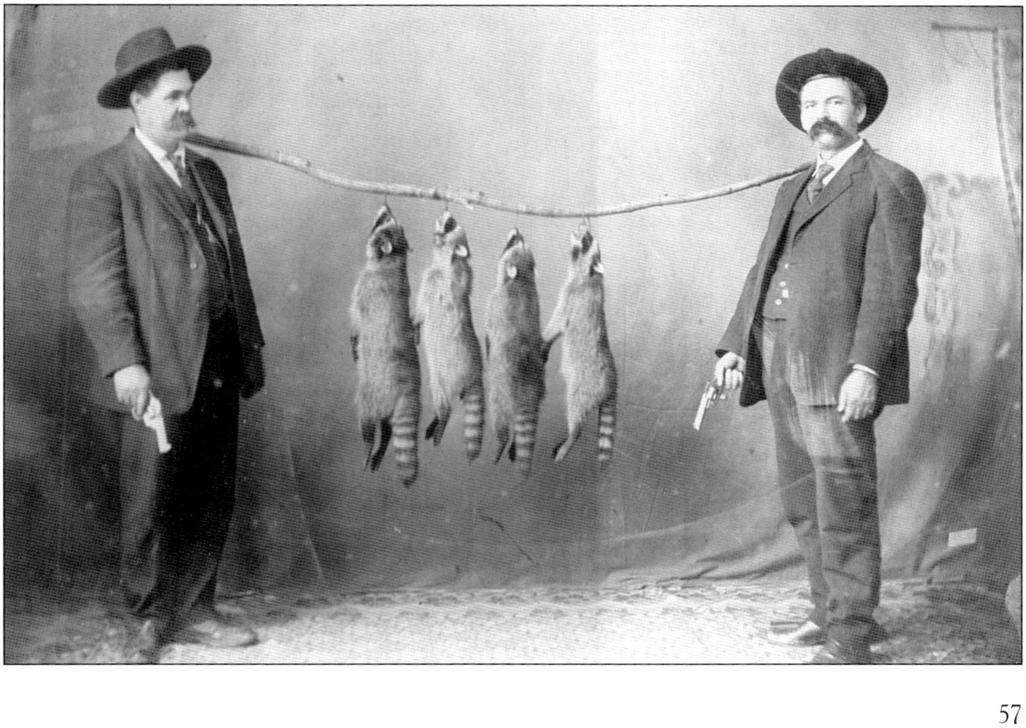

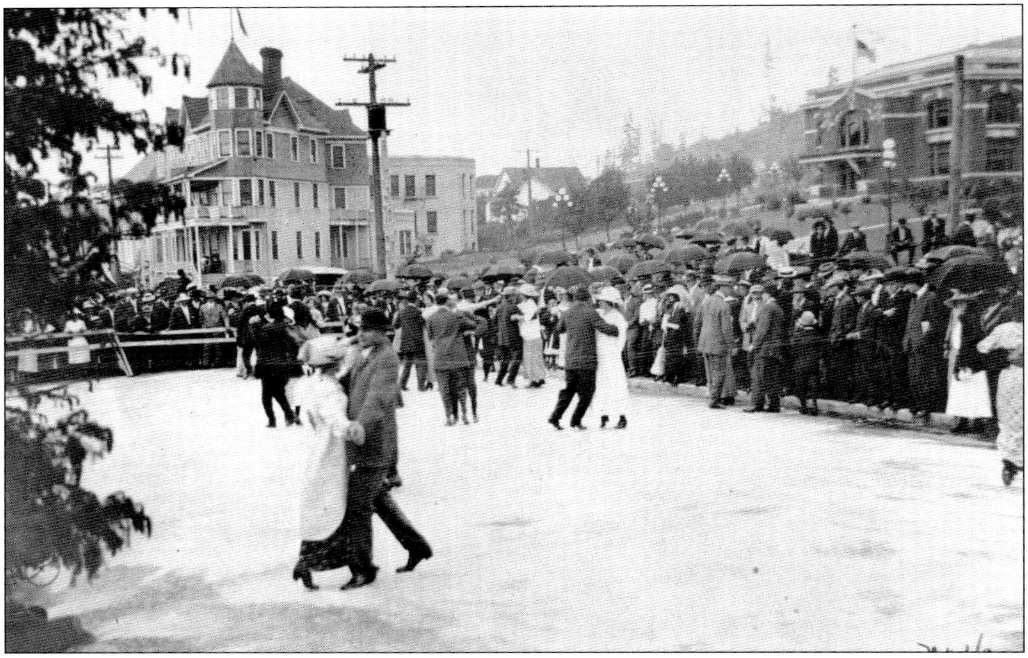

Couples brave wet weather to dance in Chehalis streets at a Chautauqua between 1910 and 1915. The women are wearing long dresses, and many people are carrying umbrellas. In the background is the St. Helens Hotel, and to the right is the city hall built in 1910. The dance took place on Market Street in front of the Westminster Presbyterian Church.

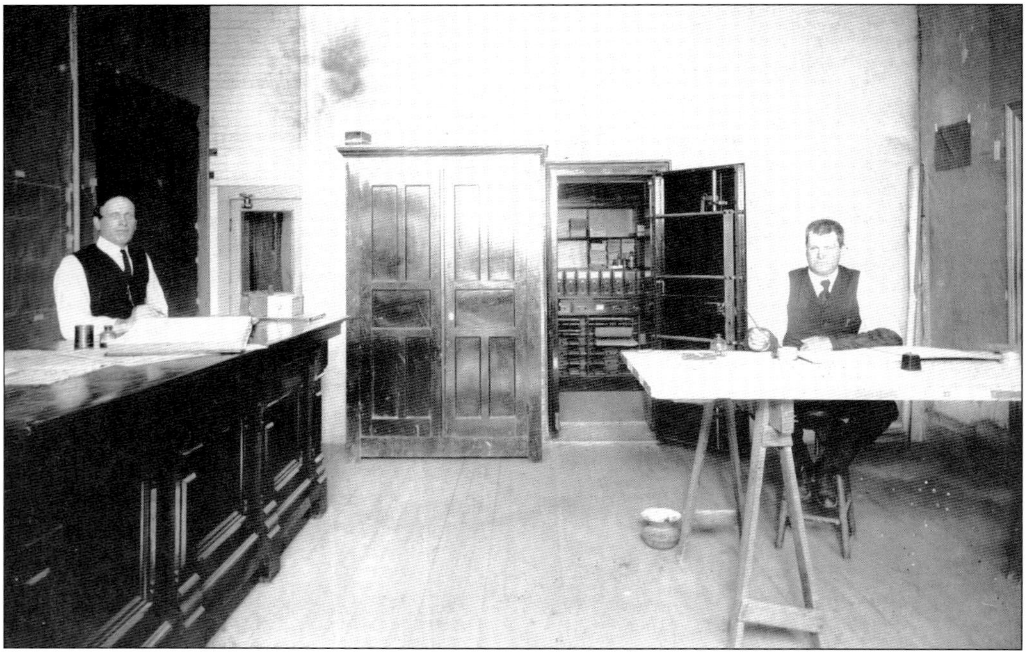

This photograph shows two men working in the Lewis County Auditor's Office in 1904, when the courthouse was in the former Grand Central Hotel, also known as the Barrett Hotel. The men are not identified, although one of them might be Joel E. Stearns, a county official who was born in 1866 and died in 1955.

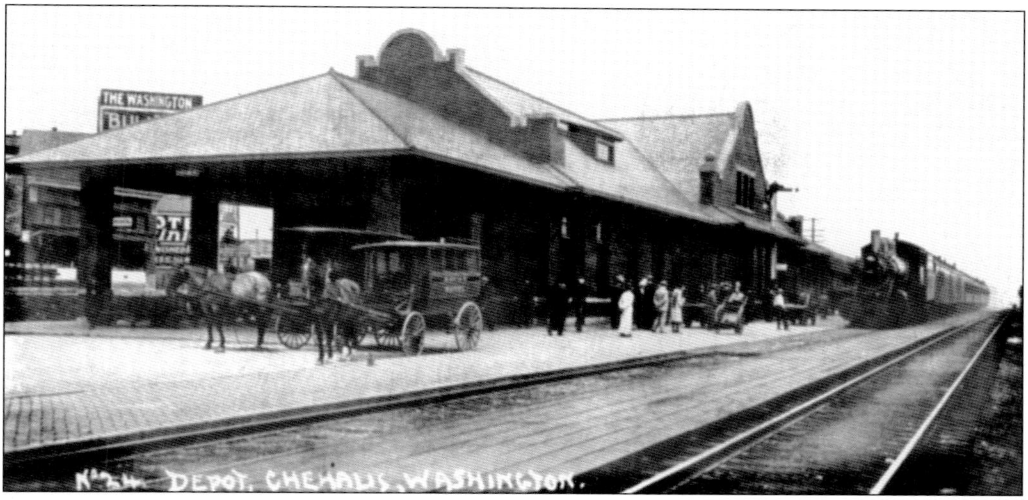

The entrance to the Chehalis Railroad Depot is pictured between 1912 and 1915, before the freight office was added. The photograph shows people with baggage carts awaiting the train's arrival. Printed on the side of one buggy pulled by a single horse are the words "Savoy Hotel," indicating it provided taxi service to passengers staying at the Savoy. The Lewis County Historical Museum used this image in its logo.

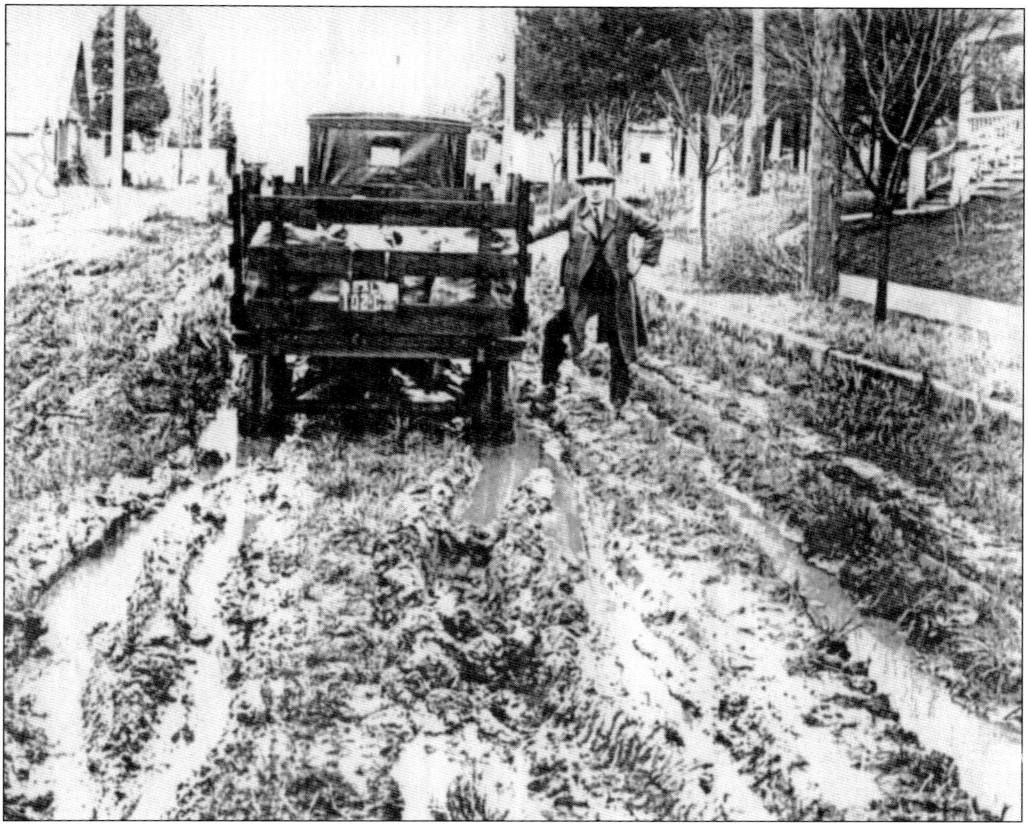

Long after the Saunders pioneers lie in their final resting places, the valley's reputation as a soggy bottomland continued. The driver of this old Model T, who is unidentified, might have been frustrated with the sloppy muck as he traveled along what used to be a dirt road.

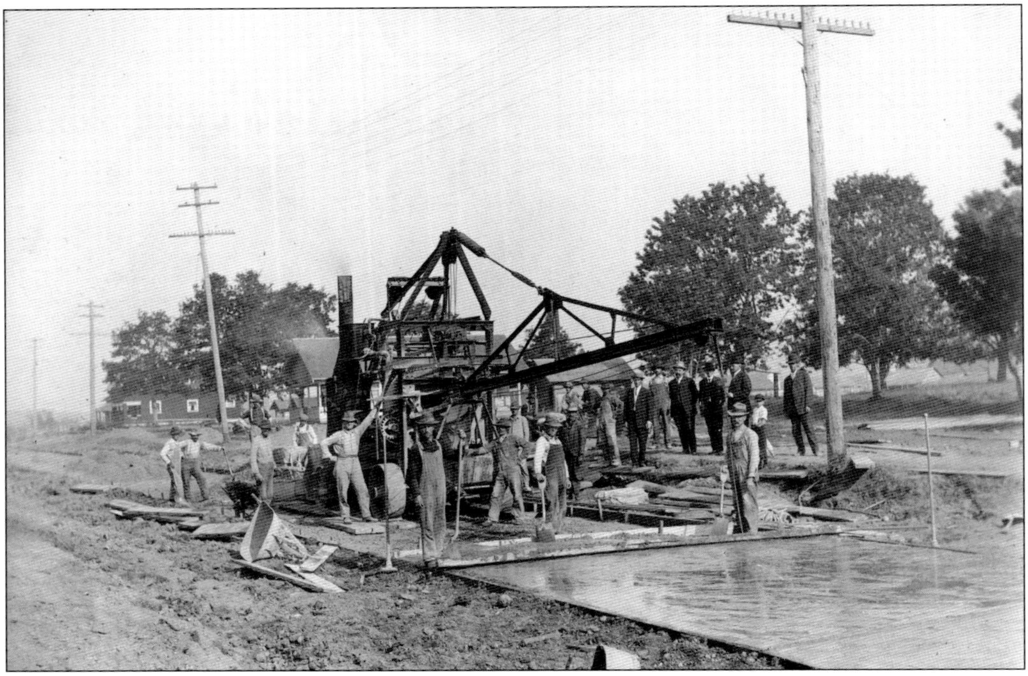

City and county officials devoted time and money to improving roads. This photograph shows the paving of Market Street or Chehalis Avenue in 1915, when the work was all done by hand. The large crew of men poured sacks of Portland cement into a large mixing machine to cover the streets. Supervising the work was F.O. Blair, city engineer. The other 1915 image shows workers doing construction on old Highway 99, now known as Jackson Highway, at the south Chehalis city limits near South Market and Twentieth Streets. Mason Greenwood Cemetery is on the hillside to the right.

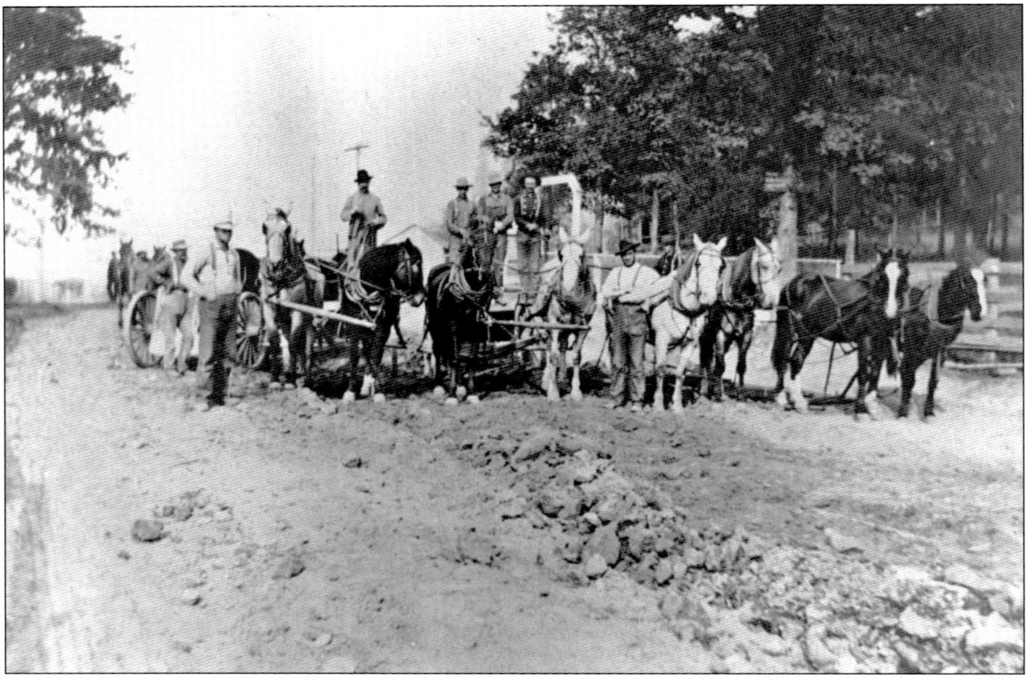

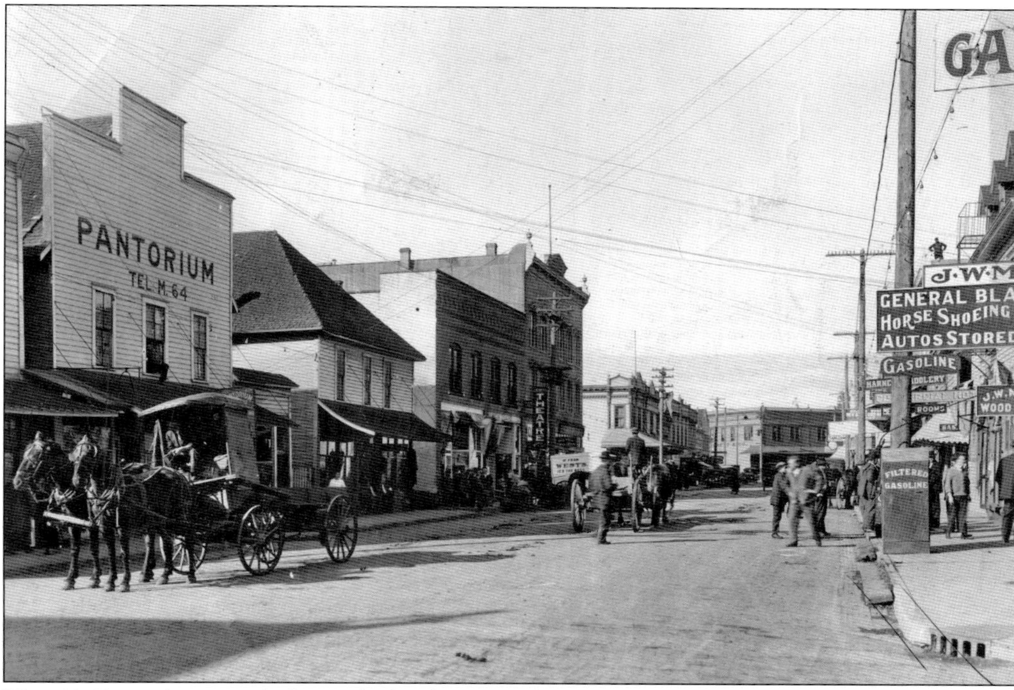

This 1915-era photograph shows the brick-surfaced Chehalis Avenue, looking northward. On the left are Pantorium Cleaners, an unidentified business, West Grocery, Empress Theatre, Brunswig Hotel, another unidentified business, and Everett Hardware Co. On the other side in the foreground is J.W. Mills, fuel, wood and blacksmithing shop; Scribner's Harness and Saddlery; the Commercial Hotel; Mulford Brothers, Second Hand Goods; and more businesses without identification.

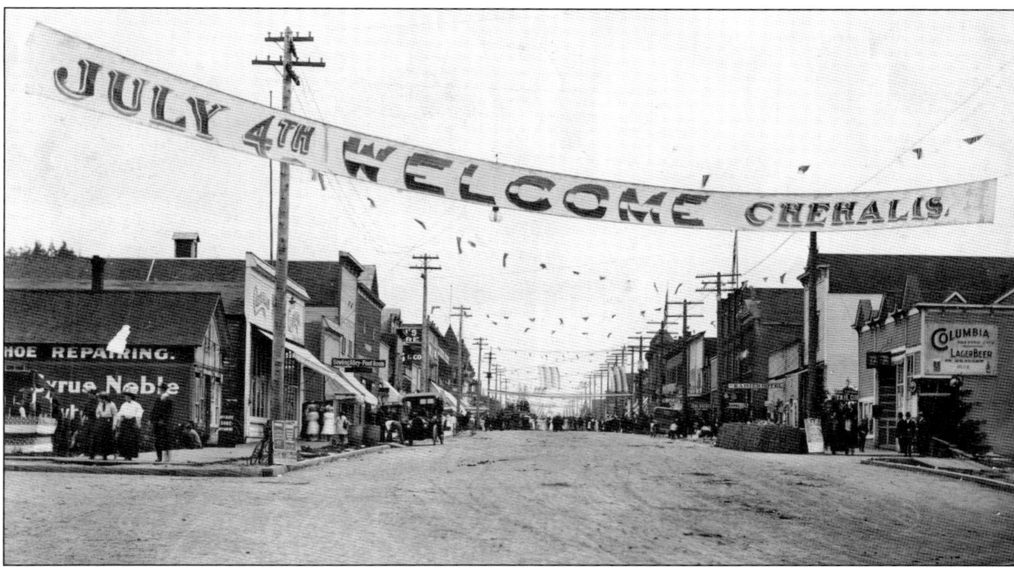

A Fourth of July banner drapes across Market Street in Chehalis around 1912 as a crowd gathers at the far end. The large pile of bricks at right indicates the plank road was being replaced by brick. Visible are Cyrus Noble's shoe repair shop, the Chehalis Garage, a bowling alley and poolroom, a bakery, a real estate office, the Rainier Hotel, Karl Teitzel's tailor shop, and the Columbia Saloon.

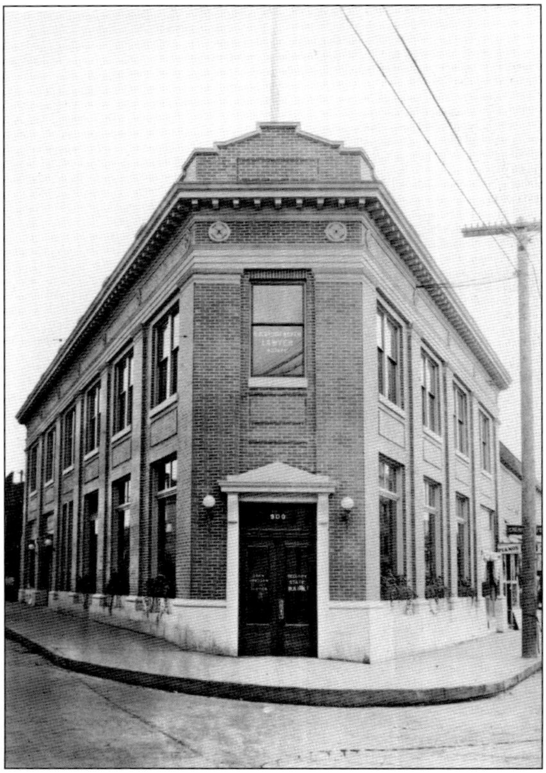

Security State Bank, founded in 1903, is seen at the corner of Northwest Pacific and Northwest Chehalis Avenues in this photograph from around 1918 or 1919. Lettering on the upstairs window advertises C.A. Studebaker, Lawyer, Notary. The Chehalis Café is at right. The president of Security State Bank was J.W. Alexander, while J.T. Alexander was vice president. They were sons of John and Margaret (Urquhart) Alexander.

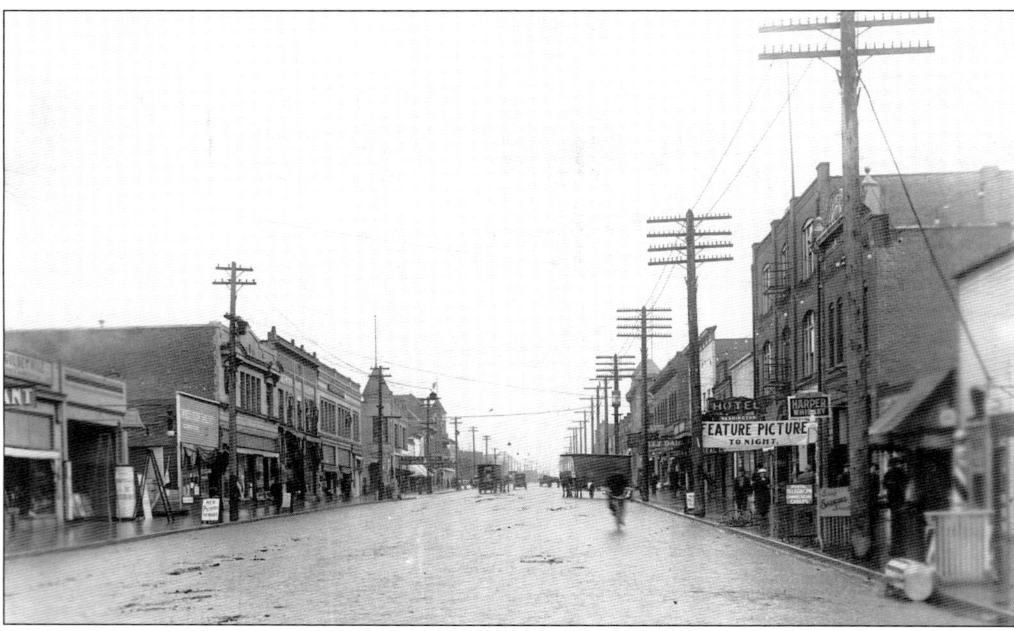

This c. 1912–1915 view of the brick-paved Market Street lined by power poles shows local businesses, including the Golden Rule Restaurant, a telephone company, tailor shop, Hartman and Nathan Big Department Store, Gem Drug Store, White and Gabel Books, 5-10-cent Store, St. Helens Hotel, Dream Theatre, a dentist office, City Bakery, a real estate office, Hotel Washington (built in 1889), a tavern, and a shoe shine stand.

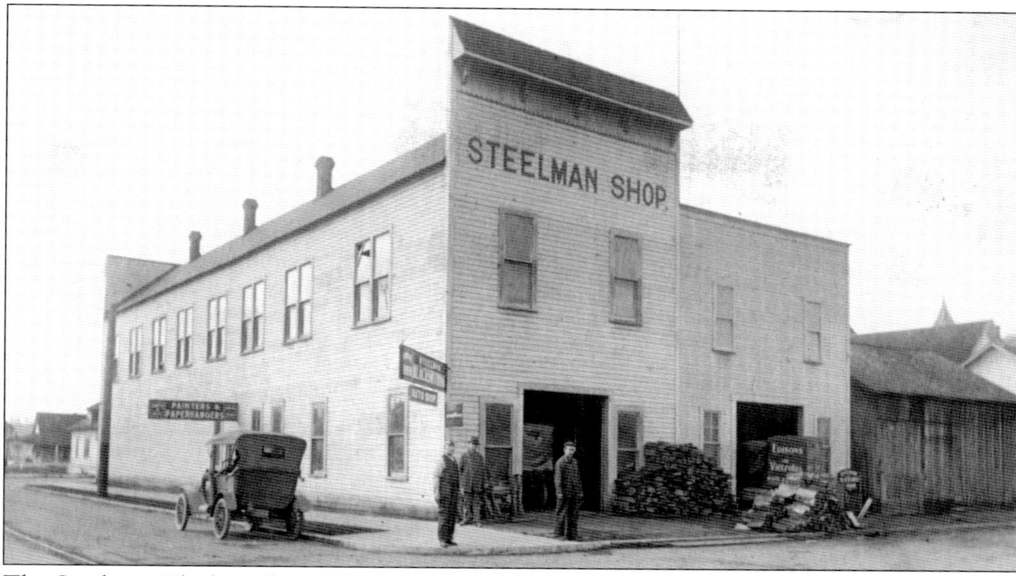

The Steelman Blacksmith and Auto Shop at the corner of Northwest North Street and Pacific Avenue met the transportation needs of both old-timers driving buggies and new motorists in automobiles. The two-story frame building, seen in 1914, also housed painters and paperhangers and the sellers of Edison Phonographs and Victrolas. A track runs along the road, which has curbs and sidewalks. A 1910 car is parked at the curb. John Steelman is seen at right, but the other men are not identified. Below, inside the Steelman Blacksmith and Auto Garage can be seen blacksmith tools, a forge, acetylene tank and gauges, and tools for working on automobiles. From left to right are Elmer Stoddard, unidentified, John L. Steelman, and Clyde Stolph, the shop's blacksmith.

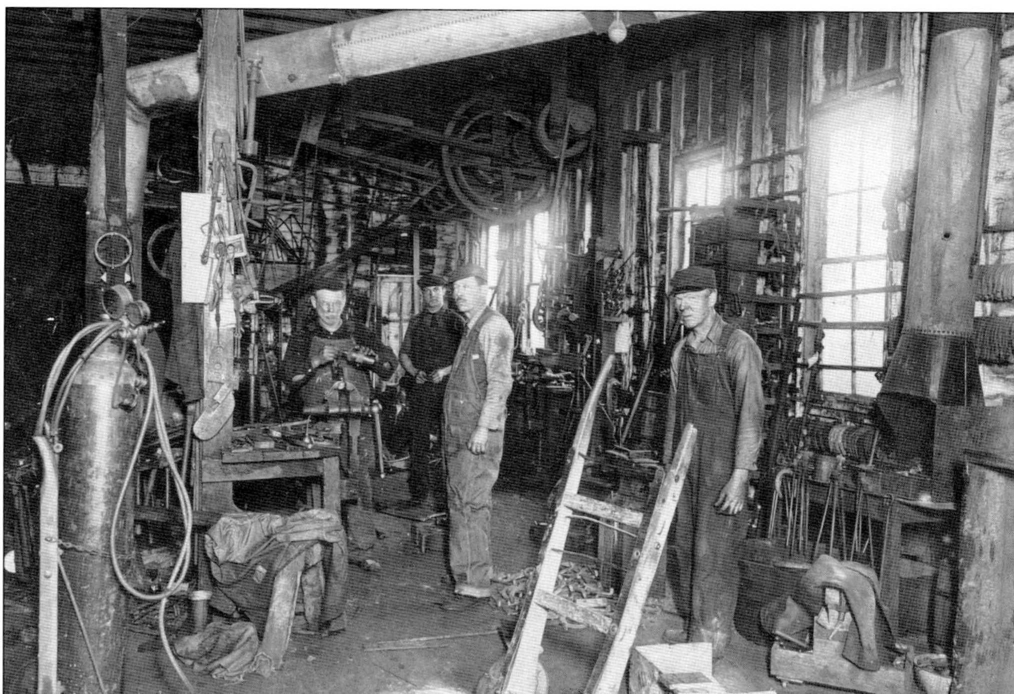

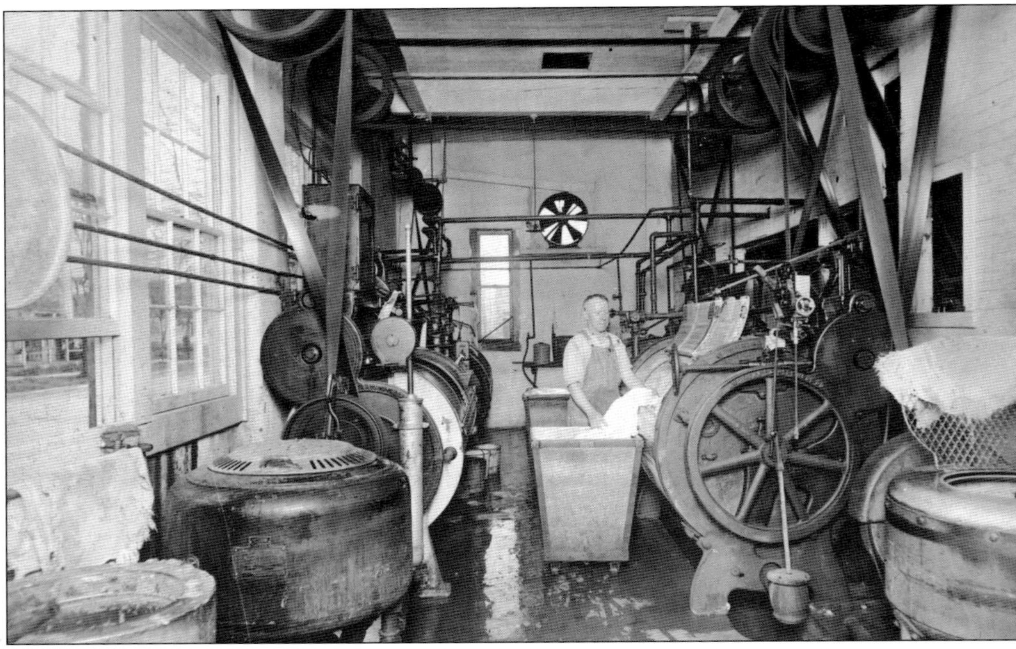

Charles E. Sonneman, who arrived in Chehalis from Kansas in 1910, owned and managed the Chehalis City Laundry erected in 1913 at Chehalis Avenue and Main Street. The man in the laundry room is unidentified, and so are the women in the drying room, seen below in 1915. The building visible outside the drying room window is most likely the Tynan Opera House. The business, in a well-equipped concrete building, collected dirty laundry and delivered clean items to clients in Chehalis, Centralia, and the rest of the county. The company also used parcel post for some deliveries, paying one-way costs. The laundry employed 12 women and three men. One department was devoted to mending, which was provided free to patrons.

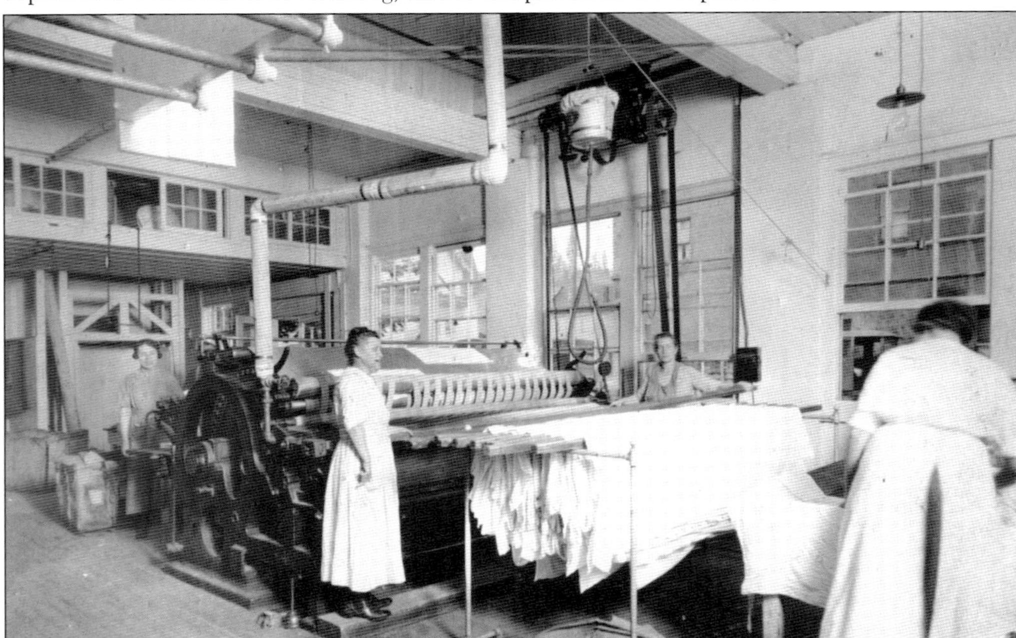

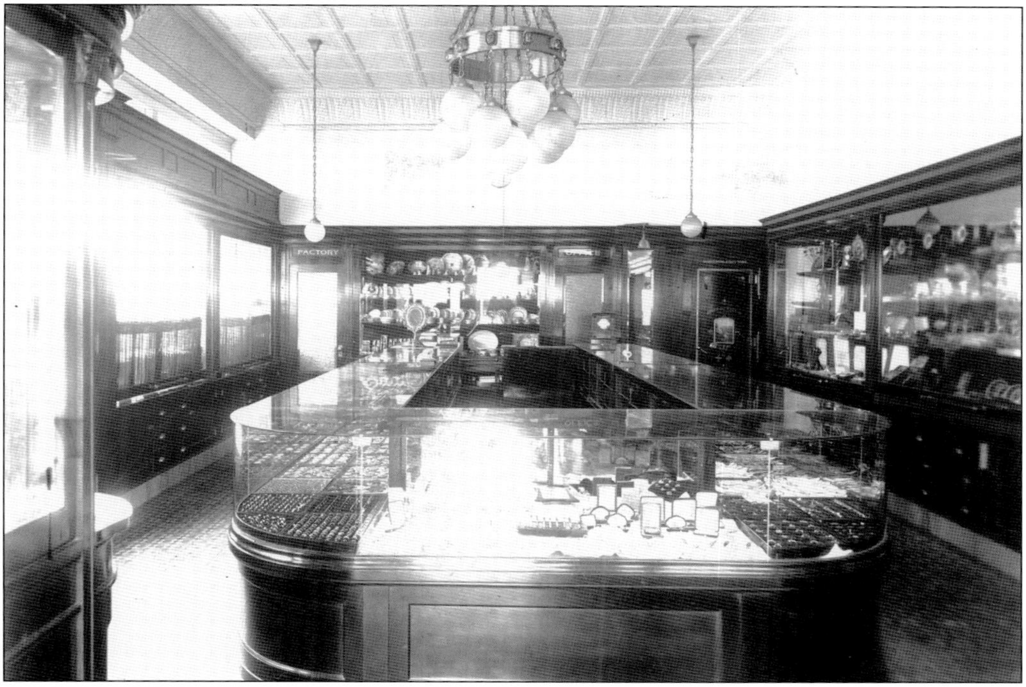

Display cases containing jewels are seen in Burnett's Jewelry Store at the corner of Market and Boistfort Streets around 1915. Morris S. Burnett owned the business, known informally as the Tiffany's of Chehalis. The Polish immigrant, who ran a jewelry store in Missouri, moved to Chehalis in 1898 and opened a store, which he operated for many years before selling to J.A. Dugaw. Burnett died June 24, 1953, at age 82.

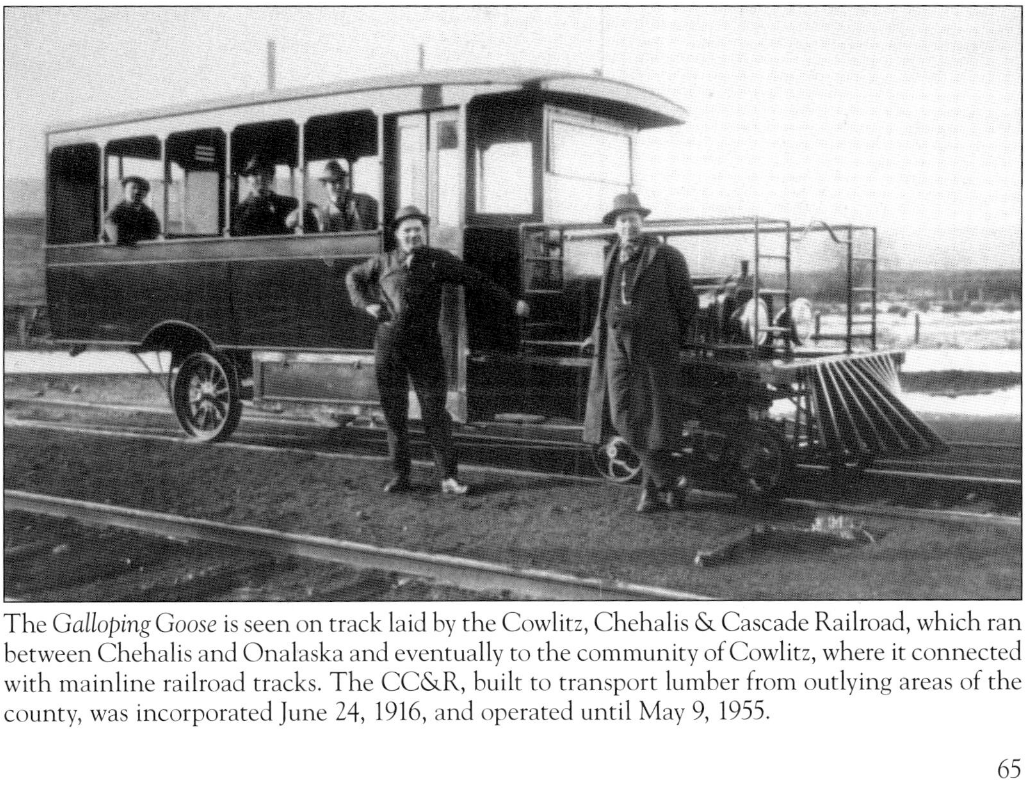

The *Galloping Goose* is seen on track laid by the Cowlitz, Chehalis & Cascade Railroad, which ran between Chehalis and Onalaska and eventually to the community of Cowlitz, where it connected with mainline railroad tracks. The CC&R, built to transport lumber from outlying areas of the county, was incorporated June 24, 1916, and operated until May 9, 1955.

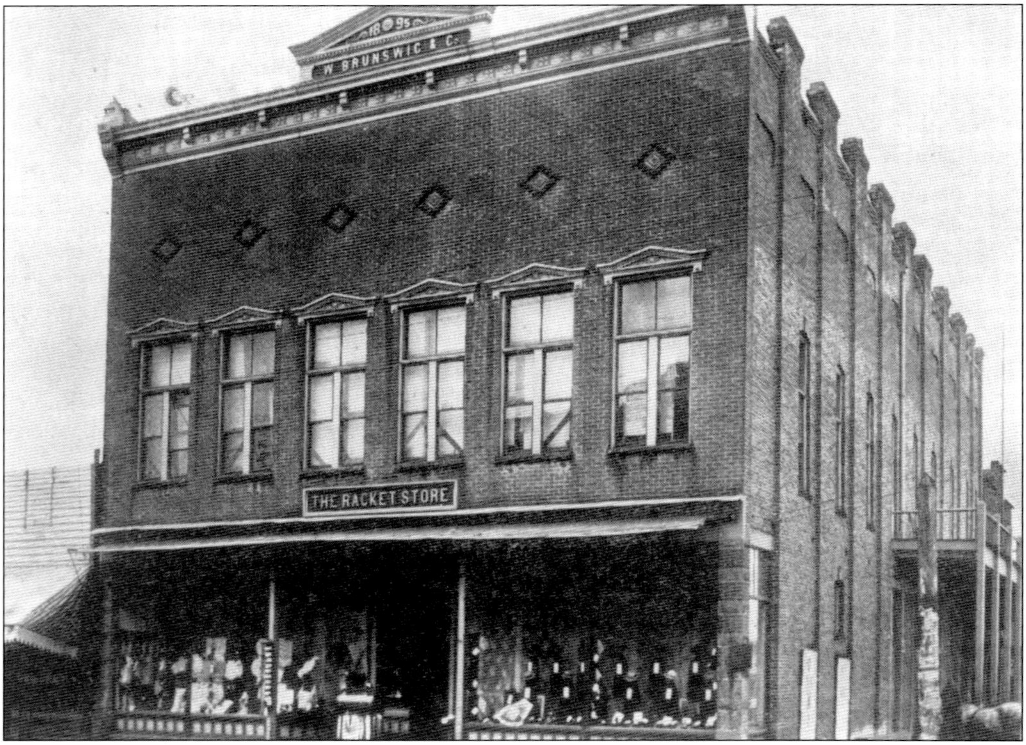

The Chehalis Opera House was built by William Brunswig, who also owned the Racket Store on Chehalis Avenue. The building was later used as apartments and offices. The German immigrant opened a variety stores at Pacific and Chehalis Avenues, known then as Thompson's Corner, in 1889. In 1895, he built the Chehalis Opera House, and in 1898, moved the Racket Store to Chehalis Avenue and Park Street. His son Norman took over when his father, who served as a city commissioner, died in 1924. Norman moved the shoe shop to Market Street in 1937. Brunswig Shoes remains in the family today.

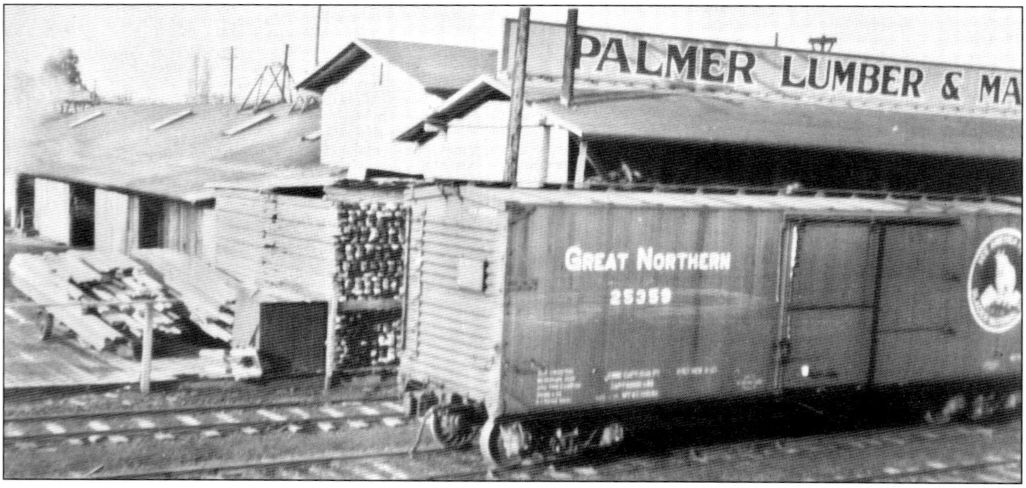

Palmer Lumber and Manufacturing Company, with offices on Prindle Street in 1915, employed 16 to 18 men with a monthly payroll of $1,000. The company reincorporated in 1915 and leased additional land for sheds. The company built made-to-order homes and building materials. State Street later ran in front of the building.

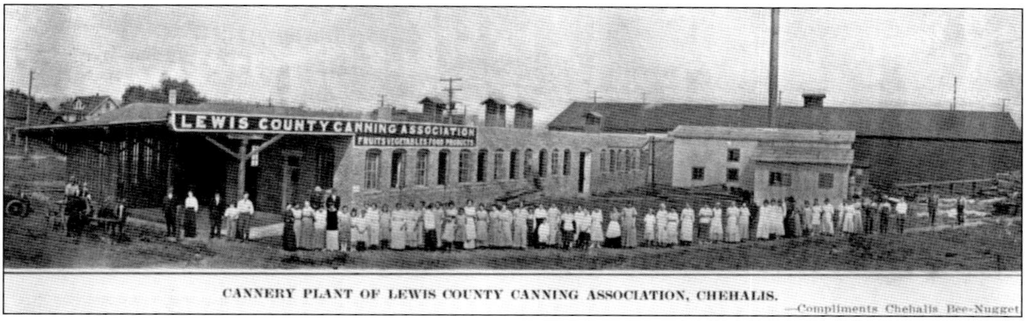

The Lewis County Canning Company on State Street in Chehalis was built by the Lewis County Canning Association, a cooperative organized after a concerted campaign by the Citizens Club, precursor to the Chamber of Commerce. The association elected nine trustees. Dan W. Bush, president of the Bee-Nugget Publishing Company, was elected president and manager. Farmers and businessmen bought stock in the fruit-and-vegetable cannery.

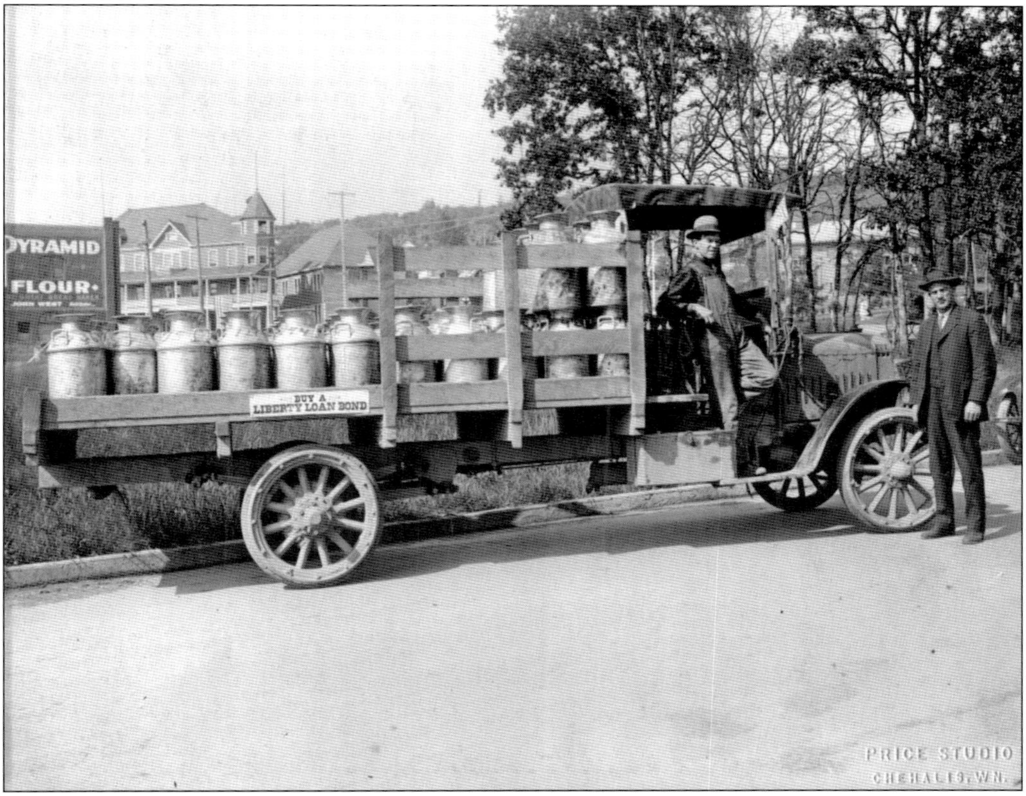

Harry B. Quick, on the right, visits with the unidentified driver of a milk truck on Whitworth Way behind the Westminster Presbyterian Church around 1917. The St. Helens Hotel, Carnegie Library, and a Pyramid Flour sign are visible. The truck was purchased from Harry B. Quick's company. A sign on the truck urges people to buy a liberty bond to support the military efforts during World War I.

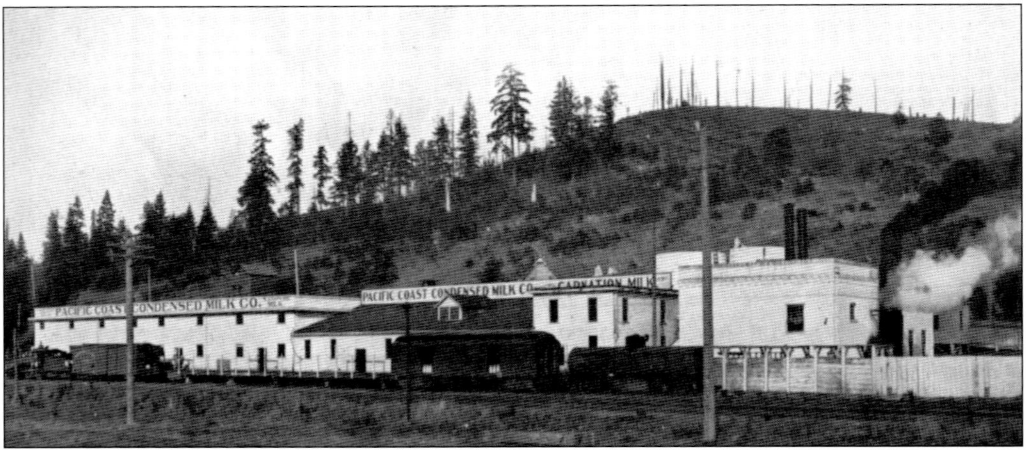

Dairy farming ruled in the region, and a large milk condensing plant provided a market for local farmers for many years. The Pacific Coast Condensed Milk Company, which produced Carnation sterilized milk, established its Chehalis plant in 1907 and, eight years later, served more than 400 farmers in the Chehalis and Newaukum River Valleys. Its name later changed to the Carnation Milk Condensery, whose employees are pictured around 1928. From left to right are J.W. Short, pan processor; A.J. Blakley, relief processor; A.D. Kain, field man; C.B. Rapier, engineer; G.R. Sibley, superintendent; W.B. Jones, sterilizing processor; Sadie Rowland, office worker; and E.L. Betts, porch foreman.

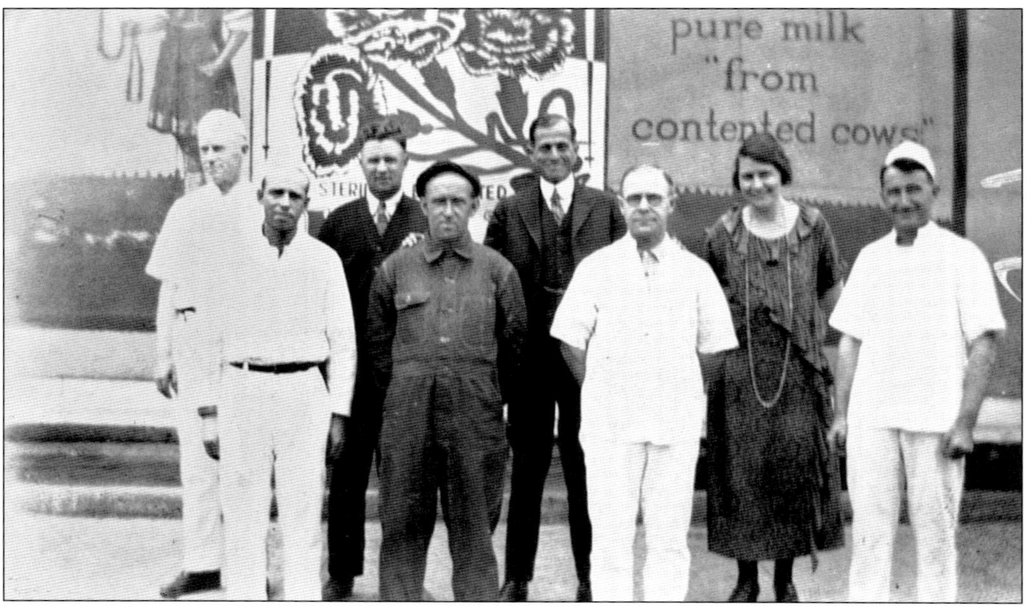

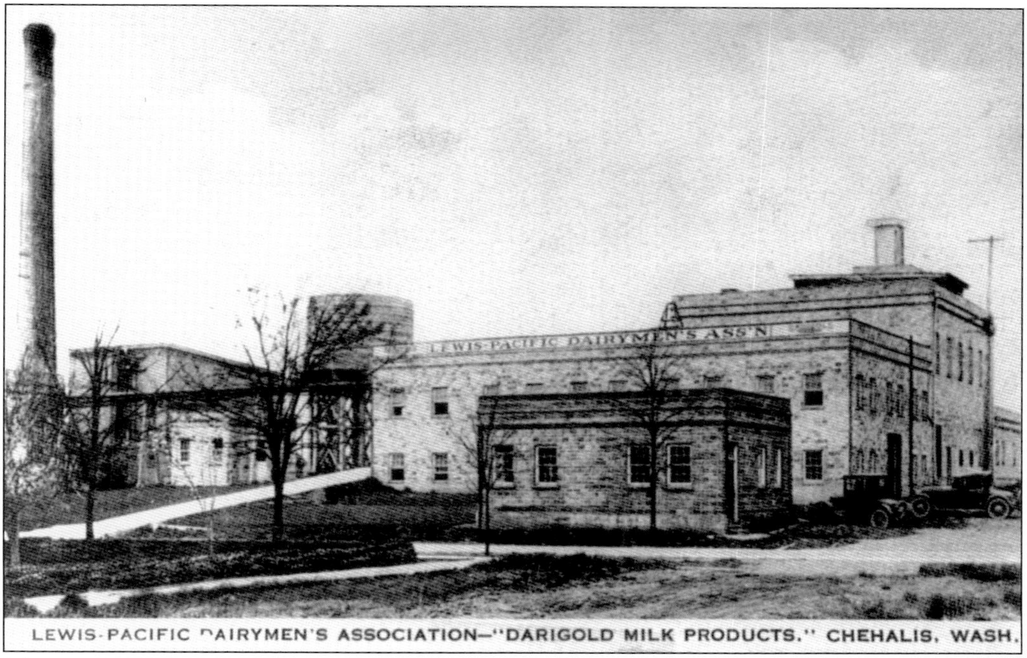

The Lewis-Pacific Dairymen's Association built a plant on Chehalis Avenue to produce Darigold Milk Products. The plant is seen in this c. 1925 artist's sketch. Darigold formed in 1918 when five Puget Sound co-ops joined forces to create the United Dairymen's Association, supported by the Lewis County Dairy Association. The other image shows three Darigold milk delivery trucks with the brick Darigold building in the background. The advertisement on the trucks reads "Lewis-Pacific Dairymen's Association" and touts its products: butter, cheese, evaporated milk, and powdered milk. The Darigold plant in Chehalis is still operating today. The company, headquartered in Seattle, operates 10 plants that serve more than 500 dairy farmers and create annual sales of more than $2 billion.

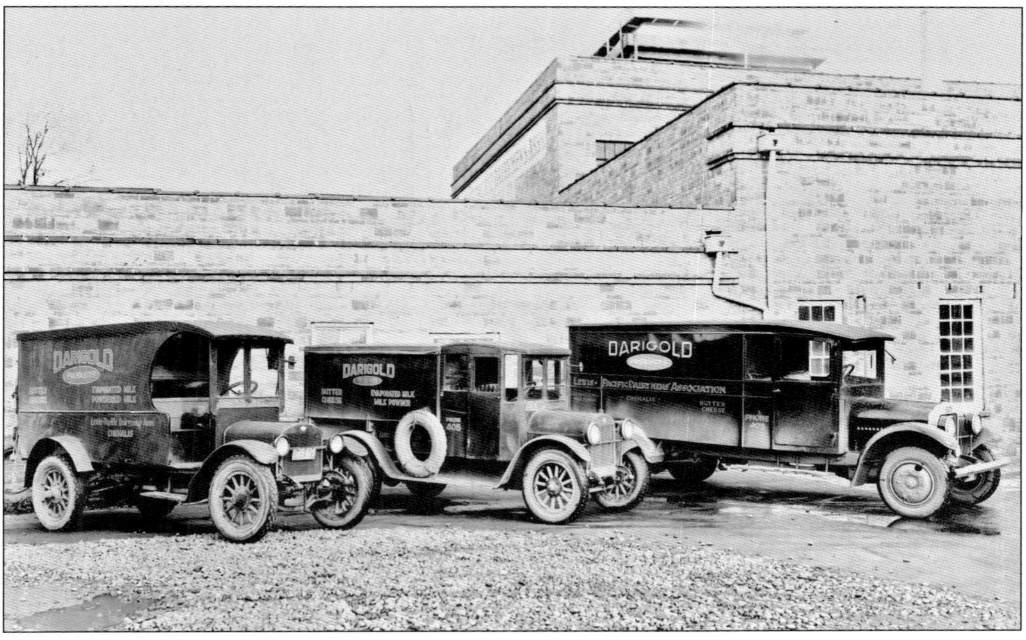

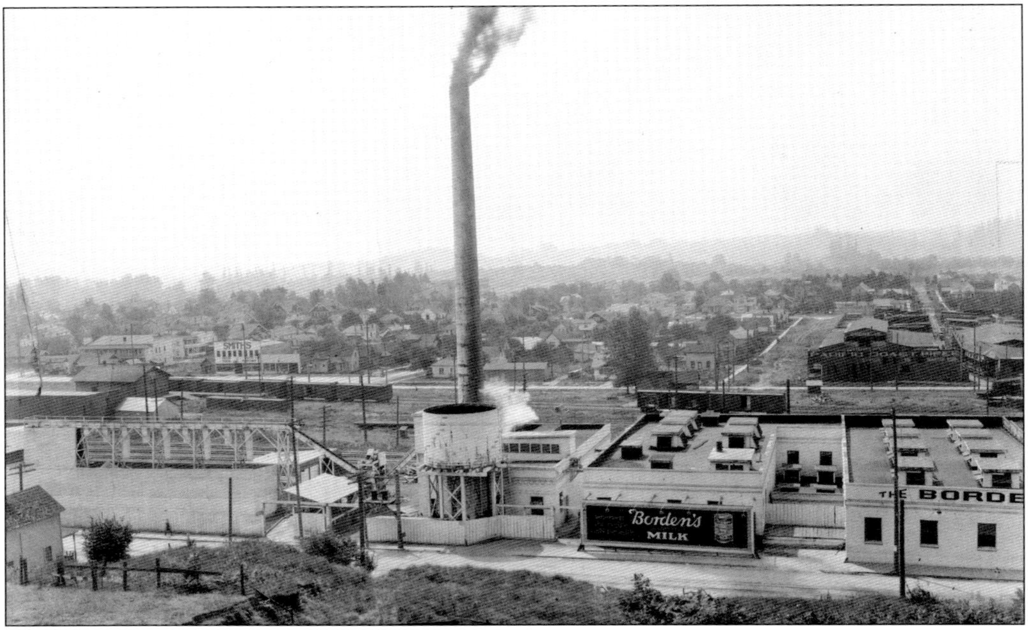

The Carnation Milk Products Company became Borden's Milk by the 1920s. The plant is seen at the north end of the Chehalis business district in 1920. Visible in the background are the Chehalis Fir Door Company, Pacific Coast Pipe Company, and Smith's Auto Painting. The business, established in 1902 as the Pacific Coast Condensed Milk Company, served more than 400 local farmers in 1912. The stack was painted in 1919 by T.H. Eatwell. Callison and Sons later located at the plant site on National Avenue. The other photograph, taken in 1939, shows the Borden milk plant on National Avenue with its landmark chimney.

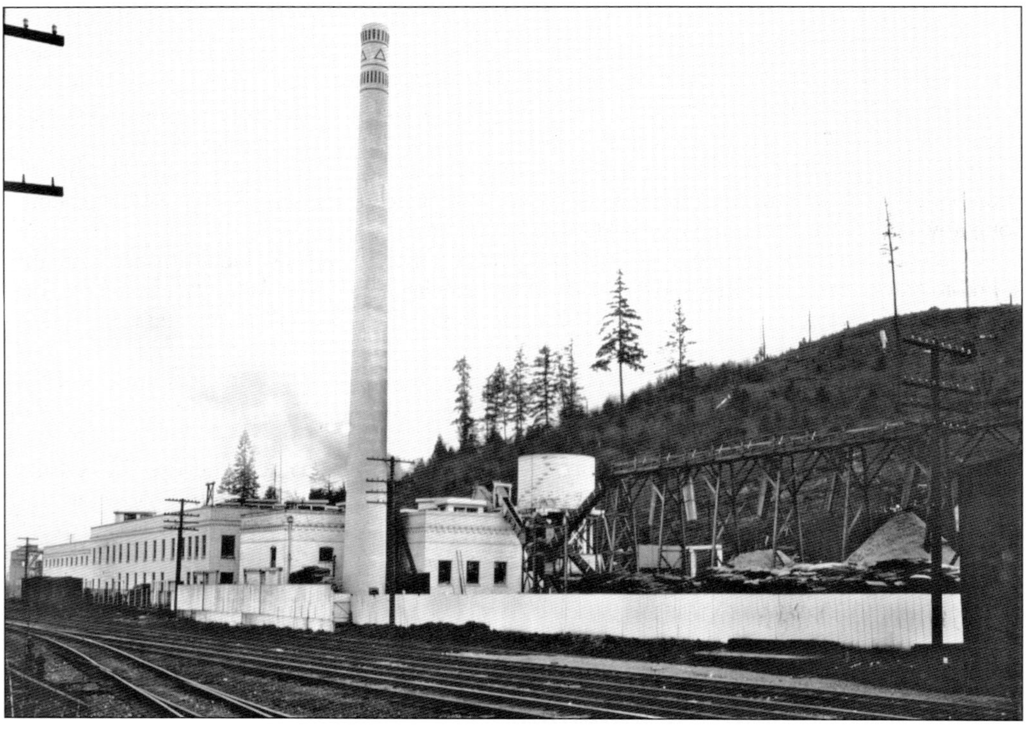

Six

The Roaring Twenties

The Roaring Twenties opened with the closure of saloons, taverns, and other places selling liquor after the passage of the 18th Amendment to the Constitution and the National Prohibition Act in 1919. Although intoxicating liquors were banned, people with thirsty palates managed to buy moonshine manufactured by bootleggers in backwoods stills. Passage of the 21st Amendment in 1933 ended Prohibition.

Many churches had opened in the 1800s—Presbyterian, Baptist, Episcopal, Missionary Alliance, Methodist, Catholic, Evangelical Lutheran, and Christian—but the early 20th century saw the construction of more places to worship. Those served followers of the Apostolic Faith, Christian Science, Peace Lutheran, Seventh-day Adventist, Pentecostal, and Assemblies of God.

By the 1920s, fewer buggies and wagons traveled Chehalis streets, with most people purchasing automobiles from the John B. Coffman Garage, St. John's Ford Garage and Twin City Automobile Company, Pollom Motor Company, or Harry Quick Auto Sales.

Streetcars carried residents in town, and the Cowlitz, Chehalis & Cascade Railroad Company laid more track outside Chehalis, over which the *Galloping Goose* rumbled. Travelers venturing farther afield boarded a motor stage, or bus, at the Central Bus Station or hopped on trains at the Chehalis depot.

The very adventurous found their way to Donahoe Field, where Arthur St. John, owner of Twin City Automobile, operated St. John Air Service and owned the *Queen of the Cowlitz,* sister ship to Charles Lindbergh's *Spirit of St. Louis.*

Dream Theatre offered vaudeville shows near the Washington Hotel, and the community gathered each summer at Alexander Park for the annual Farmers and Merchants Picnic where, in 1928, the Daily Bread Shop unveiled the World's Largest Strawberry Shortcake.

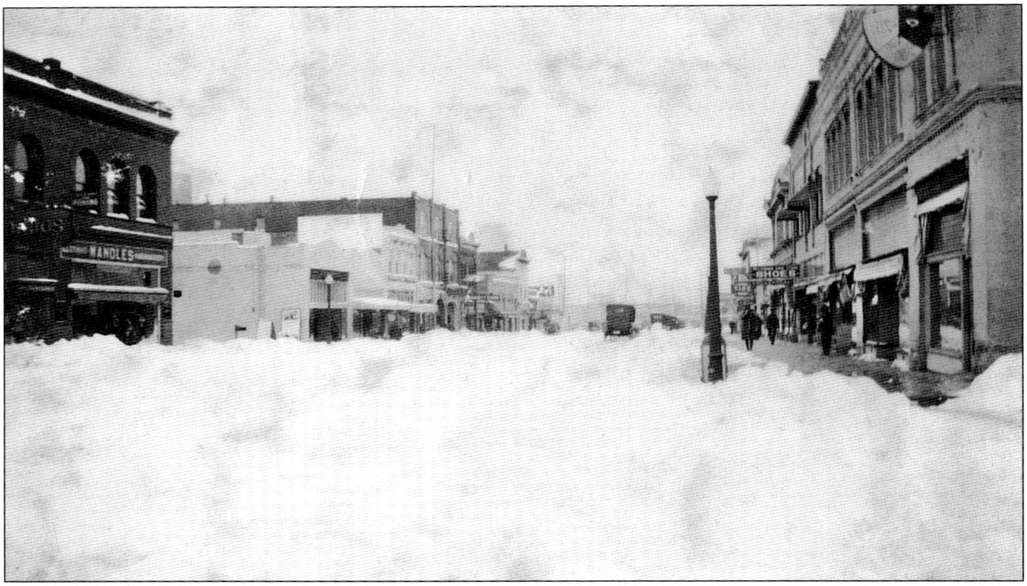

The decade began with deep snow blanketing Chehalis in December 1921. Only a few motorists traveled downtown on unplowed streets. The sidewalk at right has been shoveled, though, and pedestrians bundled themselves in warm clothes to visit merchants. At left is Mandles, a store selling such items as smart Kuppenheimer clothing, faultlessly tailored Griffon suits and overcoats, Florsheim or Just Wright shoes, and peerless Stetson and Gordon hats. Henry "Hy" Mandles, a former newspaperman, arrived in Chehalis from Colorado around 1911 and opened the clothing store. The other photograph, taken December 18, 1921, from Market Street, shows snow covering trees and homes. St. Helen Hospital is at the center.

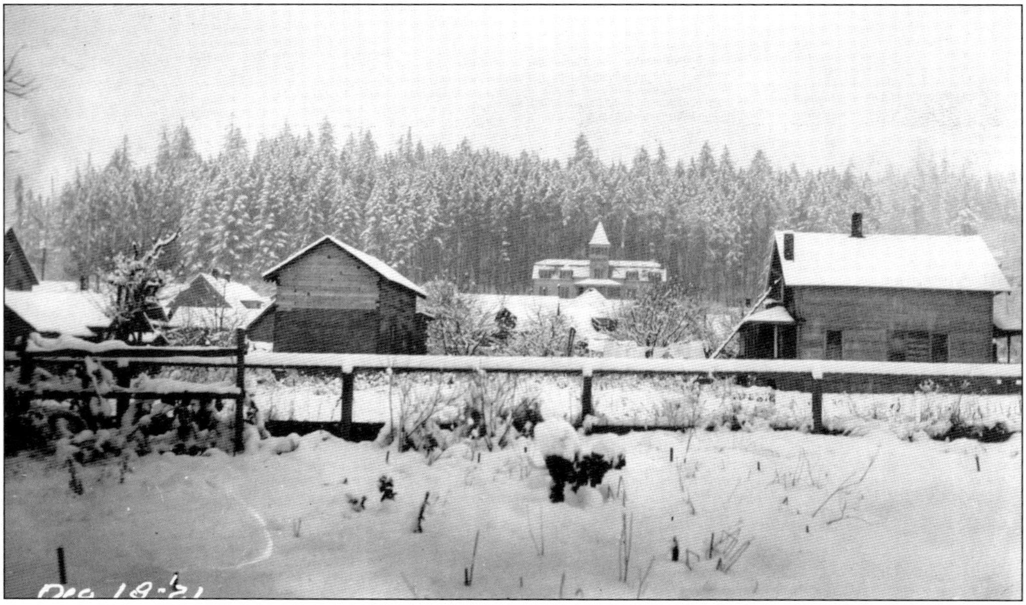

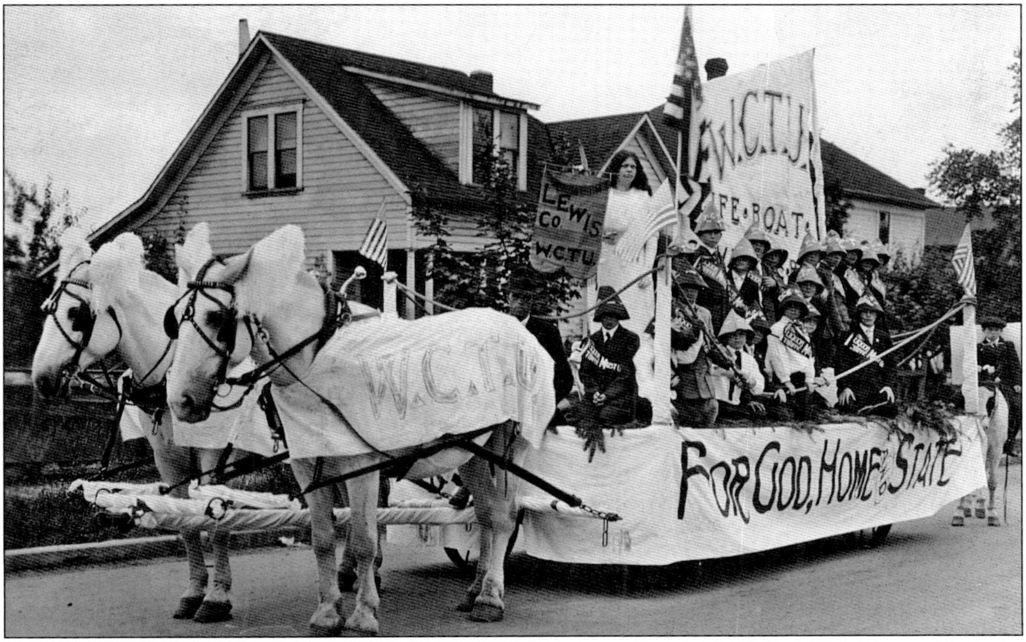

Members of the Lewis County Woman's Christian Temperance Union ride on a float in a Chehalis parade before 1920. The people on the decorated "Life Boat" float pulled by two horses are unidentified. The large banner reads, "For God, Home and State," while the children, members of the Youth Christian Temperance Union, wear YCTU hats and sashes stating, "Liquor Traffic Must Go!" In the other photograph, taken by Dan Bush around 1927, Lewis County sheriff Edward Deggeller and his deputies arrest bootleggers at the site of a still in an unknown location about 1927.

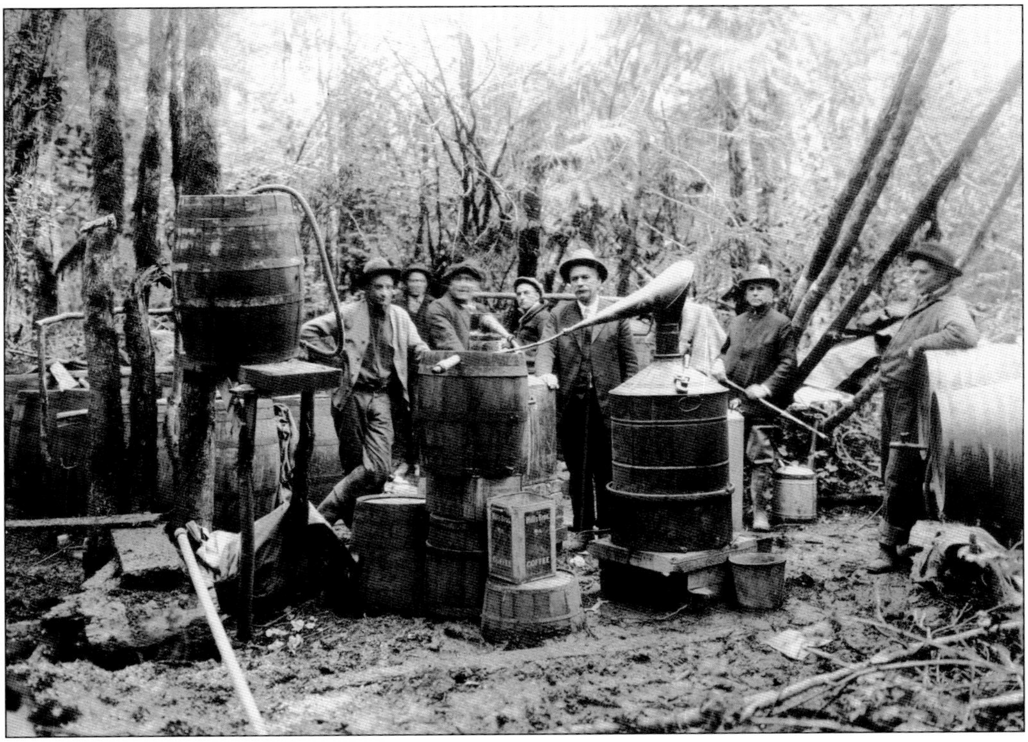

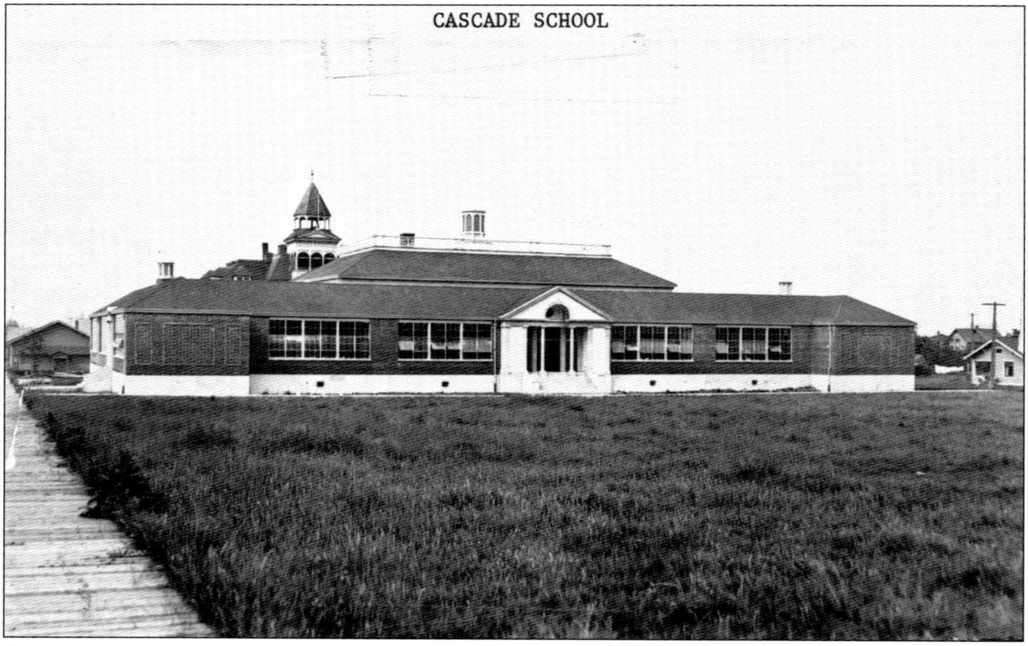

Cascade School in Chehalis was built around 1922. This photograph shows the wooden sidewalk on the left, where Third Street is today. The building in the background with the tower is the old original East Side School, which was moved to that location from a downtown lot in the School Block about 1912.

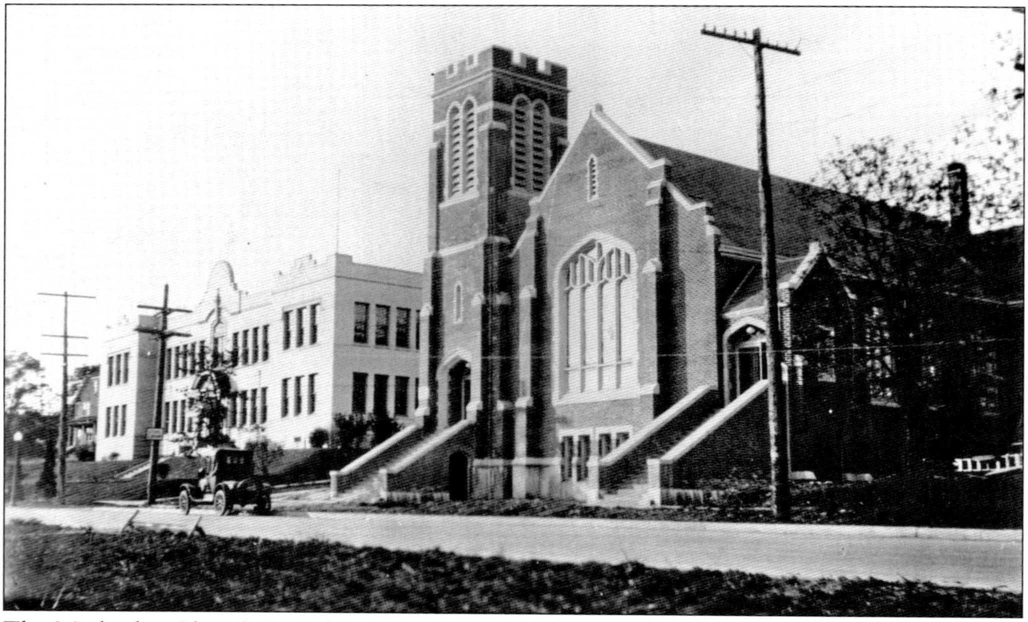

The Methodist Church (now known as the United Methodist Church) was constructed at the corner of Market and East Main Streets in Chehalis during the early 1920s and completed in January 1923. The photograph, taken around October 1922, also shows the Chehalis High School, at left, built in 1909.

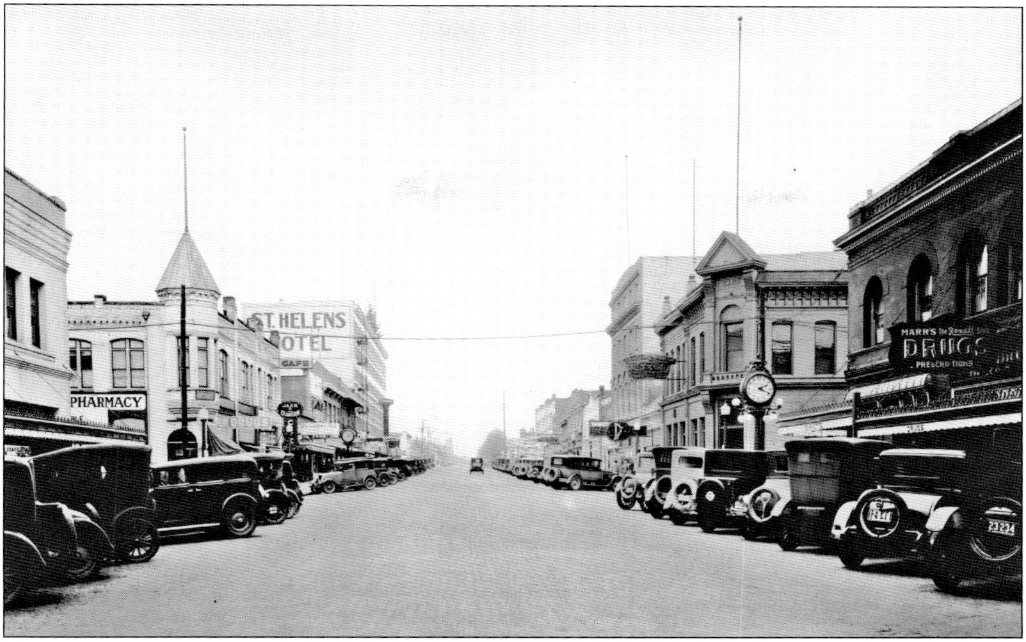

The photograph above, taken in about 1927, shows Market Street when it was the Pacific Highway, which later became Highway 99. The St. Helens Hotel underwent changes through the decades, evolving into the brick building seen on the left toward the center of the image.

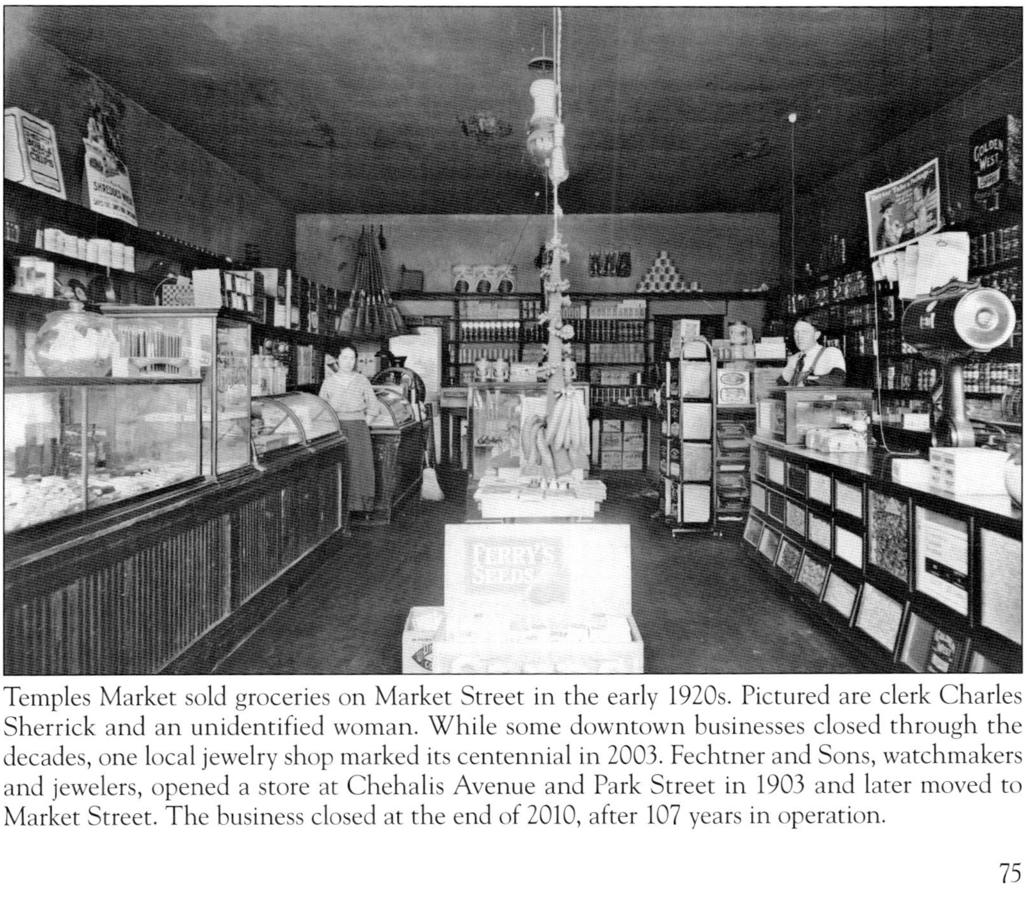

Temples Market sold groceries on Market Street in the early 1920s. Pictured are clerk Charles Sherrick and an unidentified woman. While some downtown businesses closed through the decades, one local jewelry shop marked its centennial in 2003. Fechtner and Sons, watchmakers and jewelers, opened a store at Chehalis Avenue and Park Street in 1903 and later moved to Market Street. The business closed at the end of 2010, after 107 years in operation.

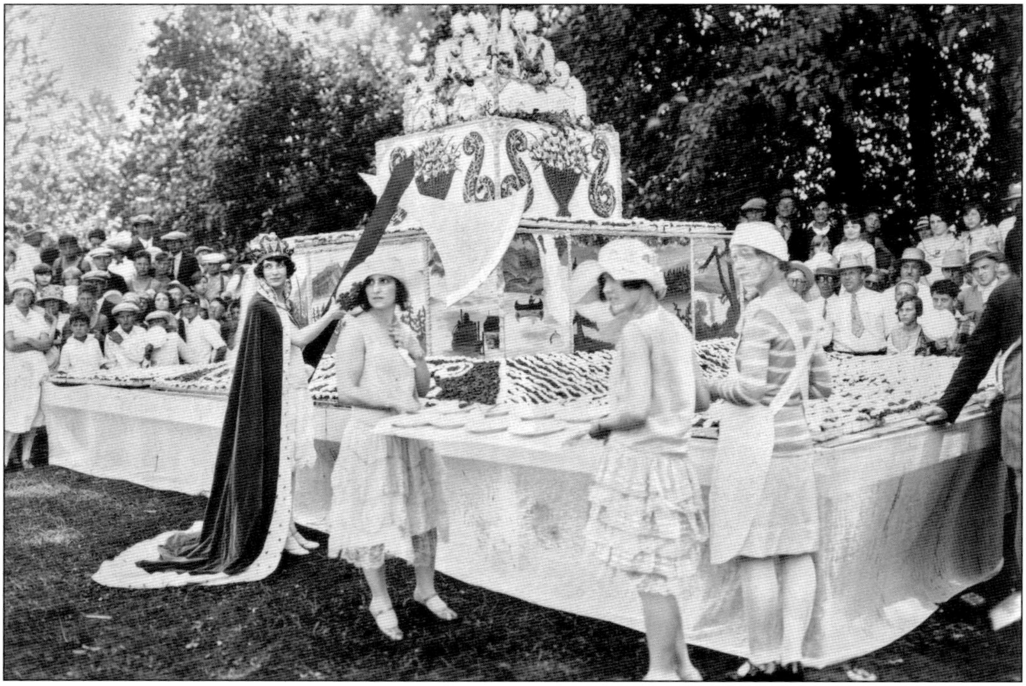

The World's Largest Strawberry Shortcake debuted on July 20, 1928, at the annual Lewis County Farmers and Merchants Picnic held at Alexander Park in Chehalis. Queen Agness Young and her court are seen near the cake, baked by the Daily Bread Shop on Market Street. In the photograph below, proprietor Ben Lutz and his crew are pictured holding a sign near the huge strawberry shortcake. The cake was baked and decorated by pastry chef G.W. Fulton, with scenes painted by his wife. From left to right are Leone Fulton, G.W. Fulton, Pete the baker, George Lutz, Garnet Lutz, proprietor Ben Lutz, and Howard Short.

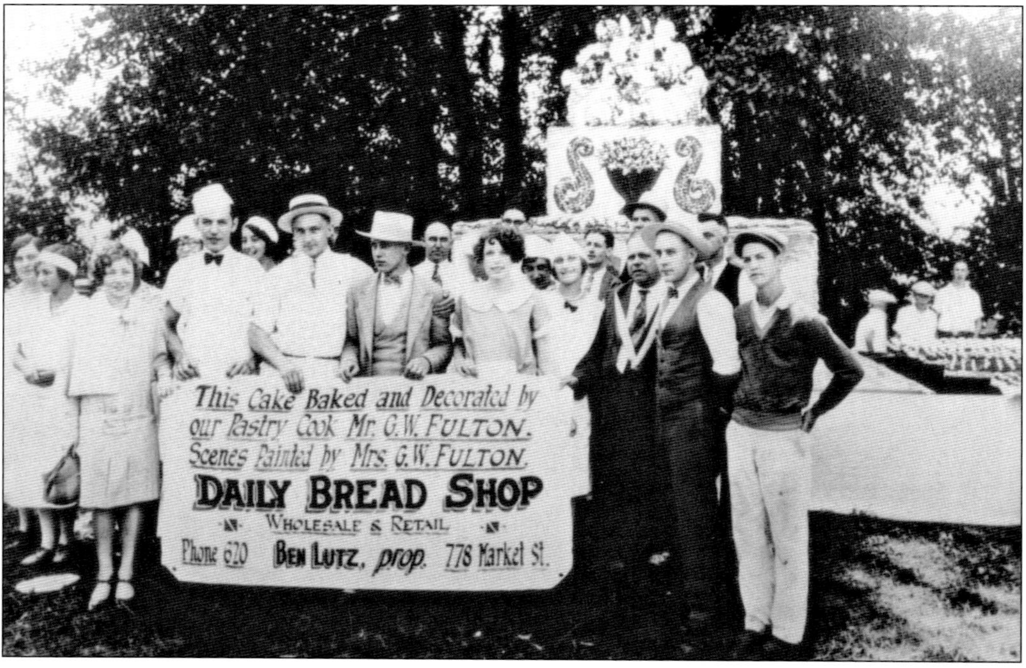

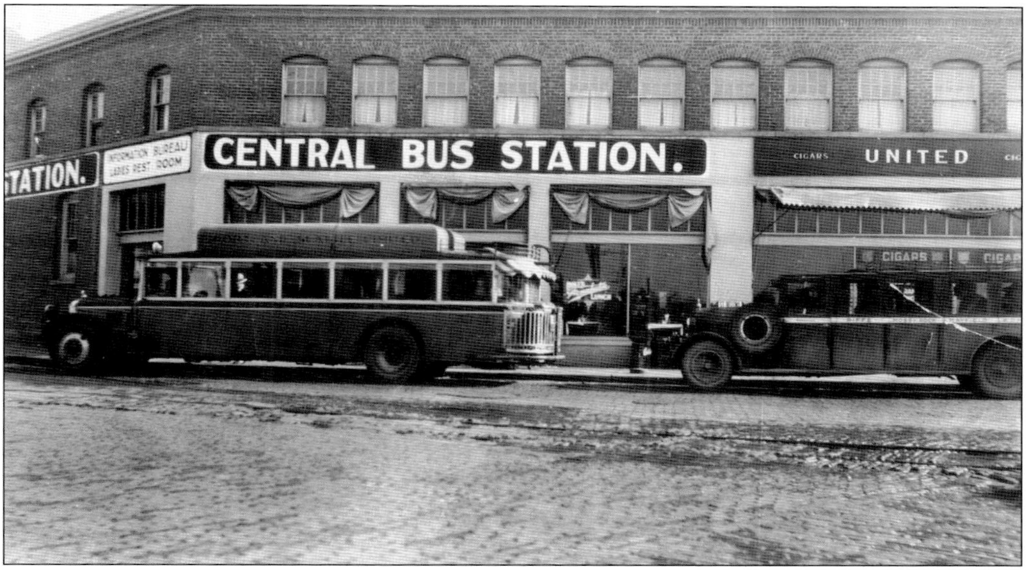

The Central Bus Station, located at the north end of Market Street in Chehalis beside a cigar shop, served as an information bureau. The latest buses, or stages, are seen at the station in 1921. The Terminal Hotel was upstairs on the second floor. In the photograph below, the Greyhound bus station at Market and Division Streets is seen in the 1950s. The Chehalis Theater is promoting the Glenn Ford movie *The Fastest Gun Alive* and *Our Miss Brooks*, starring Eve Arden, both released in 1956. The St. Helens Hotel is visible down the street.

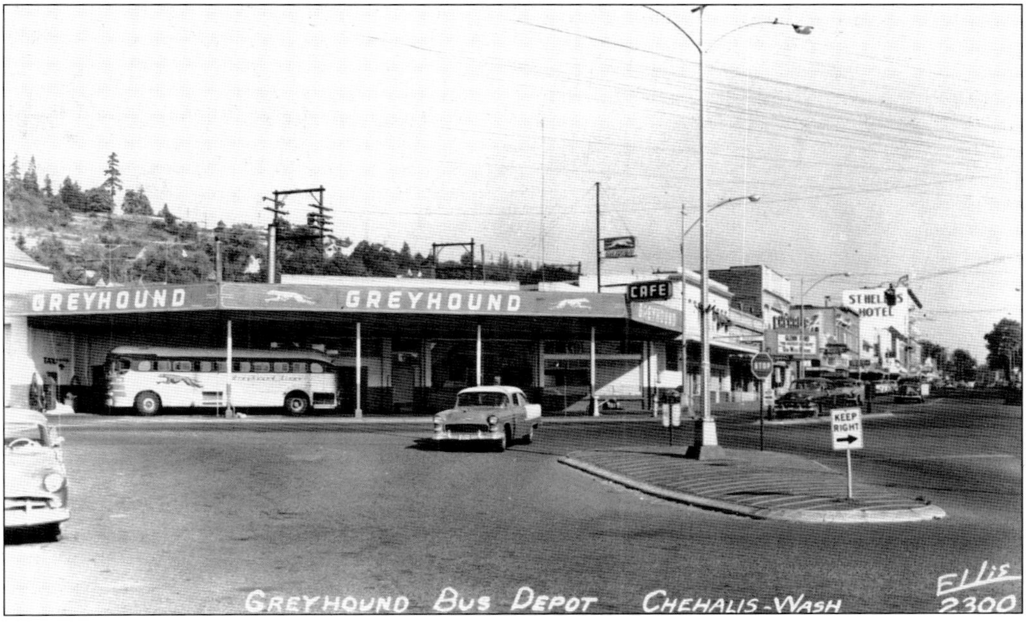

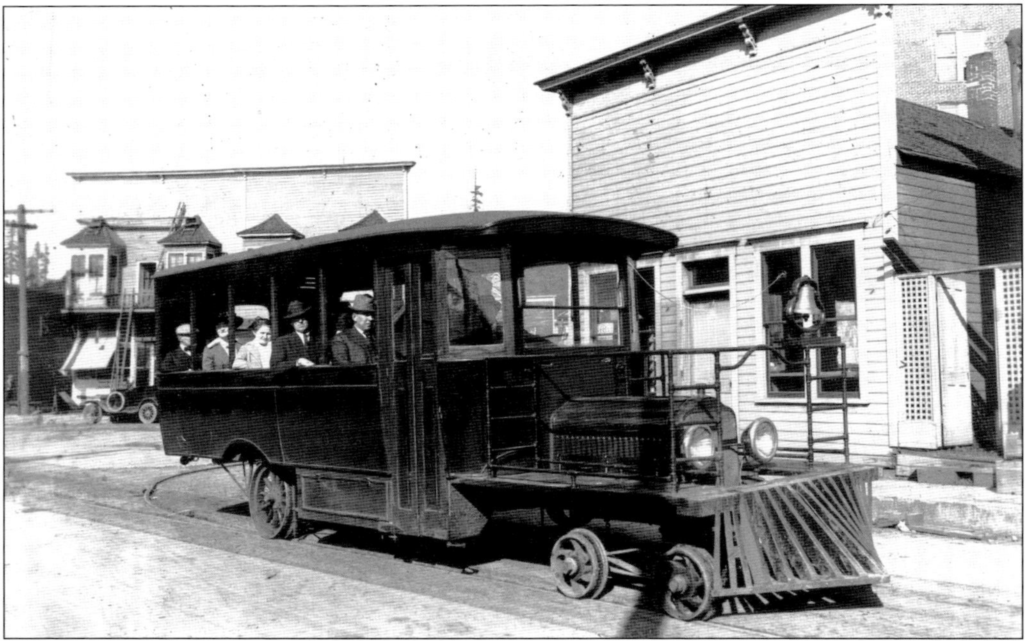

The open-air streetcar running on tracks down the streets of Chehalis in the 1930s had a cowcatcher on the front and a bell rung by a string to warn pedestrians and others. The passengers and buildings are unidentified. The cowcatcher, with slanted grating and pointed prow, was attached to the front below the headlights to clear obstacles from the tracks.

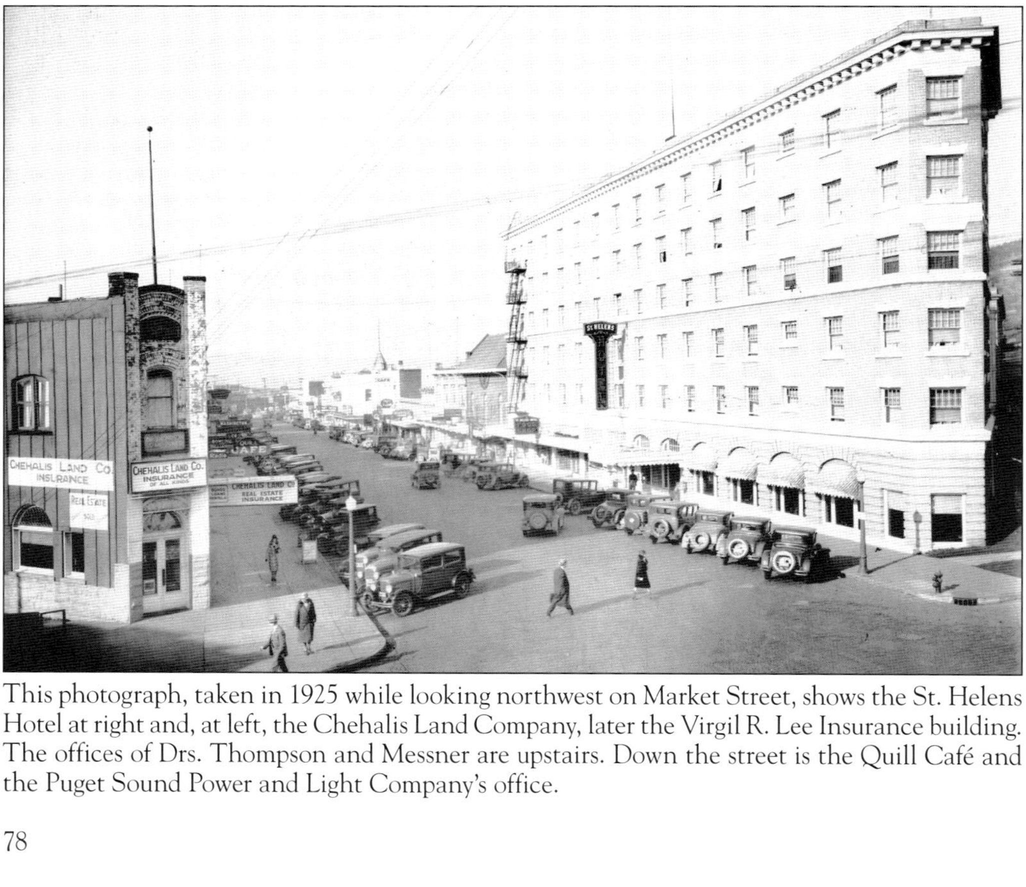

This photograph, taken in 1925 while looking northwest on Market Street, shows the St. Helens Hotel at right and, at left, the Chehalis Land Company, later the Virgil R. Lee Insurance building. The offices of Drs. Thompson and Messner are upstairs. Down the street is the Quill Café and the Puget Sound Power and Light Company's office.

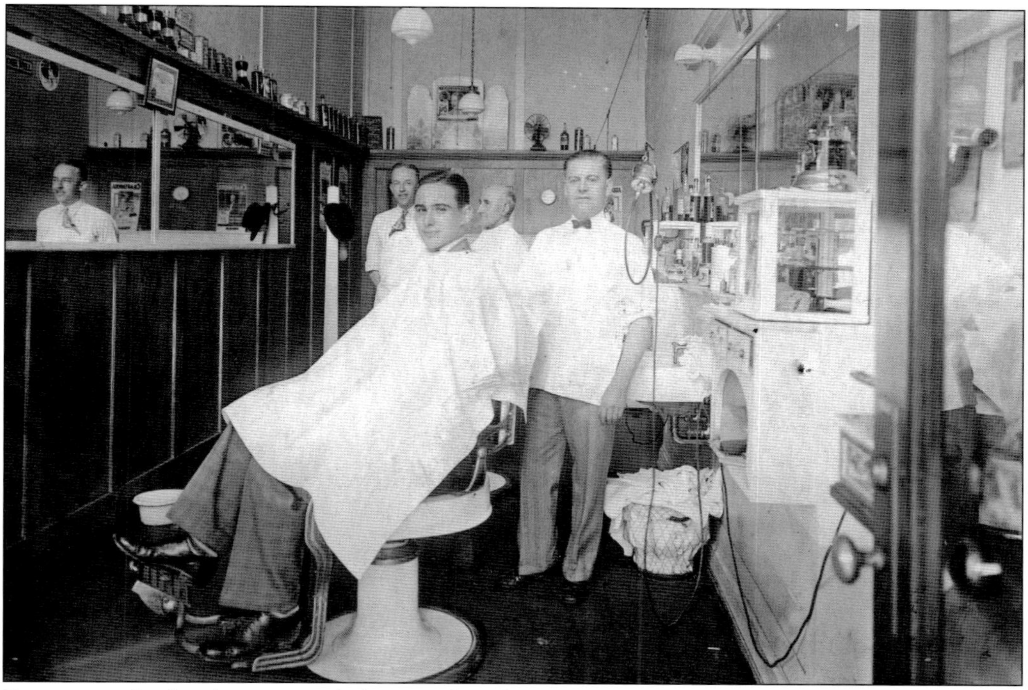

Downtown barbershops provided more than haircuts as patrons caught up on news and the goings-on of city residents. The proprietors of Terminal Barber Shop at 774 Market Street clipped the cowlicks of several generations of men. Seen in the late 1920s are barbers Charlie Osborne, left, and Guy L. Dunavan, wearing ties as they trimmed and styled the hair of unidentified customers. Osborne retired in 1972, after 45 years in the barber business, and died August 25, 1983. Dunavan worked 47 years in the business and died November 6, 1970. In the photograph below, barber James Clampitt is seen in his shop at 842 Market Street around 1927 or 1928. His customer is unidentified.

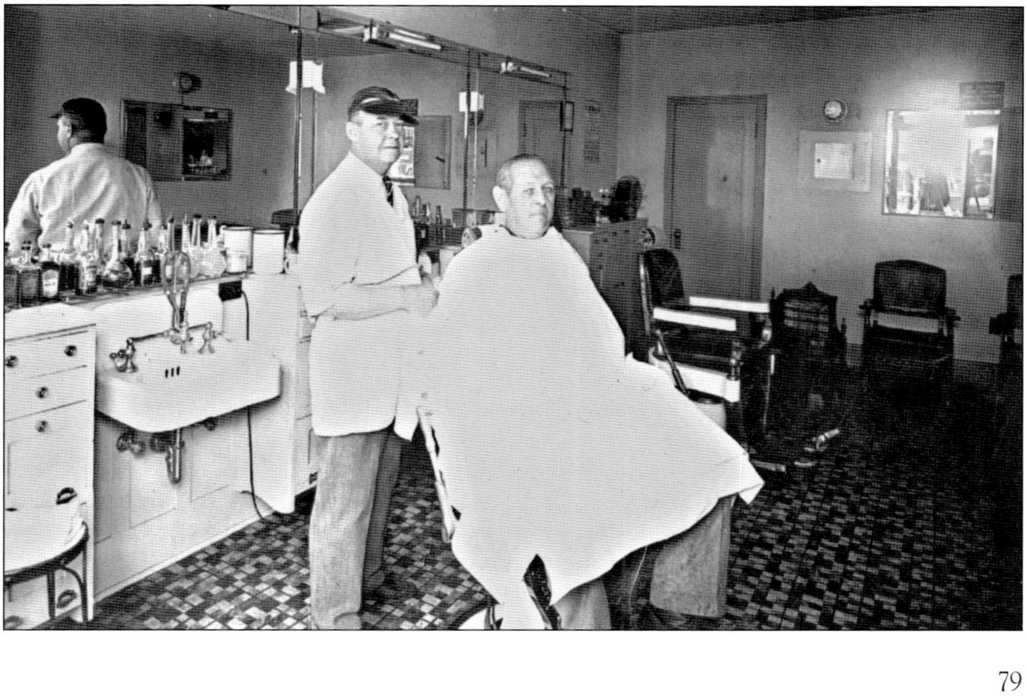

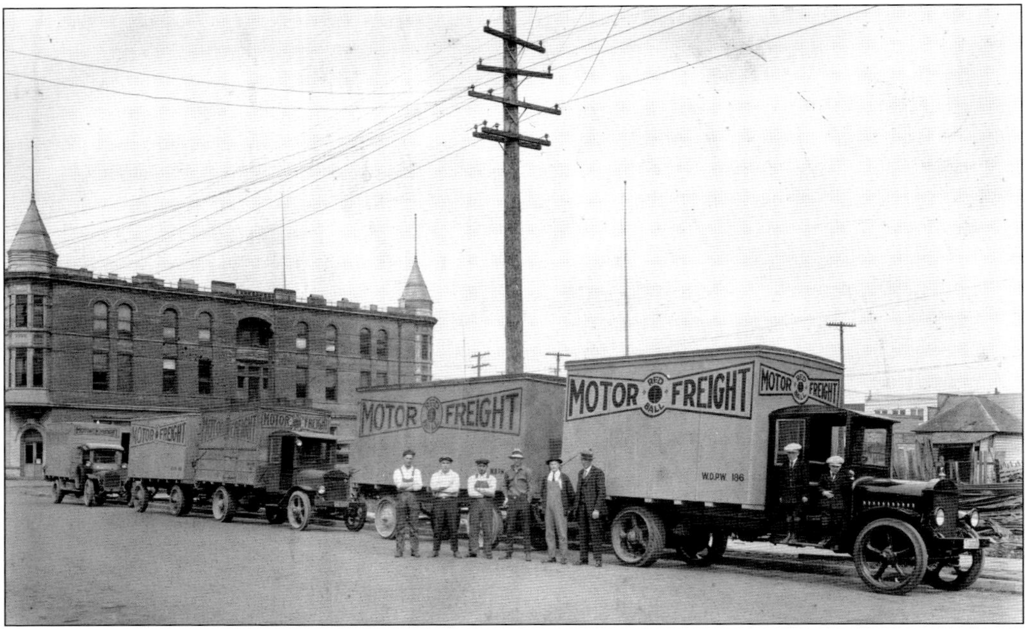

A 1924 fleet of Red Ball Motor Freight trucks is seen on Main Street in Chehalis. The company was owned by Earl Leigh Middaugh. Drivers, from left to right, are Roy Leason, Revere S. Epperson, Roy LaDue, Walt Logan, Kenneth Chase, and Earl "Pat" Middaugh. On the running board are Wyman and Don Middaugh, and in the background is the Grand Central Hotel built by Eliza (Tynan) Saunders Barrett.

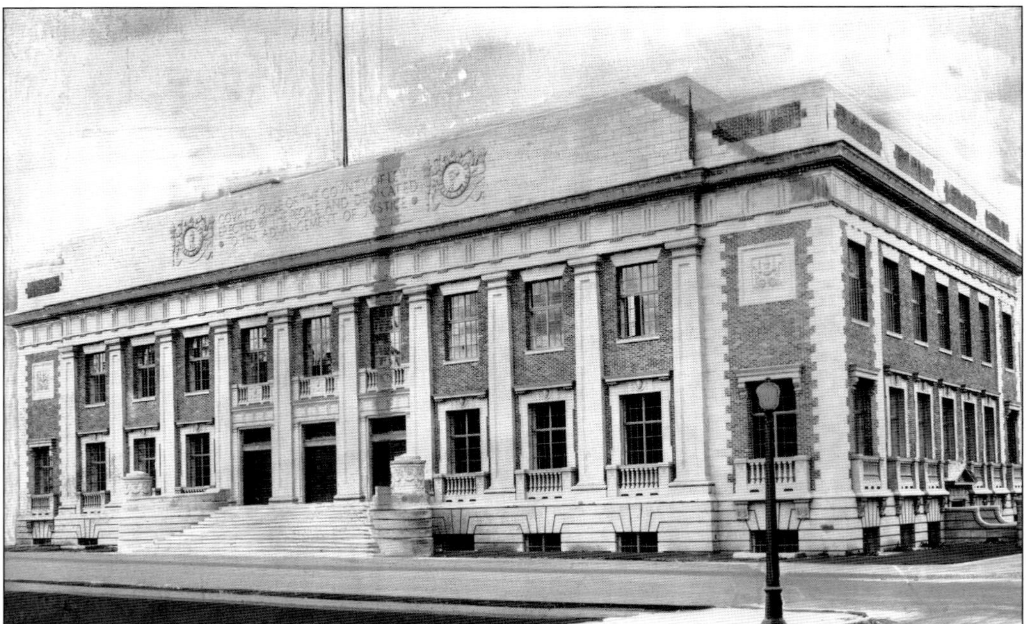

The Red Ball trucks are on the south side of the street, where a new courthouse was constructed in 1927. At that time, the county offices moved out of the old Grand Central Hotel, which had been used as a bank and business building before holding county offices. An annex was built across Main Street in 1977.

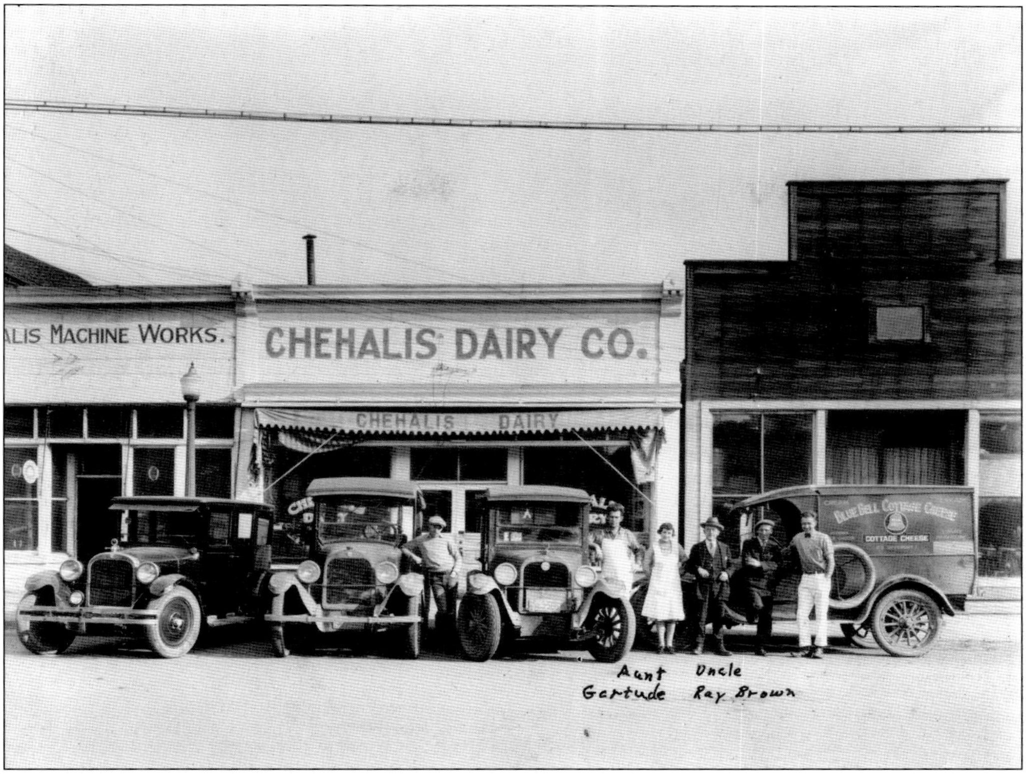

Gertrude Myer Brown (third from left), daughter of Theo and Elizabeth Myer of Alpha, and her husband, Ray C. Brown (on Gertrude's right), are seen in front of their Chehalis Dairy Company at 1066 Chehalis Avenue between 1920 and 1940. No other identification is available.

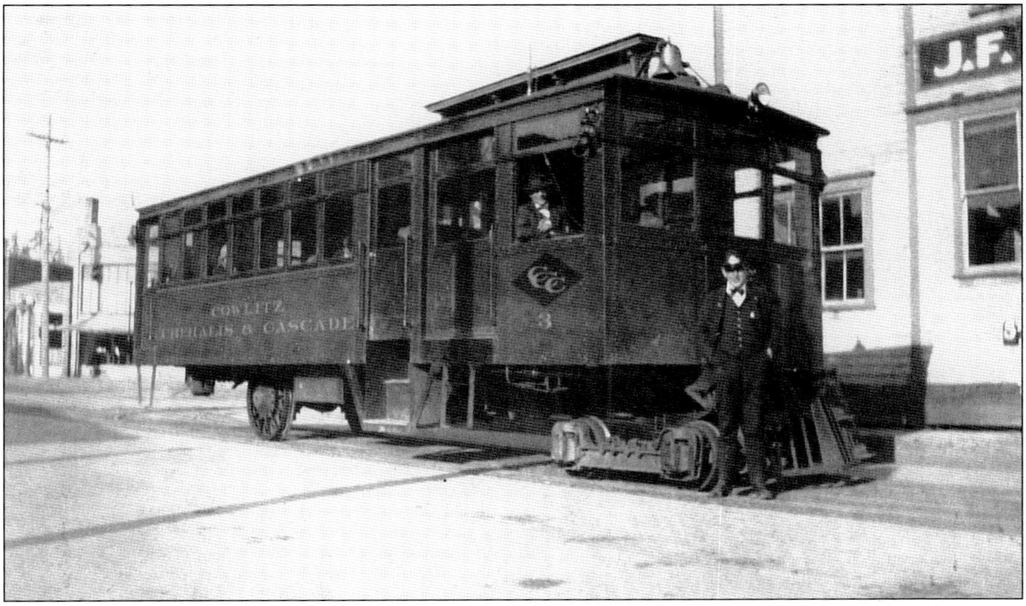

The *Galloping Goose* was a vehicle made of a truck chassis and a passenger cab that ran between Chehalis and Onalaska from 1912 to 1925 on track laid by the Cowlitz, Chehalis & Cascade Railroad. The people are unidentified.

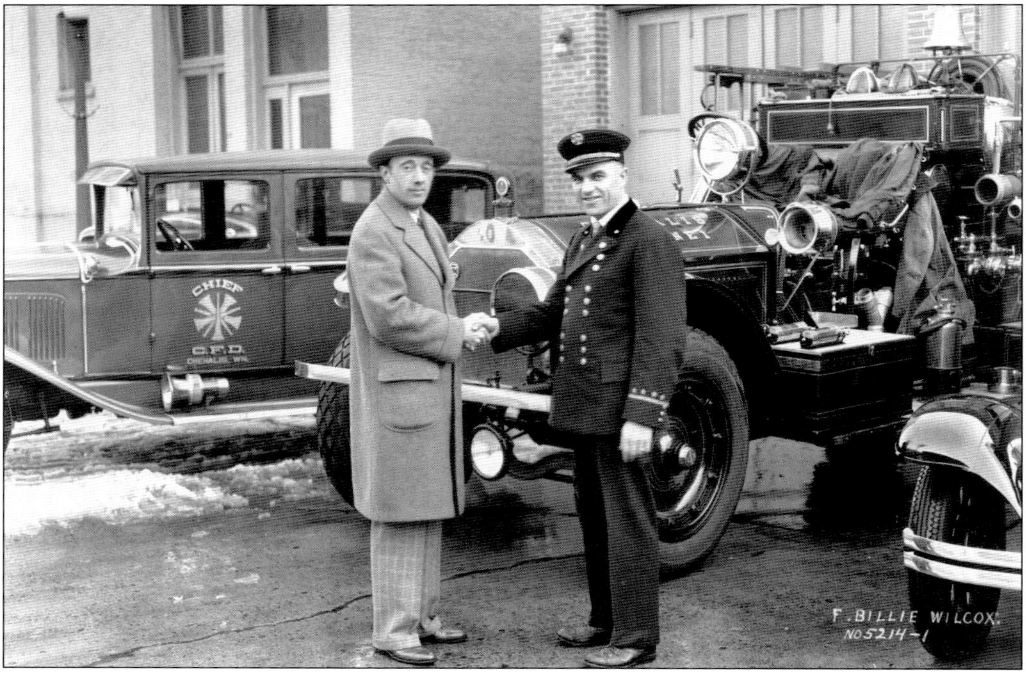

Chehalis fire chief E.C. Kuehner is seen in 1923 with a car dealer who sold the city its first chief's car, a DeSoto. The fire truck was the first pumper owned by the city. According to information at the Lewis County Historical Museum, the car dealer shaking the chief's hand "was crooked, and left Chehalis one jump ahead of the sheriff." The Chehalis Fire Department's building, crew, and engines are seen in a 1920s photograph below, with the police station and a train in the background. Pictured from left to right are Ernie Kuehner, Bill Thompson, Len Kuehner, Percy Connick, Elton Walters, two unidentified men, and Mayor John West at the far right. The department sold its old white truck to the Longview Junior Chamber for $29.

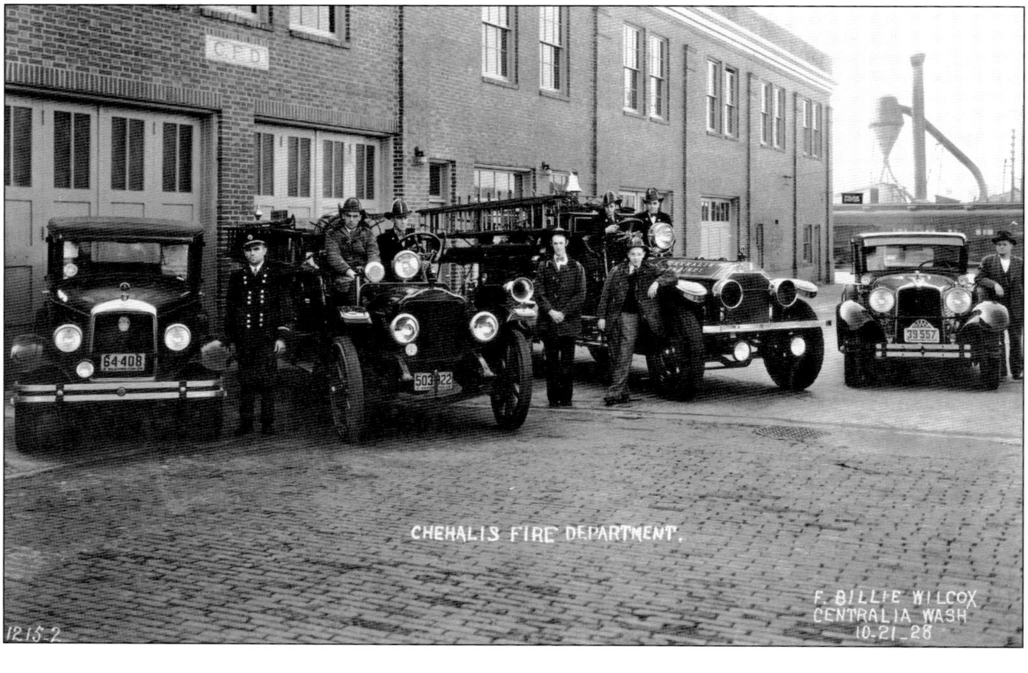

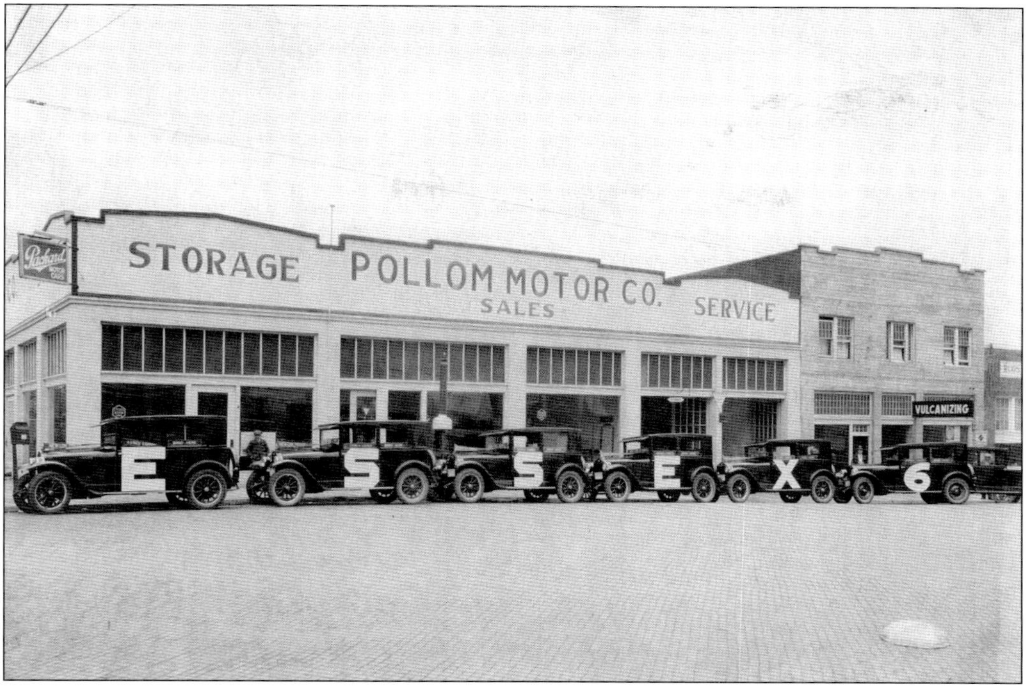

Pictured between 1922 and 1927 is Pollom Motor Company, Sales and Service near where Northeast Park Street and Northwest Cascade Avenue intersect with North Market Street. A row of Essex autos is parked at the curb in front of the salesroom.

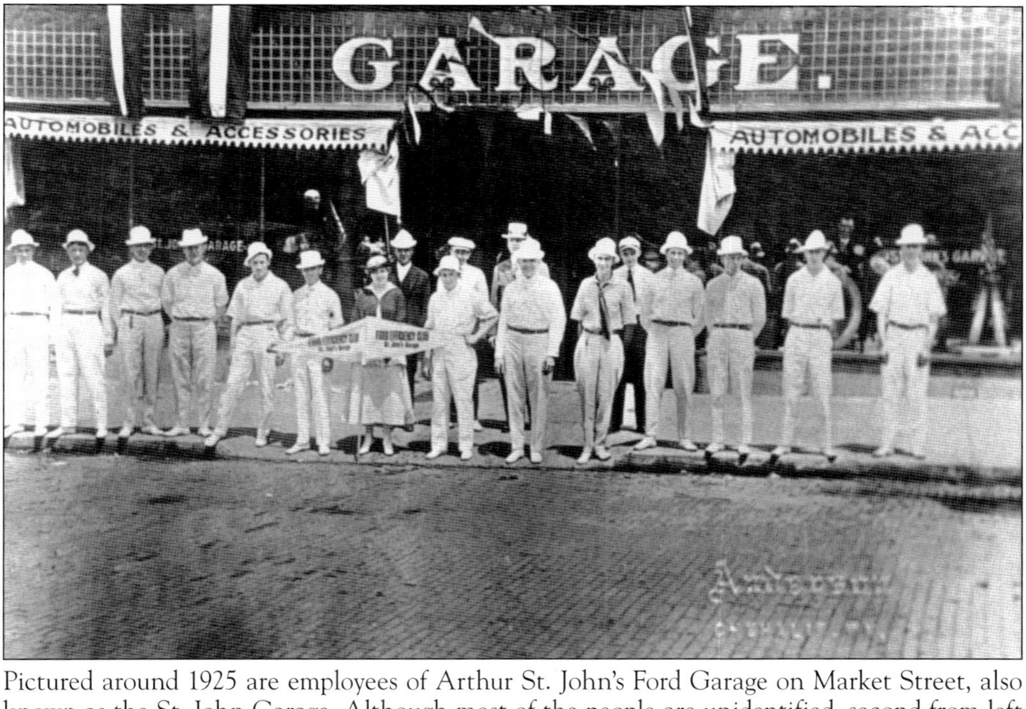

Pictured around 1925 are employees of Arthur St. John's Ford Garage on Market Street, also known as the St. John Garage. Although most of the people are unidentified, second from left in the back row and wearing a flat cap is Frank Lipscomb. The tall man to the right of Lipscomb is owner Arthur St. John.

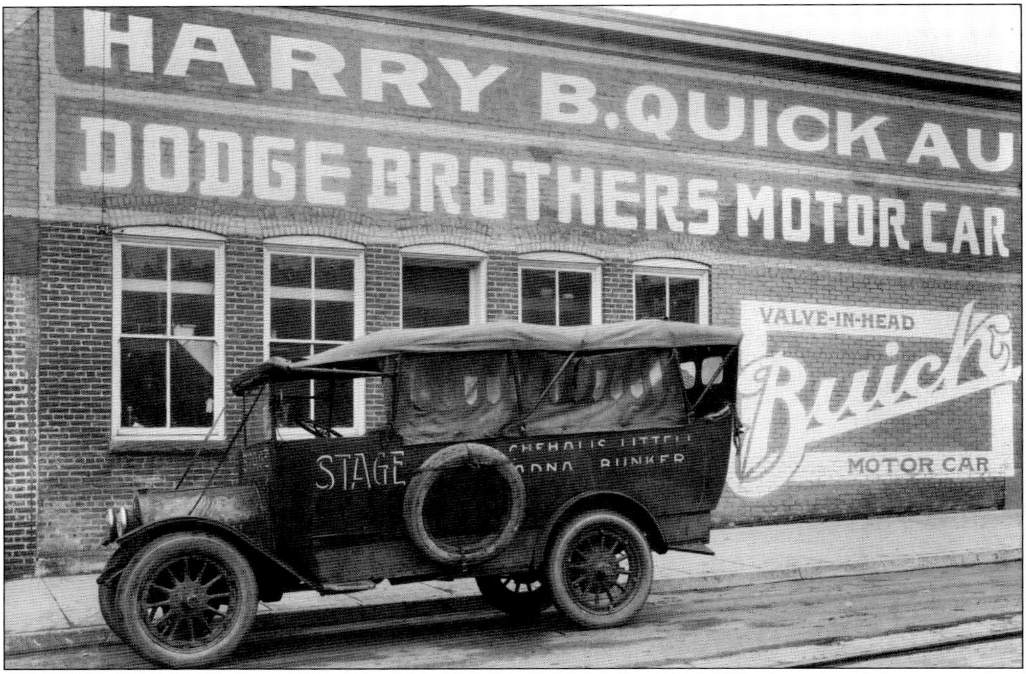

Harry B. Quick, a well-known sportsman and county official, operated a harness and saddlery shop that sold automobiles and sporting goods at the corner of Northeast Park Street and Northwest Pacific Avenue. He also ran a motor stage serving Chehalis, Littell, Adna, and Bunker in a revamped touring car with side curtains. An October 1929 advertisement in the *Chehalis Bee-Nugget* reported "he pushed the last buggy out of his shop and took on the Buick agency."

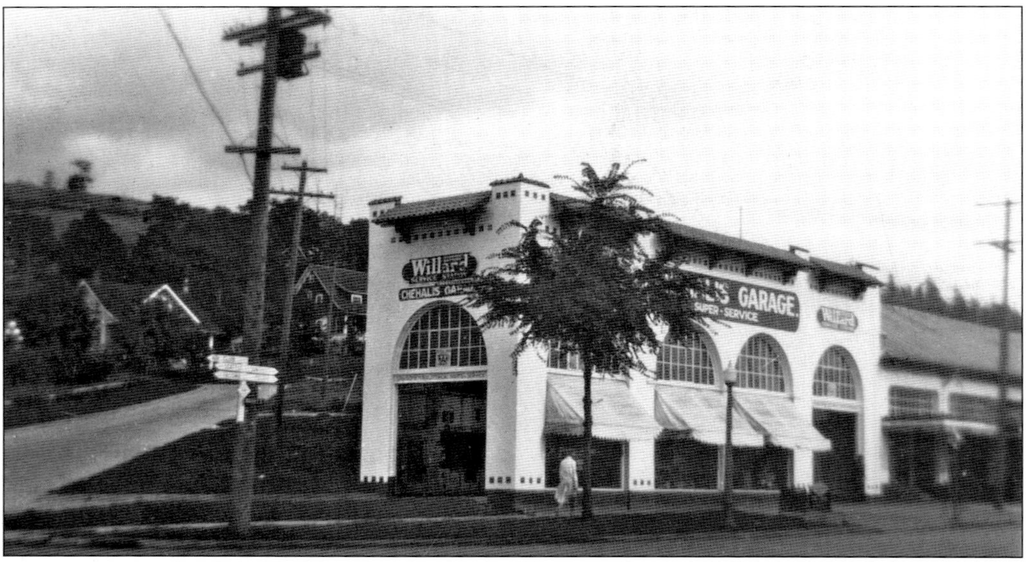

The John B. Coffman Garage, known as the Chehalis Garage, was built in 1919 at the intersection of Northeast Park and Market Streets. Coffman, who remained company president until 1957, carried a full line of auto accessories, such as tires, lights, and batteries, and operated the Chrysler and Plymouth dealership. In 1955, he sold out to Ralph Mauel, who operated it until moving out in 1969. Evergreen Savings later bought the property. Chehalis City Hall now occupies the bank building.

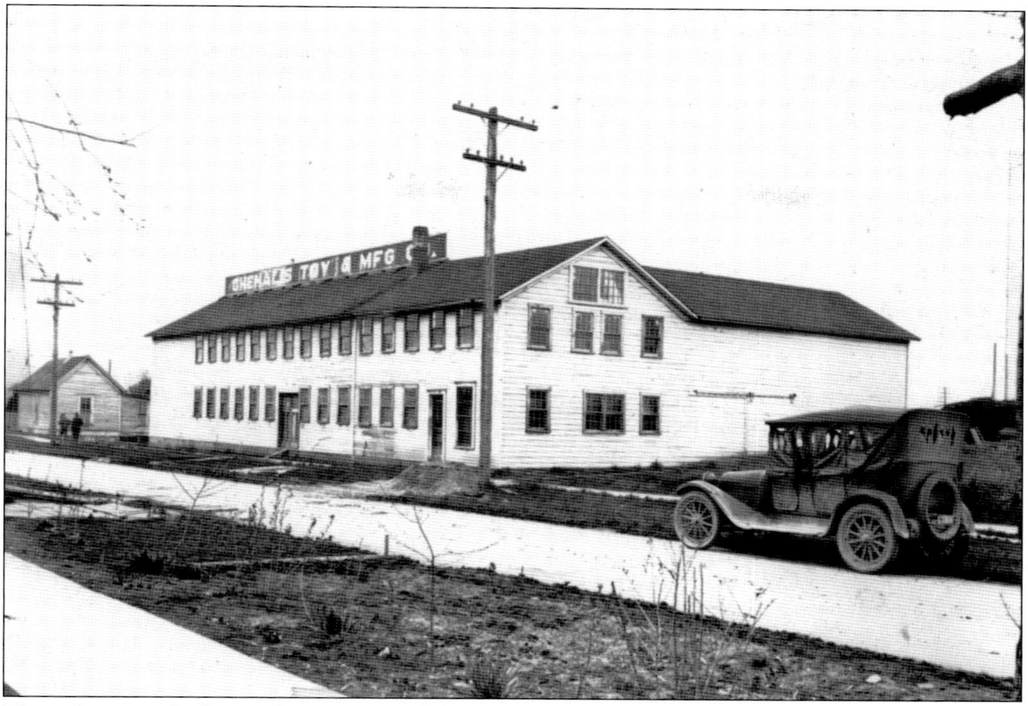

This photograph shows the exterior of the Chehalis Toy & Manufacturing Company, owned in 1922 and 1923 by William Van Woert, at 1279 Chehalis Avenue. The car may be a 1916 to 1920 Dodge.

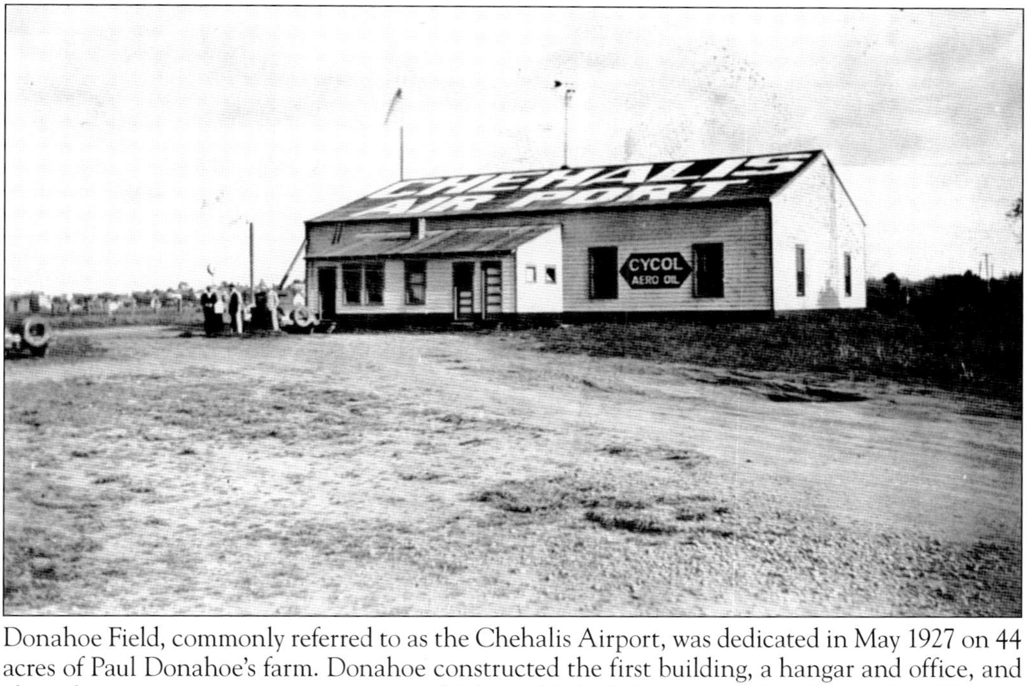

Donahoe Field, commonly referred to as the Chehalis Airport, was dedicated in May 1927 on 44 acres of Paul Donahoe's farm. Donahoe constructed the first building, a hangar and office, and cleared a grass runway. Lewis County, which established the airport, bought another 50 acres in 1928. A year later, the federal government recognized the airport as among "The Best in the West." The men outside the building in this 1928 photograph are unidentified.

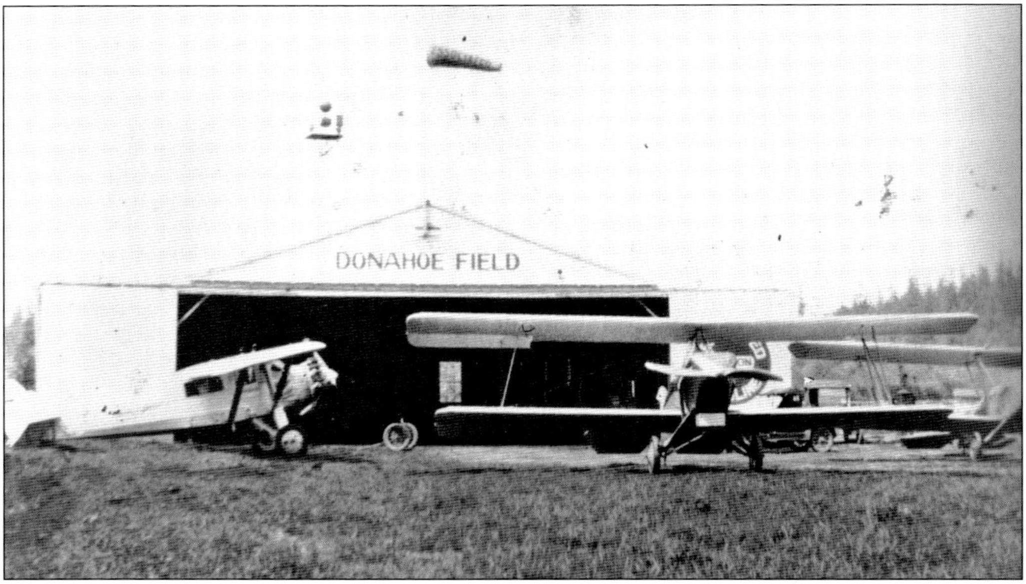

Three early planes are seen in front of the hangar at Donahoe Airport. The City of Chehalis joined with the county in joint ownership of the airport, which became known as City-County Airport. During World War II, the military took over the airport temporarily, and the government spent nearly $800,000 to develop two, 5,000-foot runways, dikes, and a drainage system. Arthur St. John, founder of St. John Air Service, owned the *Queen of the Cowlitz*, a Ryan airplane and sister ship to Charles Lindbergh's *Spirit of St. Louis*. Pictured near the airplane are John West, Chehalis mayor (left), and Arthur St. John. The men in the back are not identified. St. John, who established St. John Motor Company in 1907, became the first president of the Central Broadcasting Company, operator of KELA radio station, and built and owned the San Juan Apartments.

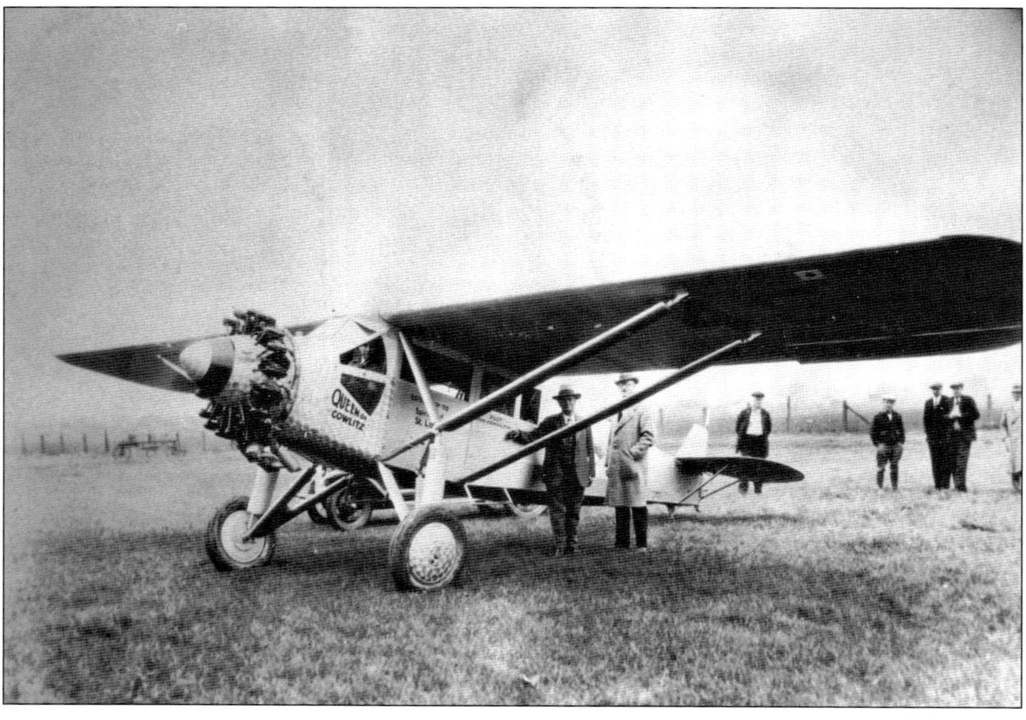

Seven

The Depression Era

After a relatively flood-free decade, heavy rains in December 1933 brought on swelling of the Chehalis and Newaukum Rivers that swept floodwaters across Alexander Park, covered the Ocean Beach Highway, and submerged the road between Centralia and Chehalis.

It rained 26 out of 31 days in December 1933, dumping 22.12 inches on Chehalis—nearly half of the average annual rainfall and still the highest monthly rainfall ever recorded in the Twin Cities. Before the flood, a wonderfully cheeky letter from E.A. Linscott appeared in the April 6, 1933, *Centralia Daily Chronicle*, in which he said it was a disgrace to have the county seat in Chehalis with so much frequent flooding. "People don't want to come in rowboats to pay their taxes," he said.

Six years later, a newspaper reported that the Elma Community Chamber planned to lead efforts to form a flood control district in Grays Harbor, Lewis, and Thurston Counties, all affected by Chehalis River flooding. Similar discussions are continuing today—more than 70 years later.

As the nation sunk into the Great Depression, and Washington's governor declared a bank holiday on March 2, 1933, the Security State Bank in Chehalis remained open. The banking supervisor declared Security State Bank to be financially sound. Conditions were bleak, though. The Lewis County treasurer reported more than $1.5 million in unpaid taxes. Chehalis citizens gathered in the city auditorium to decide what to do. After organizing committees to review local government expenses, they slashed more than $300,000 a year from county and school budgets.

Although demand for lumber slowed and agricultural prices plummeted in the 1930s, most residents planted gardens in the spring and canned fruits and vegetables to feed their families in winter. If they could scrape together two bits, they could see a movie at the St. Helens Theater. Or, in the late 1930s, they spent Saturday evenings dancing at the Playquato Ballroom.

The New Deal implemented by Pres. Franklin D. Roosevelt generated jobs for local workers during the 1930s. The Works Progress Administration (WPA) spent $45,000 renovating the fairgrounds and constructing a horse barn. The Civil Works Administration built an addition at the rear of the Carnegie Library for a children's room. And the WPA constructed the Chehalis post office on Cascade Avenue and the Chehalis Scout Lodge at Southeast Third Street and Southeast Adams Avenue in Dobson Park.

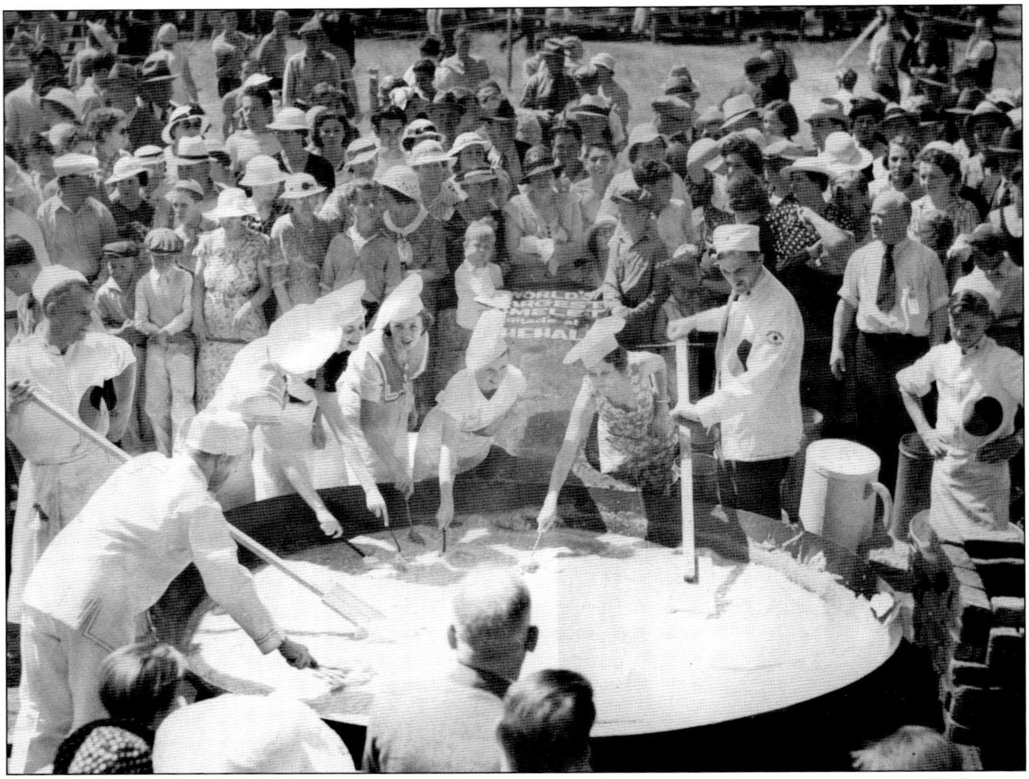

Businesses shut their doors at 11:00 a.m. July 24, 1931, as citizens from around the county gathered at Alexander Park for the annual Farmers and Merchants Picnic, where William Nelson and another Northern Pacific Railroad dining car chef from Seattle made the World's Largest Omelet using 10,000 eggs. The specially made frying pan, eight feet in diameter, later hung outside a museum at Long Beach on the Washington coast.

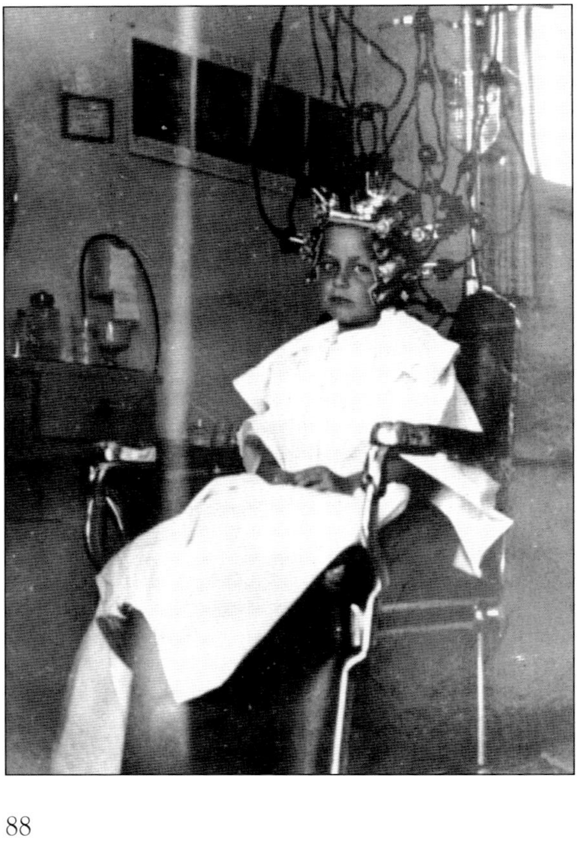

This child looks a tad unhappy hooked to a permanent wave machine at a beauty shop in the 1930s or 1940s. Perhaps she's worried about being electrocuted. The hairdresser rolled hair in curls clamped to wires that hooked into the machine. Heat dried the curls and gave them a long-lasting wave.

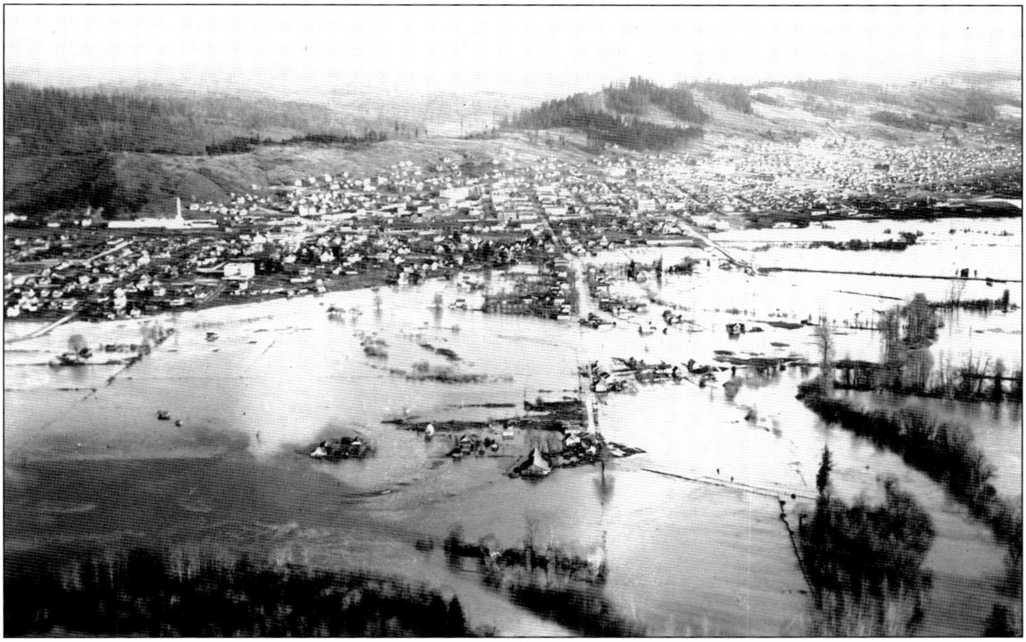

Saunders Bottom retained its soggy reputation as more flooding occurred in Chehalis during 1933, inundating roads, railroad tracks, and parks. The aerial photograph shows Chehalis on December 23, 1933, after heavy rainfall. It rained nearly every day that month. The December rainfall in Chehalis of 22.12 inches accounted for more than a third of the year's total rainfall of 59.29 inches. Floodwaters swamped Alexander Park, where the top part of a building shows amid the tree trunks. For the first time in 25 years, Chehalis was "mail-less" when floodwater kept trains out of the city for 33 hours. Washington State sustained $150,000 in damages to roads and bridges, while Lewis County's damage was between $35,000 and $50,000.

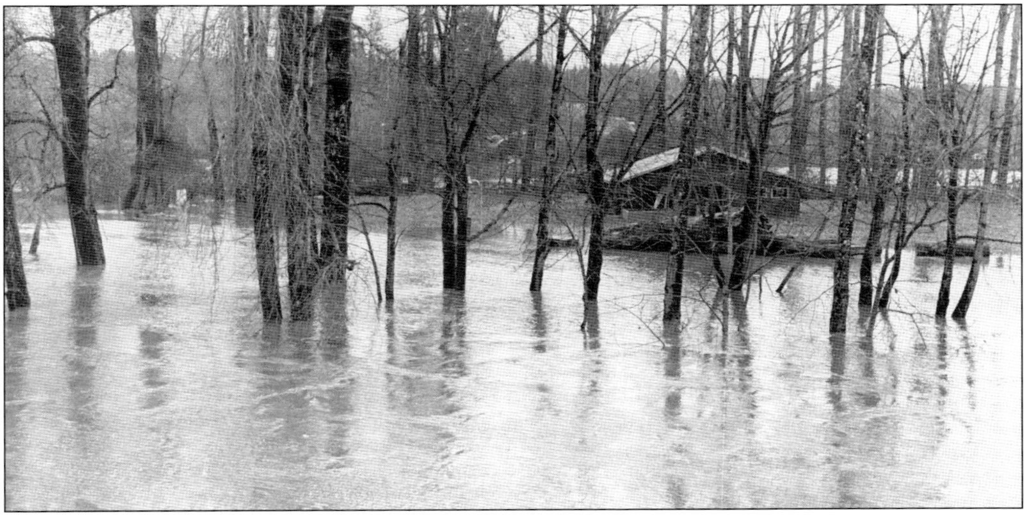

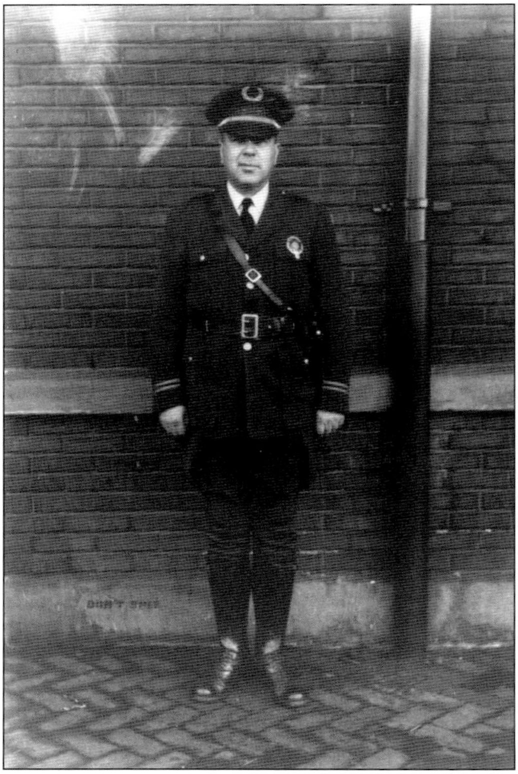

Chehalis police chief Thomas Murray, seen in 1939, served the city as a police officer for eight years and as chief for 24. He was born in England in 1889, retired around 1961, and passed away in 1975.

Local law enforcement officers and others pictured here around 1930 are, from left to right, (first row) Nort Wynn, deputy sheriff; Edward Deggeller, county sheriff; Perry W. North, Chehalis police chief; and Dave Mathis, Chehalis police traffic patrolman; (second row) Louis Lund, deputy sheriff; E.L. Coleman, deputy sheriff; John West, Chehalis mayor from 1923 to 1936; and an unidentified jailer; (third row) an unidentified reporter; J.A. Blankenship, deputy sheriff; James Sareault, prosecuting attorney; and John Parr, police patrolman.

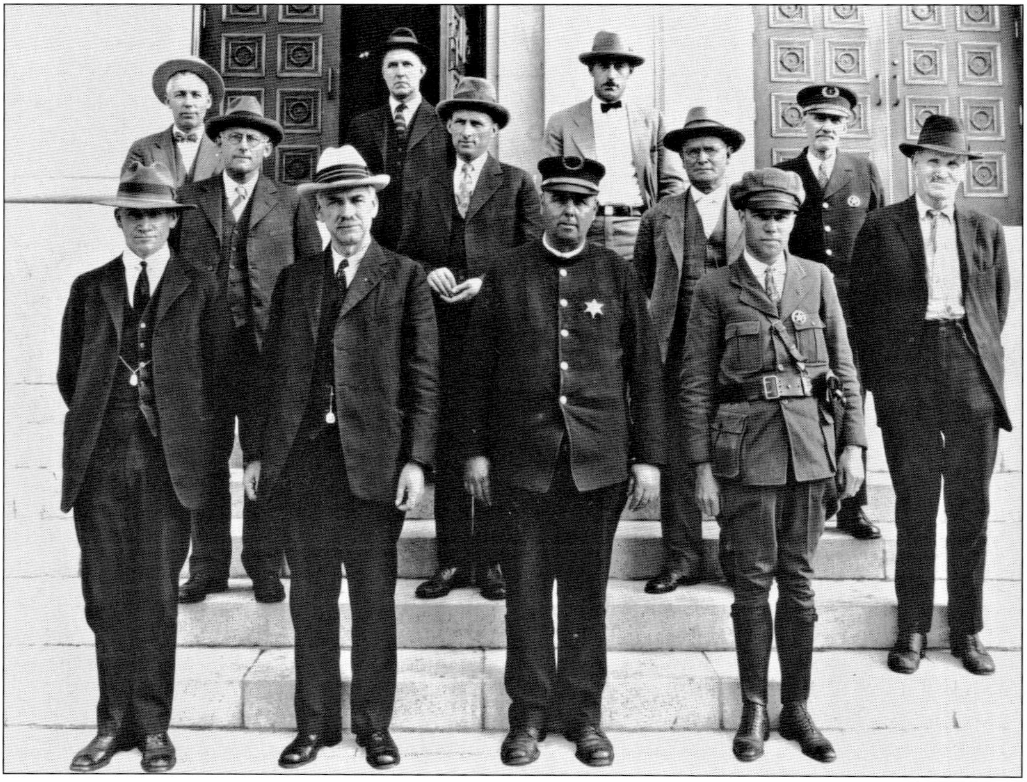

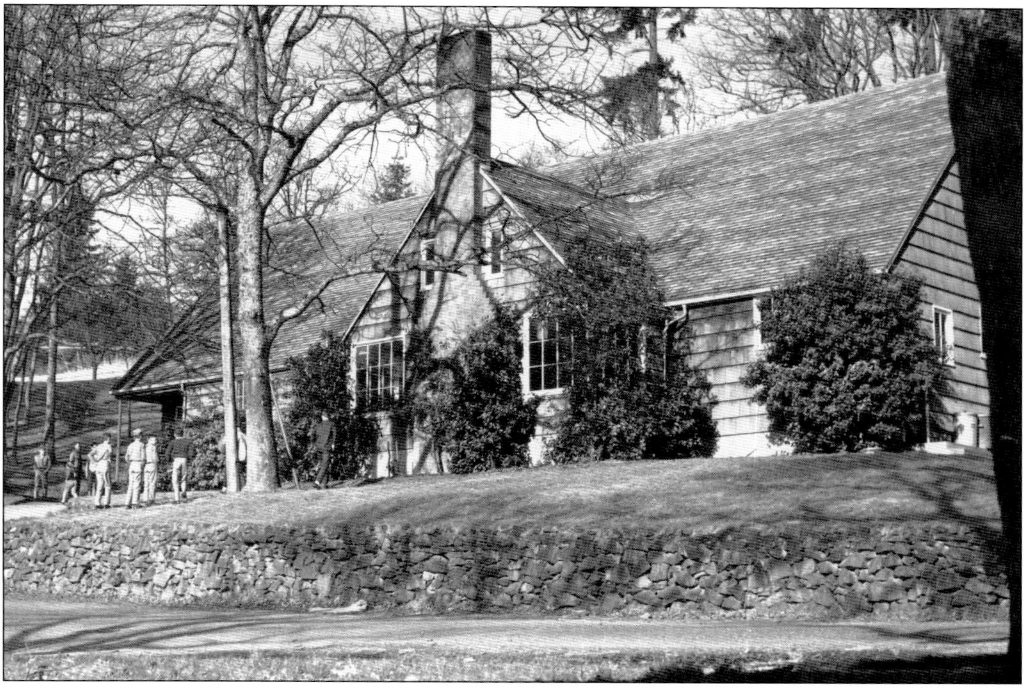

As part of the New Deal in the 1930s, the Works Progress Administration built the Chehalis Scout Lodge at Southeast Third Street and Southeast Adams Avenue in Dobson Park. The Assembly of God Church gathered in the meeting hall there from 1942 to 1951. The city owns the historic one-and-a-half-story building, which is still used today by the Boy Scouts, Girl Scouts, the Civil Air Patrol, and for city functions.

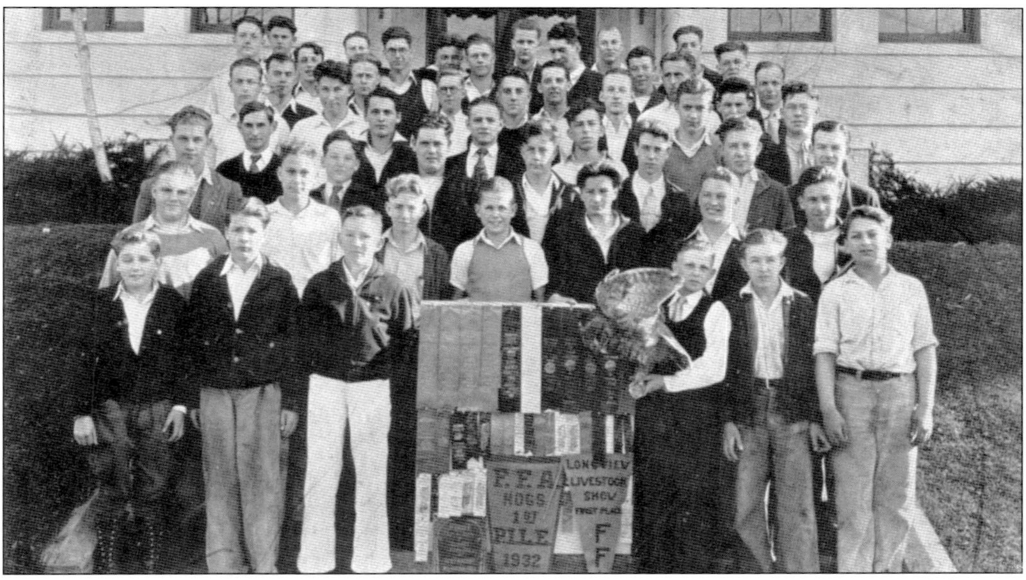

Although Chehalis continued to develop as a city, the surrounding countryside remained devoted to farming and logging. As such, the Southwest Washington Fair played an important role in the community, as did the Future Farmers of America (FFA). Students in the FFA are seen during a conference at Chehalis High School in the mid-1930s. Instructor Henry Porter is in the third row from the back, outside right. Jack Bennett holds the eagle in front.

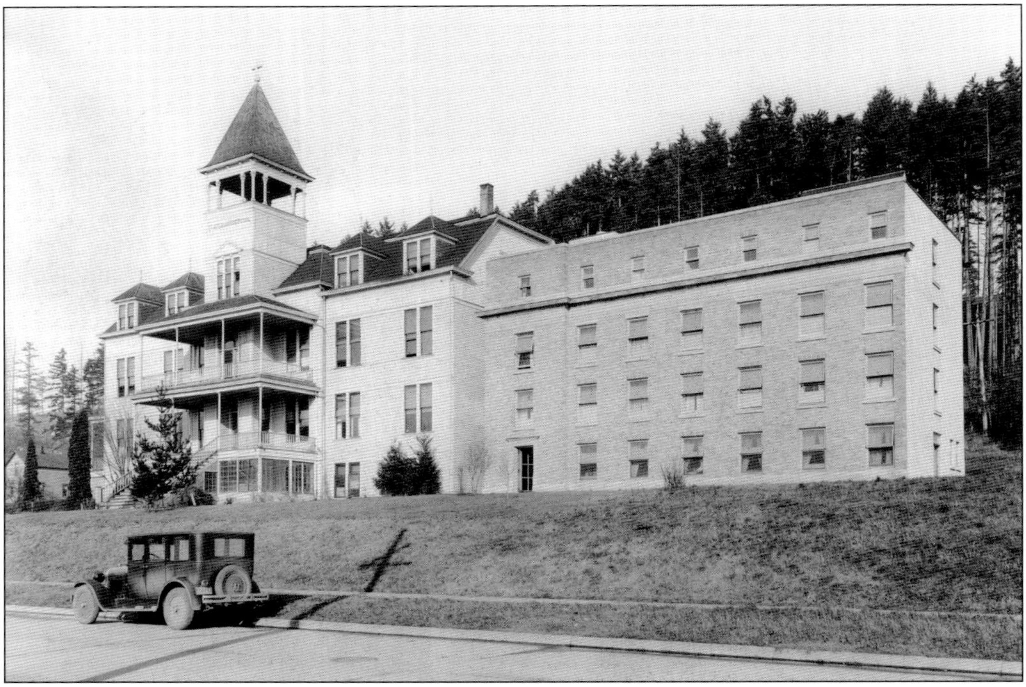

The St. Helen Hospital, initially constructed in 1907, was expanded during the 1920s. The original wooden building stands at left, beside the first brick addition on the right. An Essex is parked on the road in front of the hospital in this 1928 photograph.

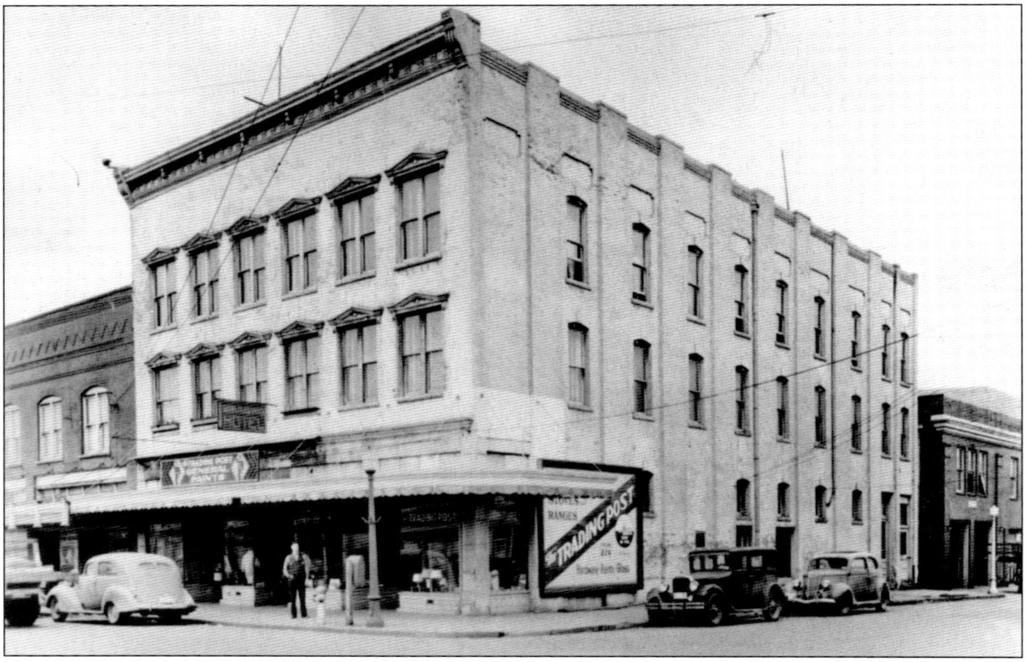

Standing in front of the Trading Post at the corner of Chehalis Avenue and Park Street in 1936 is Dan Harper. Upstairs, the Brunswig Hotel, originally the Chehalis Opera House, featured 48 apartments with hall bathrooms on each floor. At right is the fire department, and at far left is the John West Building, with the Eagle's Hall upstairs.

The marquee on the Fox St. Helens Theatre advertised the movie *Dawn Patrol* featuring Dick Barthelmess and released in 1930. The building was originally constructed by Arthur St. John for his Ford dealership, the St. John Motor Company. The theater opened May 12, 1924, with a tagline touting it as the "House of Hits." It closed in 1954.

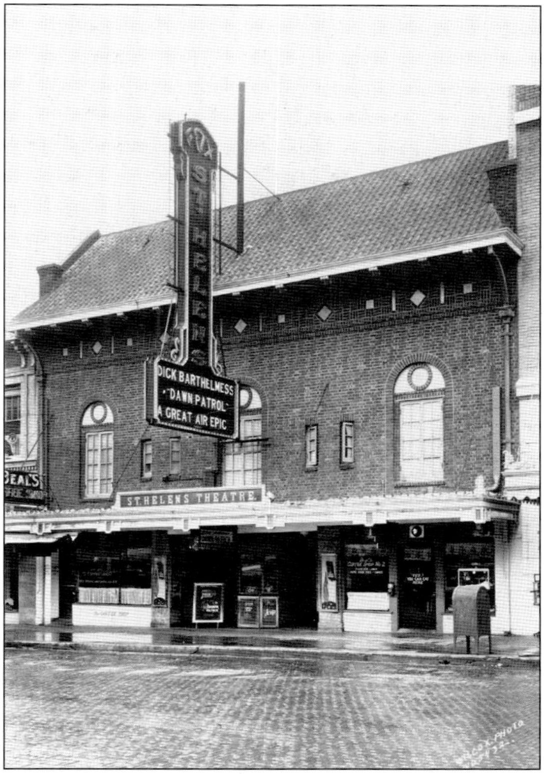

A glimpse inside the St. Helens Coffee Shop in the 1930s shows one of the community's most remembered native sons—Bill West, owner of the hotel and donor of property for construction of the W.F. West High School in Chehalis. From left to right, the waitresses are Lois Willett and Amy Clampitt, and the men are Claude Whitehead and Bill West.

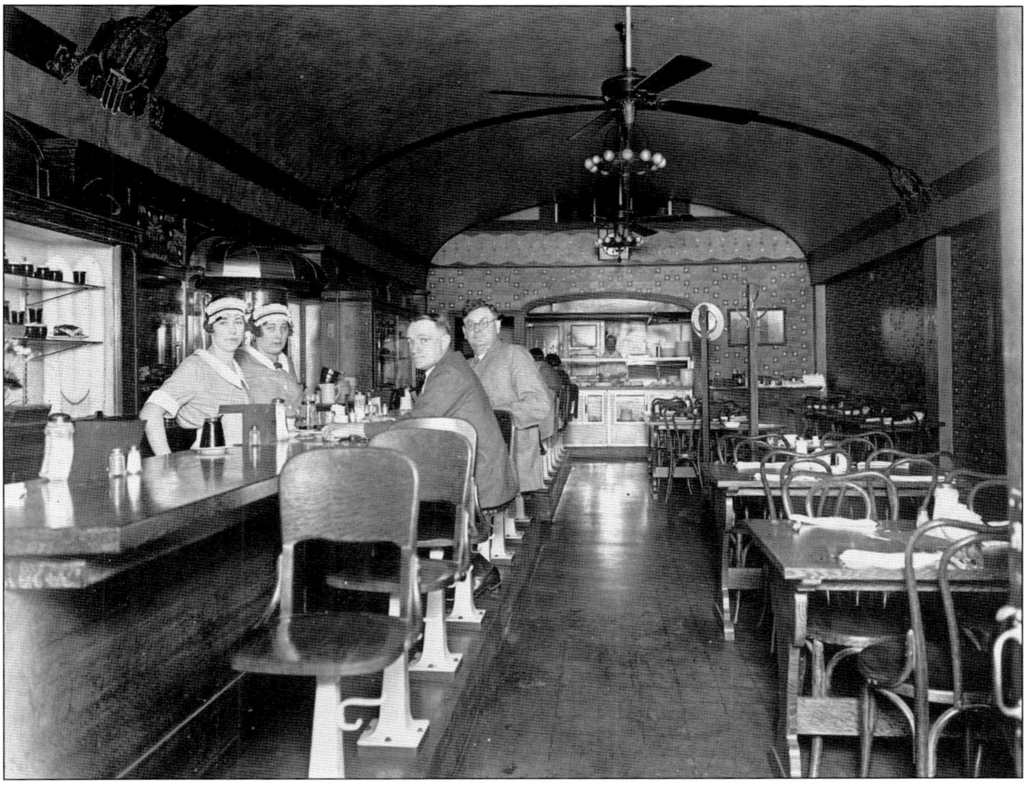

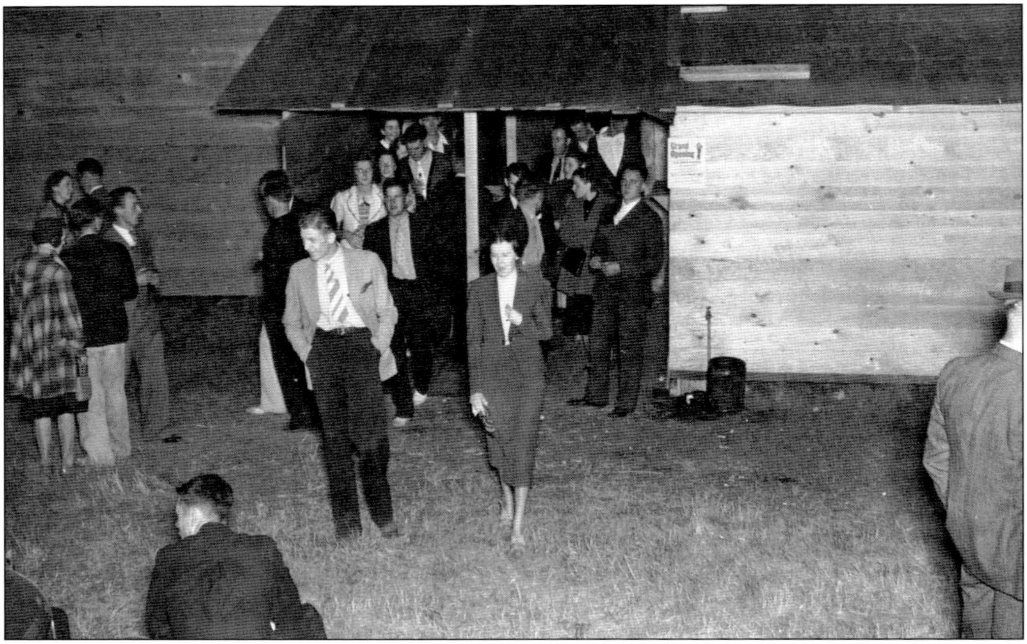

The Playquato Ballroom at Claquato opened in July 1938 as a dance hall and showcase for musical bands. The photograph shows a sign noting that this was the "Grand Opening." The image below shows members of a local band performing at the Playquato Ballroom. In the back are Leo Milanowski on trombone and Margaret Milanowski at piano. Standing at the front is Gunnar Halgren on violin. No other identification is available. The dance hall featured local talent into the early 1970s, when fire destroyed the building. A fiddle instrumental called the "Playquato Waltz," performed by local artist Chris Guenther, pays tribute to the legendary dance hall.

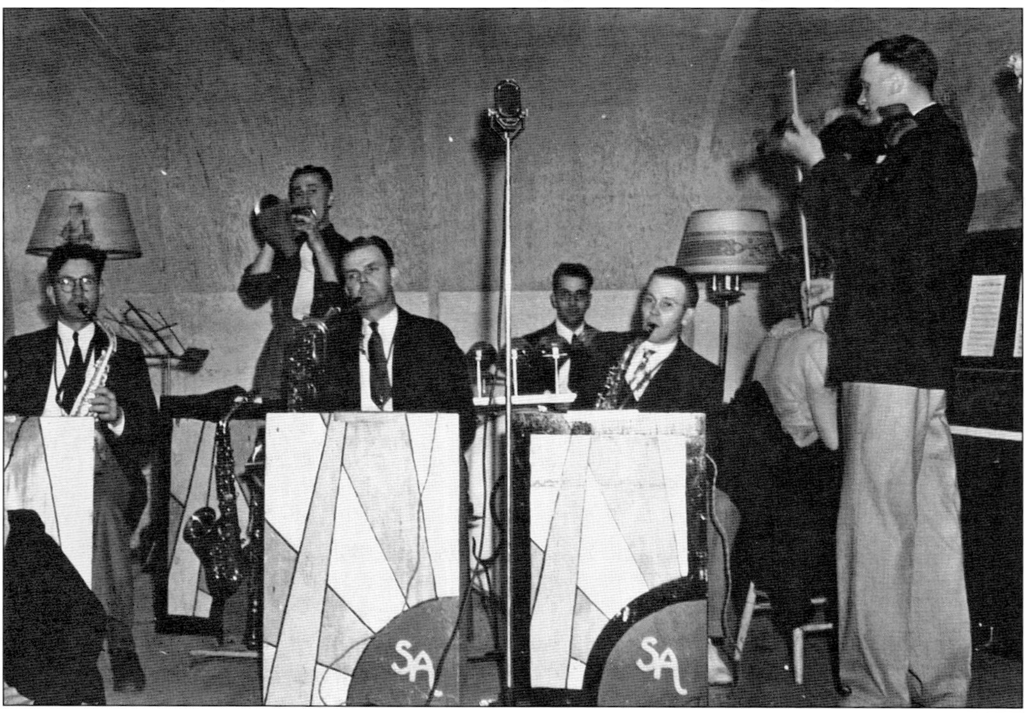

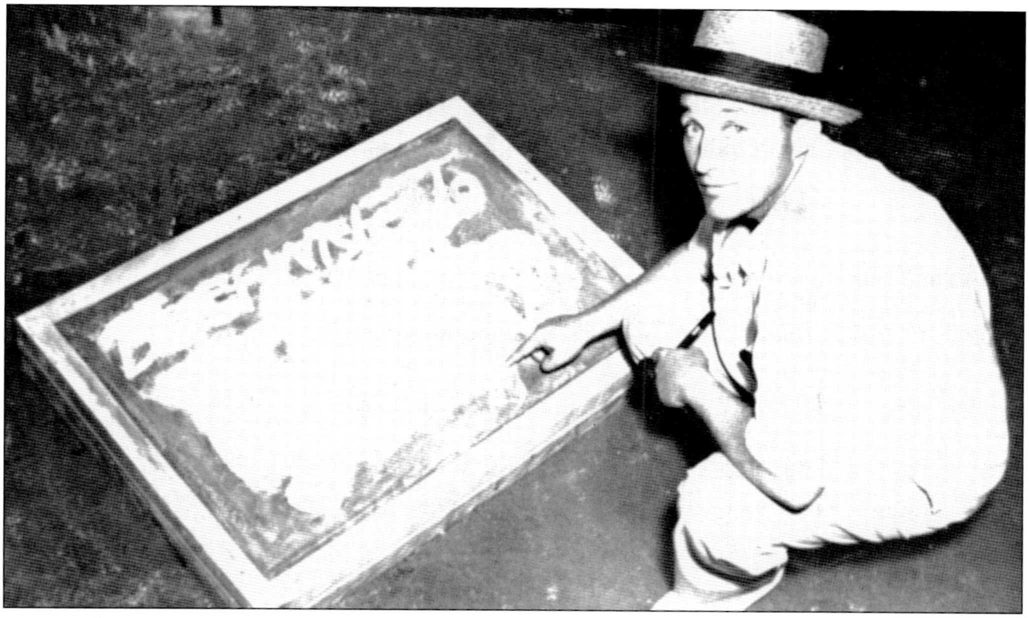

In 1932, famous American singer and actor Bing Crosby, seen here, wrote "Best Wishes" in cement at the first radio broadcasting station in Lewis County, which was established by J. Elroy McCaw, Cecil Gwinn, and Arthur St. John. Joe Chytil purchased the station in 1965, and it was later operated by his son Ted. The commemorative slab is still at the KELA radio station.

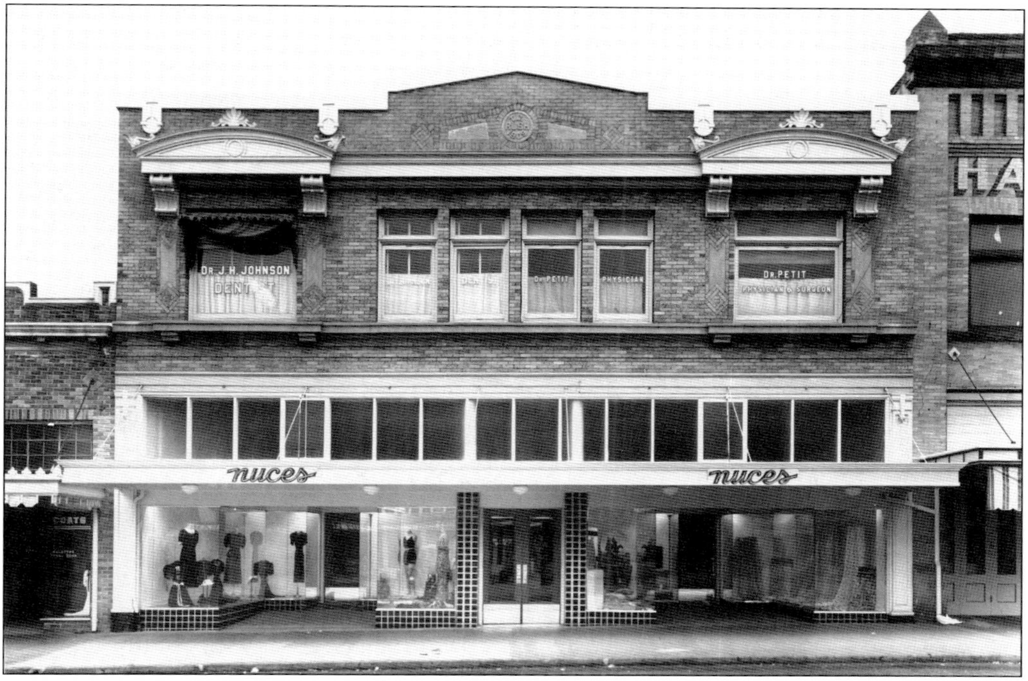

Nuce's Department Store at 834 Market Street carried ladies' and children's ready-to-wear clothing, as well as dry goods and bedding. This May 1937 photograph shows Nuce's new storefront in the Rush Building. Upstairs were the offices of Dr. J.H. Johnson, a dentist, and Dr. Petit, a physician and surgeon. Nuce Nathan, who moved to Chehalis in 1891, operated the department store for 58 years. He died October 7, 1949, at age 82.

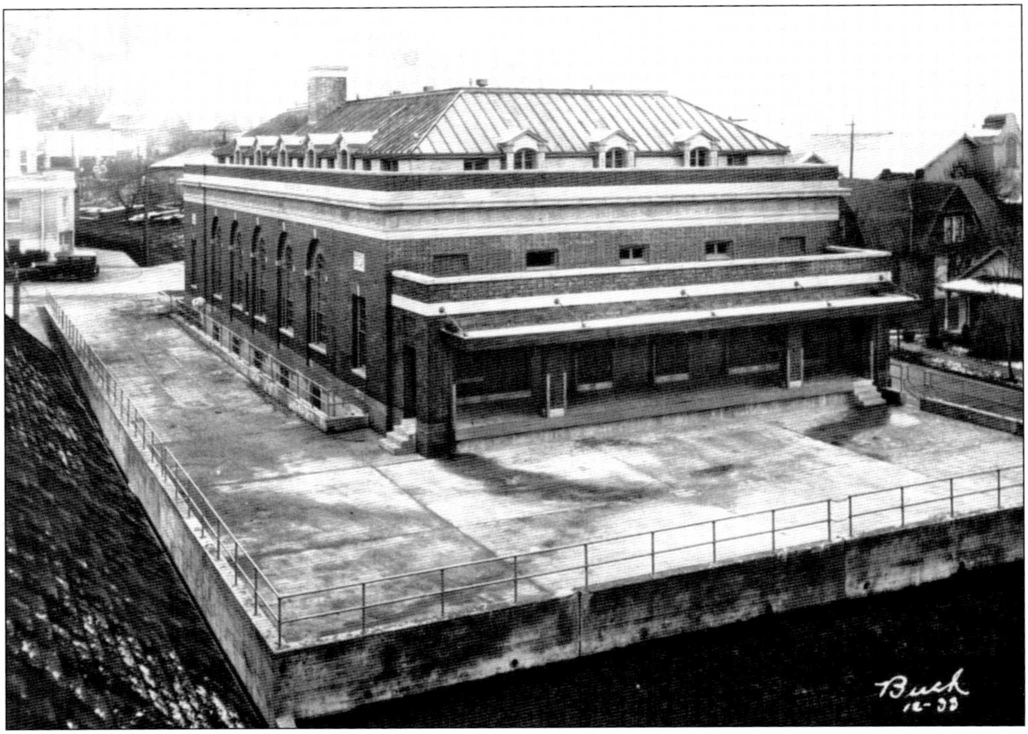

In 1933, the Works Progress Administration also erected the post office building at 225 Northwest Cascade Avenue. The construction photograph shows the newly completed loading dock. Visible above the rooftop is the Baptist Church's steeple. The post office building, listed in the National Register of Historic Places, was dedicated around January 1934.

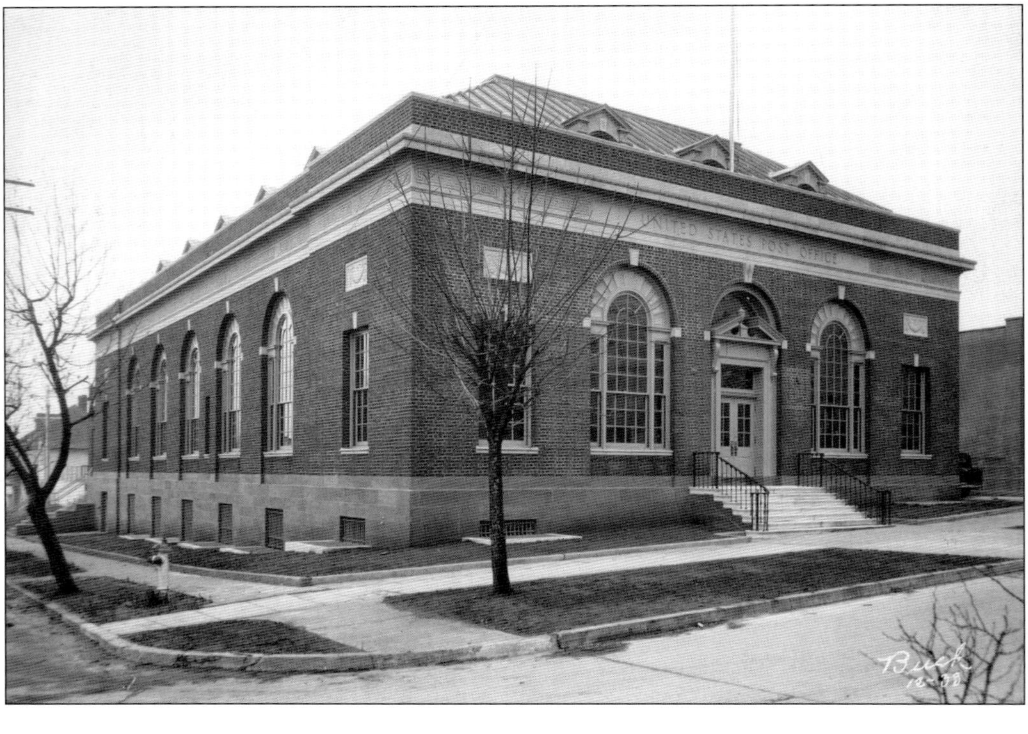

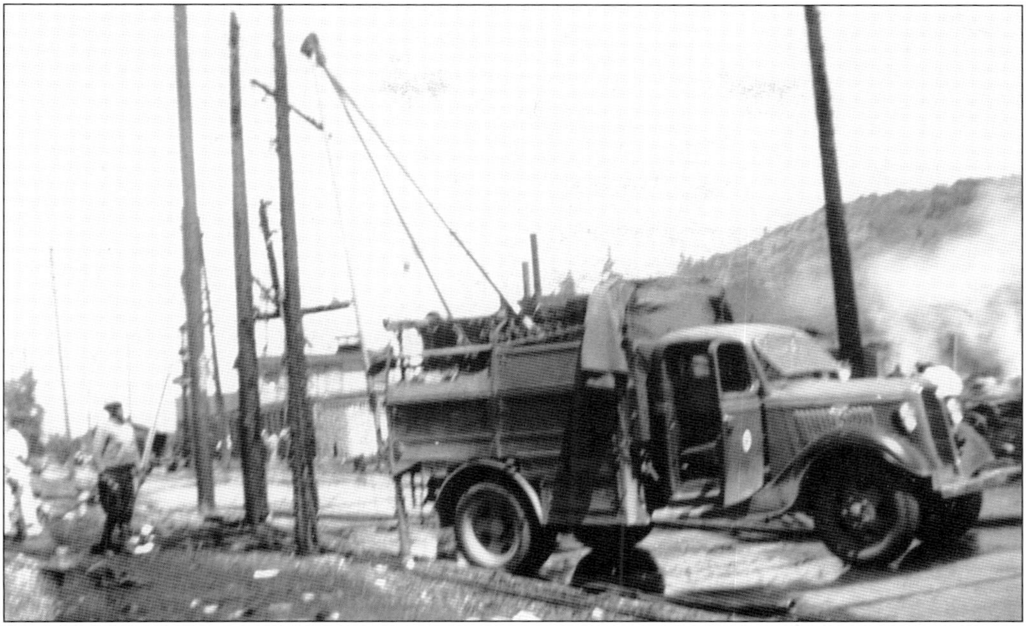

A devastating fire, described in the *Centralia Daily Chronicle* as "the most disastrous fire to ever hit the city of Chehalis," began in the finish sheds of Palmer Lumber and Manufacturing July 25, 1939, and quickly spread to three other businesses. The smoldering remains of the company are seen here, along with a Puget Sound Power and Light Company truck. Palmer Lumber sustained $50,000 in damage to the finishing and storage sheds and another $50,000 to the contents. The fire then raced across the street and consumed the O.R. Kirk fern plant owned by the National Fruit Canning Company, as well as Forget-Me-Not Products and Gustavsson Iron Works.

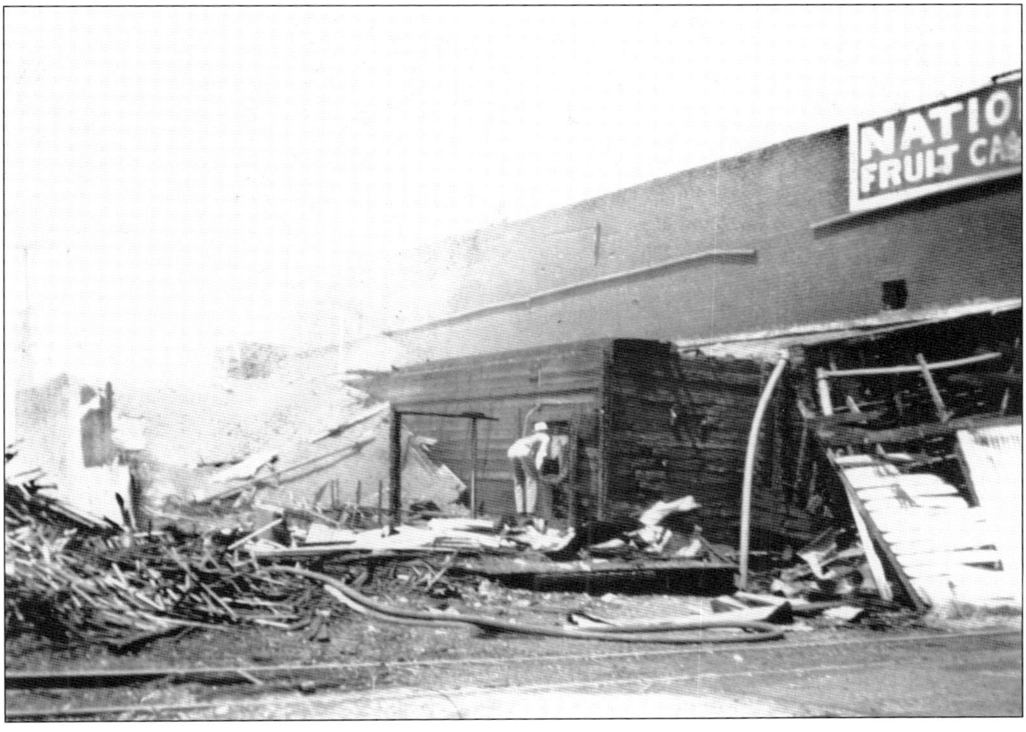

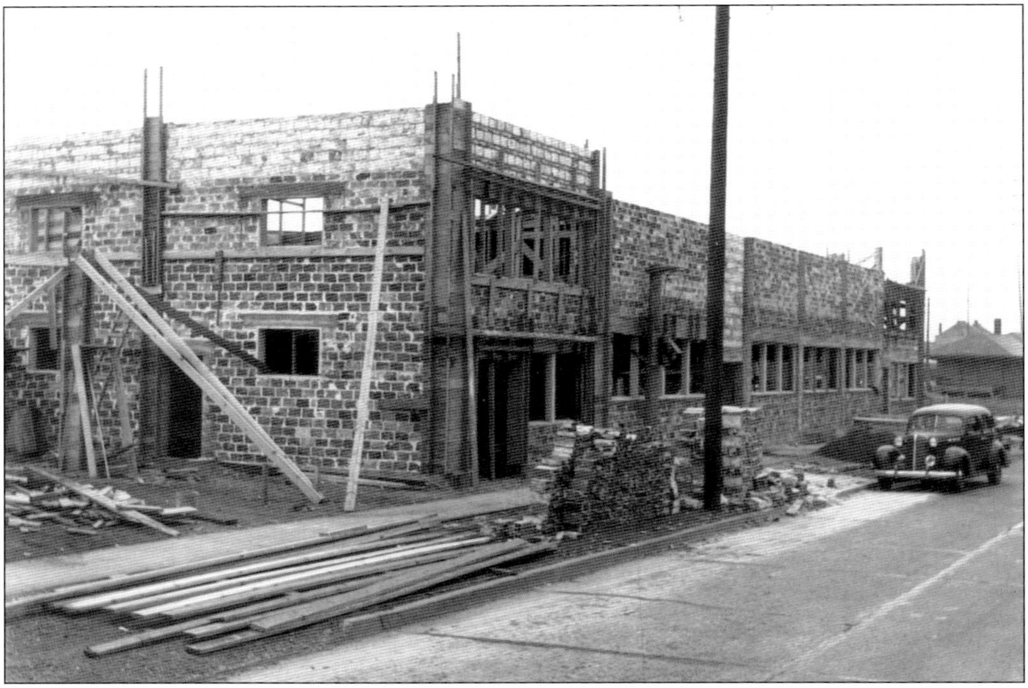

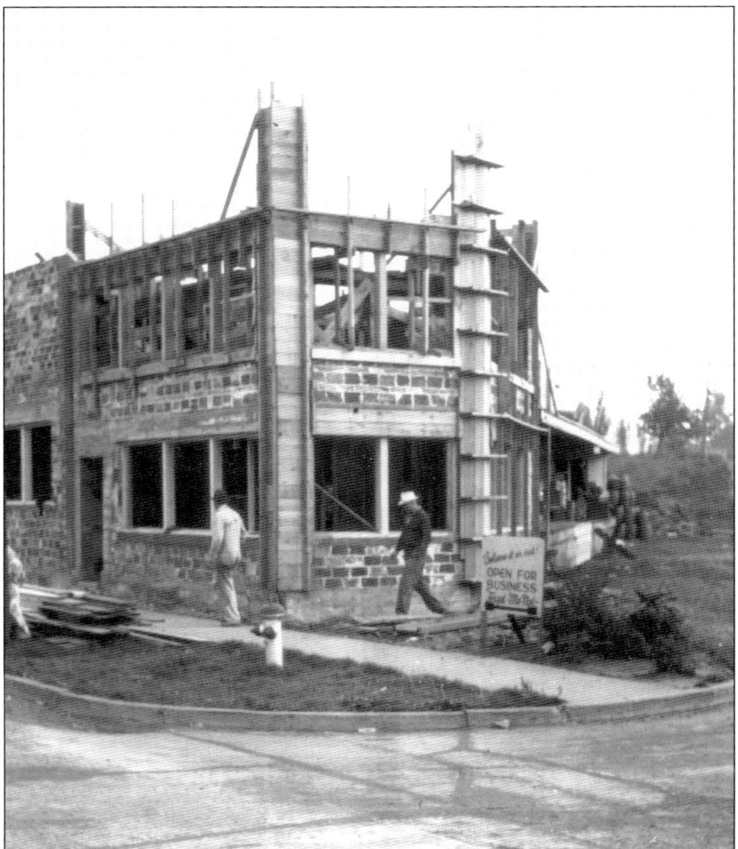

Altogether, damage from the July 1939 fire reached nearly $200,000, which would equate to a $3.13 million loss in 2011 dollars. Firefighters from Chehalis, Centralia, and Winlock joined forces to battle the State Street blaze, which broke out after 10:00 p.m. It caused an estimated $40,000 in damage to Forget-Me-Not Products, $20,000 to Gustavsson Iron Works, $10,000 to National Fruit Canning Company property, and $4,000 to Puget Sound Power and Light Company property. In these photographs, workers begin to rebuild the Forget-Me-Not plant at 867 State Street after the fire.

Eight

A World at War

Life in Chehalis, as in other American communities, changed overnight with the Japanese attack on Pearl Harbor on December 7, 1941.

Men enlisted in the military, the government instituted rationing of gasoline, food, and clothing, and Japanese-American residents found themselves detained as a potential threat to their country. Tom Sato, a Japanese-American farmer in Adna who delivered fruits and vegetables to stores in Chehalis and Centralia, was ordered to take his family and board a train to Tule Lake, an internment camp in California. The family spent three years behind barbed wire until the war ended in August 1945, when they returned to Adna. However, Tom's wife, Hanako, died in the camp shortly after giving birth to her fifth child.

Scrambling to build airplanes for the military, Boeing Aircraft Company found itself short of manpower, so it recruited workers in smaller communities, providing training and high wages to entice people to Seattle. After training sessions in Chehalis, many people moved north to work at Boeing. Even those efforts didn't provide enough workers, so in 1943, Boeing opened branch plants in half a dozen smaller cities, including Chehalis. Those plants manufactured B-17 and B-29 parts that were shipped to Seattle for assembly. The Chehalis plant opened November 15, 1943, in a building now occupied by the Lewis County Public Utility District. The plant employed 700 people who made parts for B-17s and B-29s, contributing to the war effort while earning good wages. The plant closed after the war ended.

Servicemen returned to Chehalis looking for jobs, and women returned to housekeeping—but not all of them. Many found employment outside the home to their liking and continued working, marking a significant change in American culture.

Returning loggers might have cut trees eventually sold through the Hemphill-O'Neill Company, a small Chehalis lumber brokerage started in 1947 by Allen Candee Hemphill and Robert Harold O'Neill. The company eventually owned three mills in Lewis County and employed hundreds of workers.

The end of the decade saw the earth literally shake in Chehalis and elsewhere in the Pacific Northwest as a 1949 earthquake measuring 7.1 on the Richter scale knocked bricks loose from buildings and killed people in several western Washington communities. Both the Chehalis High School and West Side School were condemned, and the Carnegie Library and city hall in the Civic Center were severely damaged.

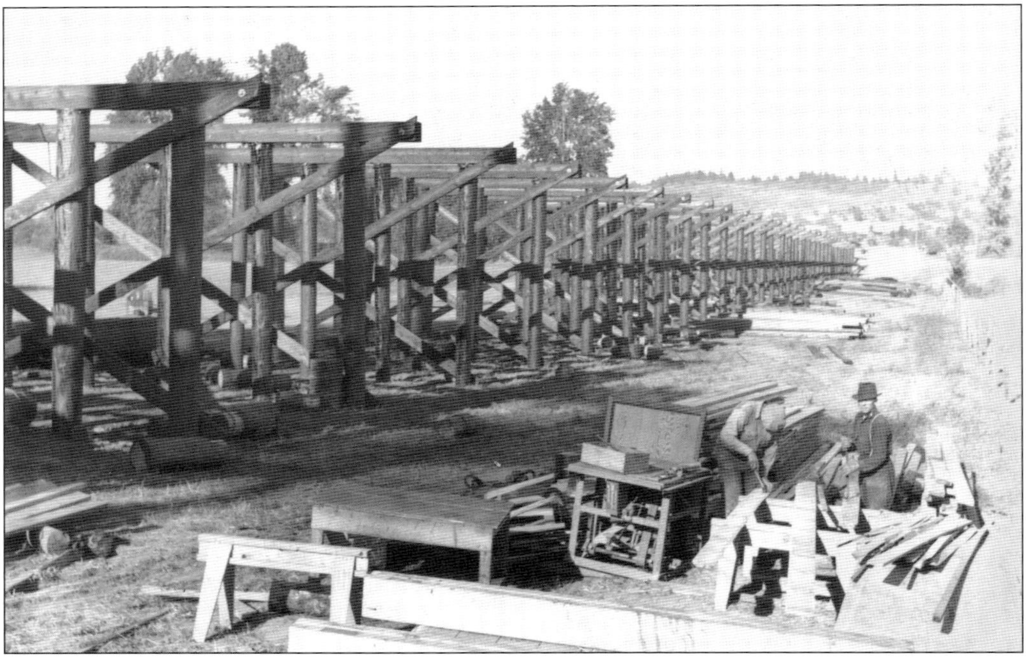

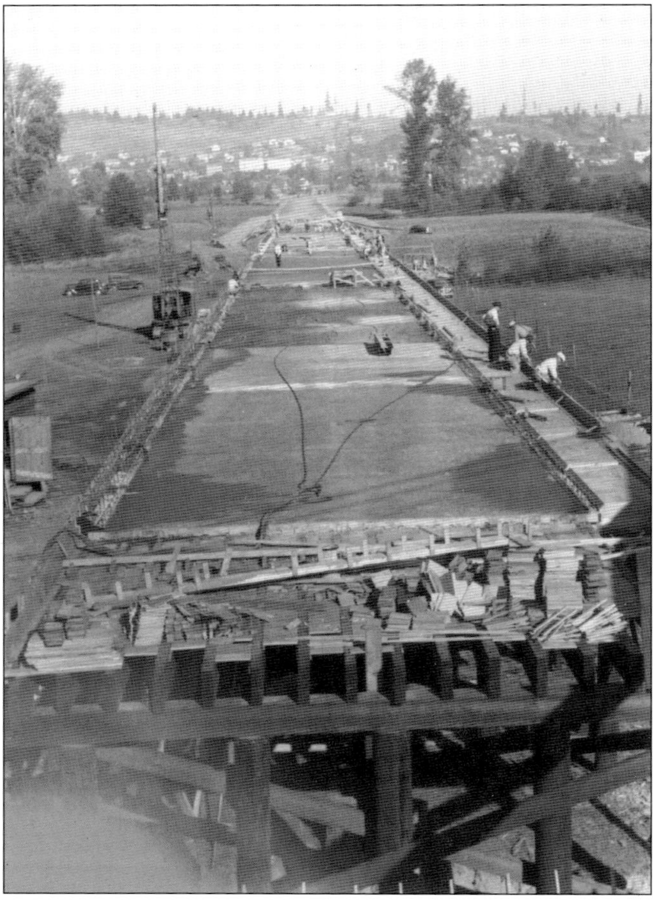

In the late 1930s, work began on the new Riverside Bridge leading from Chehalis to Pe Ell after the old highway bridge was condemned as unsafe. Construction was halted in late 1939 as workers waited for a delayed shipment of steel to arrive. It resumed in early 1940. Here, piling is aligned like a formation of soldiers as Riverside Bridge takes shape in 1939. The other photograph was taken looking toward Chehalis from the west side of the bridge. Money to pay for the $150,000 bridge was appropriated by the state legislature when it approved the State Highway Department's budget.

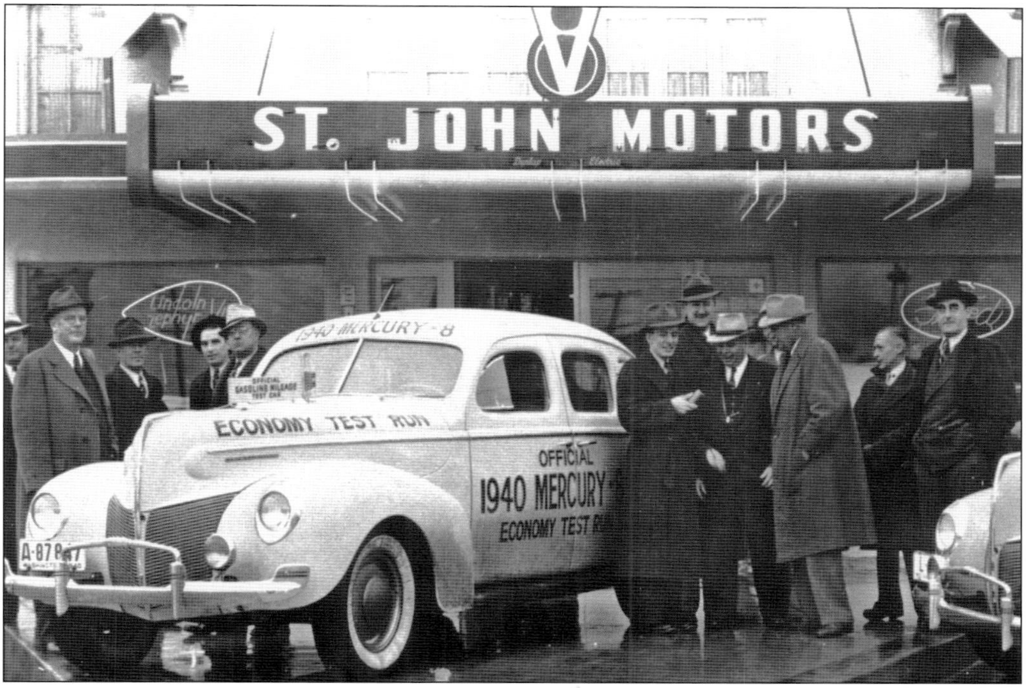

The St. John Motor Company Ford garage in Chehalis displays a new 1940 Mercury sedan offering an economy test run. The company's founder and owner, Arthur St. John, is nearest the front fender on the left side. On the right side of the car, from left to right, are unidentified, Norman Brunswig, Louis Vimont, unidentified, Lloyd Sullivan, and George Sears.

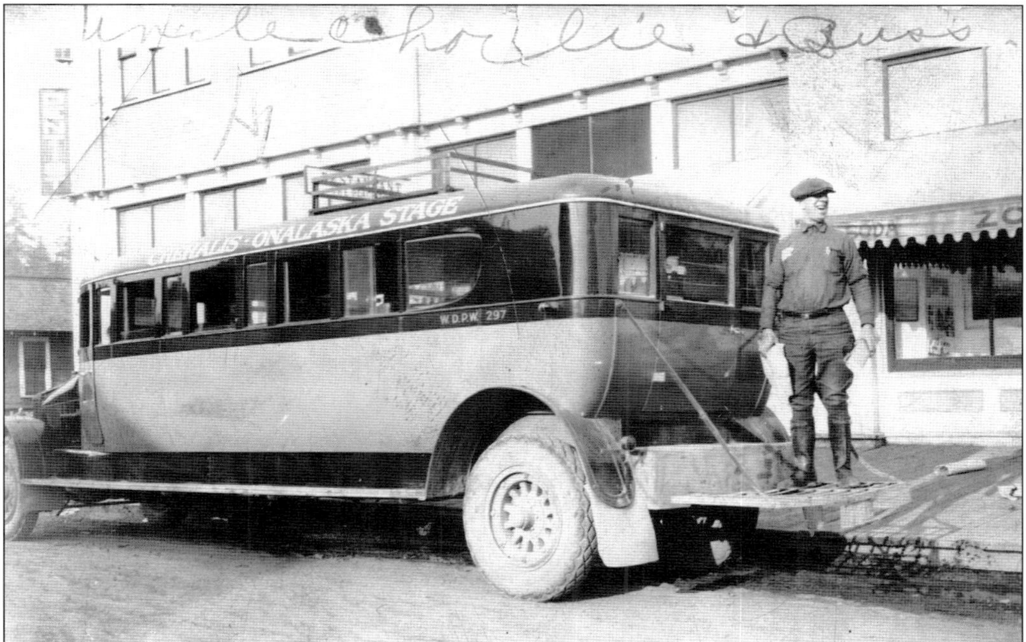

Charlie Sitton is shown with his bus in this image taken in front of his bowling alley in Chehalis. In November 1931, as reported in the *Centralia Daily Chronicle*, Sitton told the Lewis County Sheriff's Office that his bus had struck a stray cow the previous night, breaking its leg.

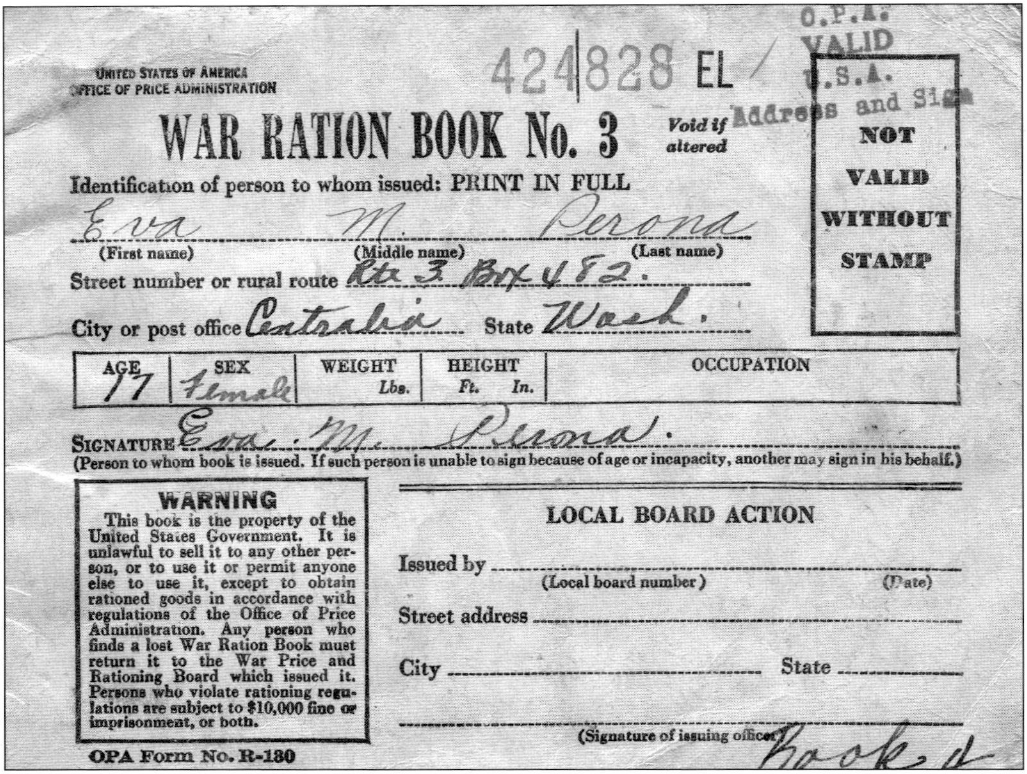

424828 EL

O.P.A. VALID U.S.A. Address and Sign

UNITED STATES OF AMERICA
OFFICE OF PRICE ADMINISTRATION

WAR RATION BOOK No. 3 *Void if altered*

NOT VALID WITHOUT STAMP

Identification of person to whom issued: PRINT IN FULL

Eva M. Perona
(First name) (Middle name) (Last name)

Street number or rural route Rte 3 Box 482.

City or post office Centralia State Wash.

AGE	SEX	WEIGHT	HEIGHT	OCCUPATION
17	Female	Lbs.	Ft. In.	

SIGNATURE Eva M. Perona.
(Person to whom book is issued. If such person is unable to sign because of age or incapacity, another may sign in his behalf.)

WARNING
This book is the property of the United States Government. It is unlawful to sell it to any other person, or to use it or permit anyone else to use it, except to obtain rationed goods in accordance with regulations of the Office of Price Administration. Any person who finds a lost War Ration Book must return it to the War Price and Rationing Board which issued it. Persons who violate rationing regulations are subject to $10,000 fine or imprisonment, or both.

LOCAL BOARD ACTION

Issued by .... (Local board number) (Date)

Street address ....

City .... State ....

.... (Signature of issuing officer)

OPA Form No. R-130

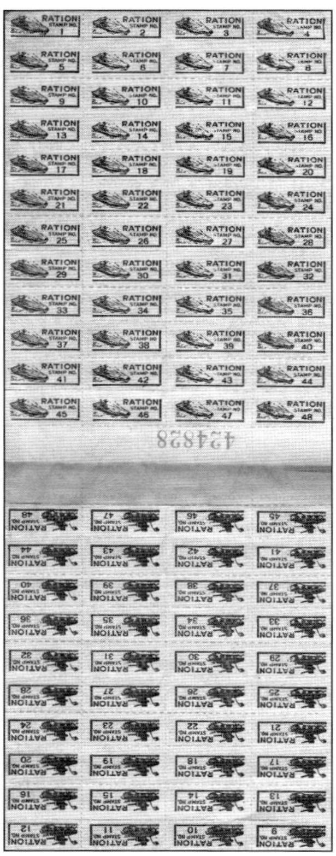

In May 1942, only months after the Japanese attack at Pearl Harbor, the US government began rationing to conserve resources for the war effort. The Office of Economic Stabilization instituted controls on farm prices, rents, wages, and salaries. Citizens received ration books and coupons that limited the amount of gasoline, coffee, sugar, meats, rubber, butter, heating oil, and shoes they could purchase. Because of rationing and shortages, consumer spending plummeted from $69 billion in 1939 to $38 billion three years later. These photographs show the ration book and coupons of Eva Perona Hauck, who worked as a C mechanic at the Chehalis Boeing plant.

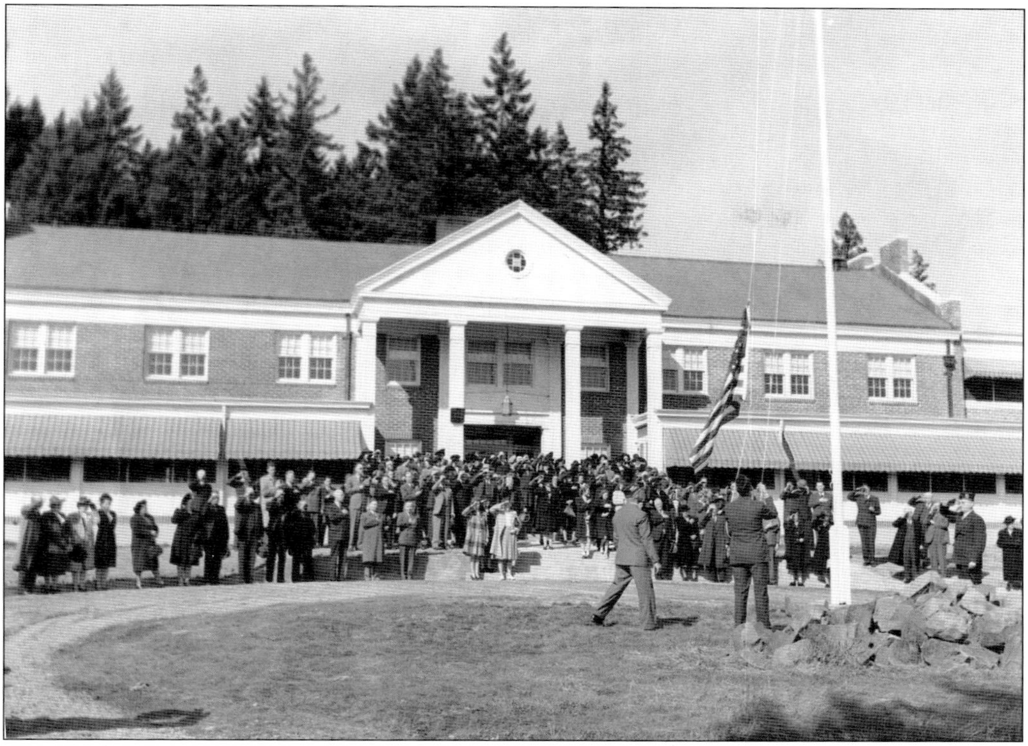

In 1931, the county poorhouse was replaced with a brick fireproof building remodeled in the 1940s and dedicated in March 1943 as the MacMillan Tuberculosis Sanatorium. Speaking at the event was Washington governor Arthur B. Langlie and, seen here, Dr. Angus MacMillan. The sanitarium, five miles south of Chehalis on Highway 99, remained open until 1954, when it became a nursing home. In 1975, the Forest Manor Retirement Home opened in the building. Today it is home to Safe Family Ministries, a transitional shelter for women and their children as the mothers rebuild their lives after making destructive lifestyle choices. The nonprofit volunteer-run shelter provides addiction counseling, vocational training, and other educational programs to help the women live productive, healthy lives.

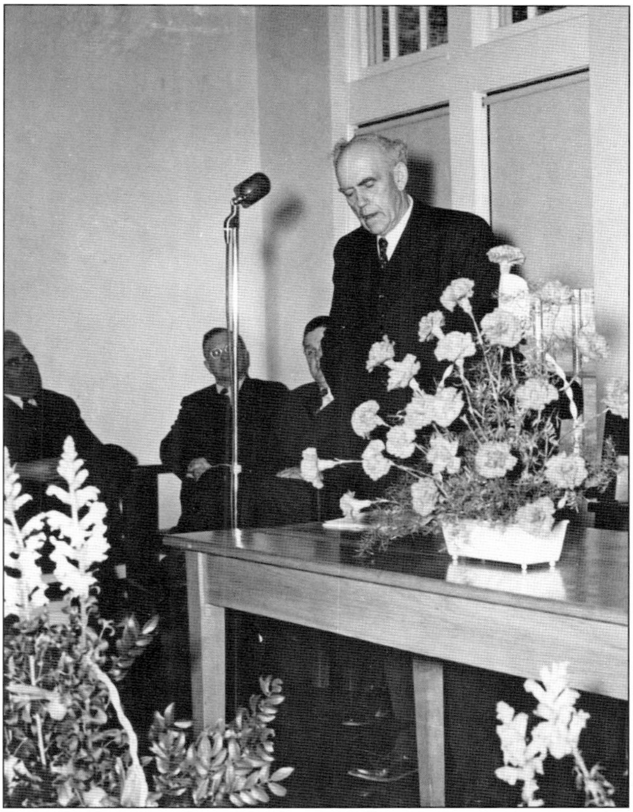

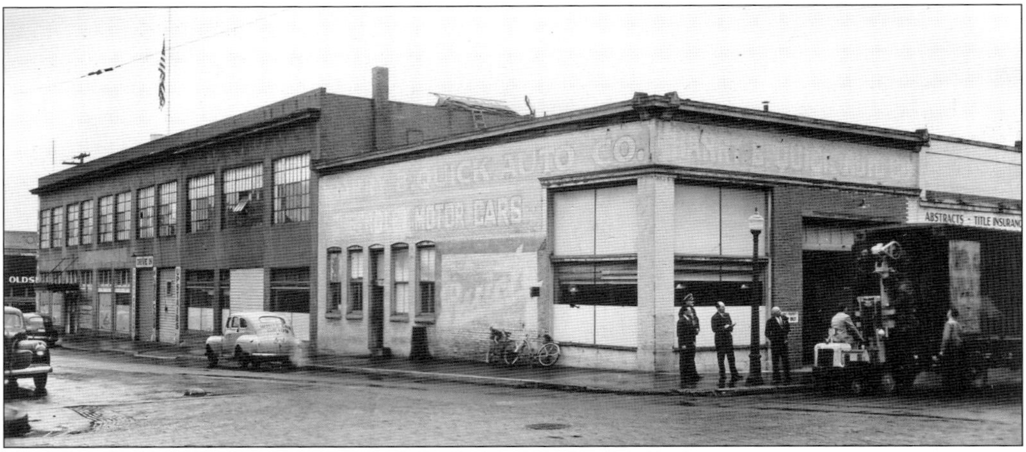

When the United States entered World War II, Boeing officials sought workers in rural communities to help build airplanes. The company offered a training session at Chehalis Junior High School, which drew loggers, mill workers, and farmers seeking higher-paying jobs. Still unable to keep up with demand in 1943, Boeing opened branch plants in smaller communities—Chehalis, Aberdeen, Bellingham, Everett, Hoquiam, North and South Everett, and North and South Tacoma—where parts for the B-17 could be made and then shipped to Seattle for assembly. Workers obtained two weeks of training while the plants were constructed. The Chehalis branch opened November 15, 1943, at the corner of Pacific Avenue and Park Street, in Harry B. Quick's building seen here. The December 1943 photograph below shows the Chehalis assembly plant floor, where workers constructed pilot and copilot seats, wings, and lower turret mounting assemblies. (Above, courtesy of Eva Perona Hauck; below, courtesy of the Boeing Company.)

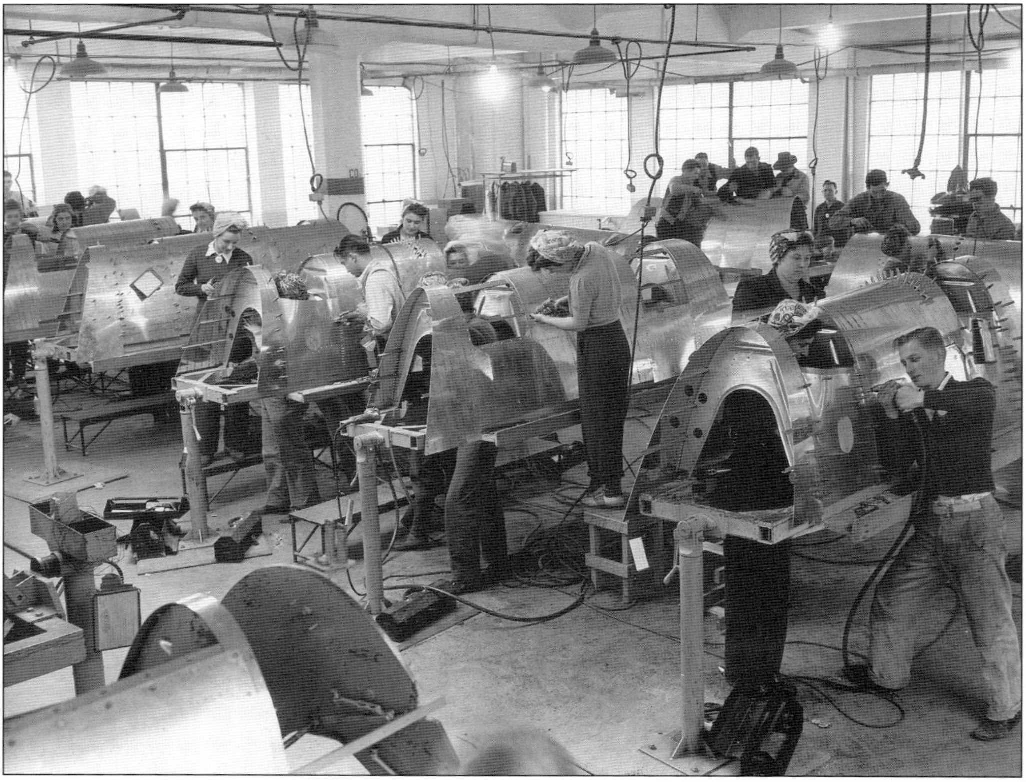

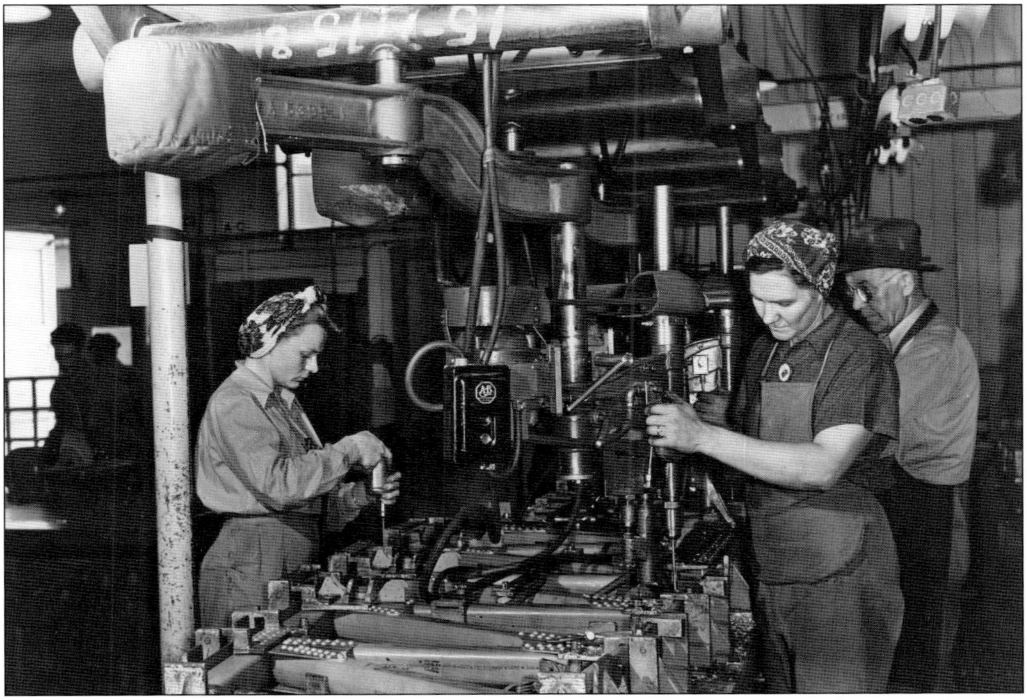

Above, Margaret (Shaver) Shields, at left, enrolled in a mechanics class at the Southwest Washington Fairgrounds in Chehalis and then applied for a job at Boeing Aircraft Company in Seattle. She transferred to Chehalis when Boeing opened its branch plant in November 1943. She is seen working with Autumn Berg Beam of Onalaska. Joyce (Markstrom) Venemon, who served on the Chehalis City Council from 1975 to 1995 and as mayor from 1982 to 1985, once told a newspaper reporter that she felt like a millionaire earning high wages as a riveter. Below, Chehalis employees had their photograph taken outside the plant after receiving the "E" award in recognition for production excellence. (Above, courtesy of Margaret Shaver Shields; below, courtesy of Dorothy McMahan Powell.)

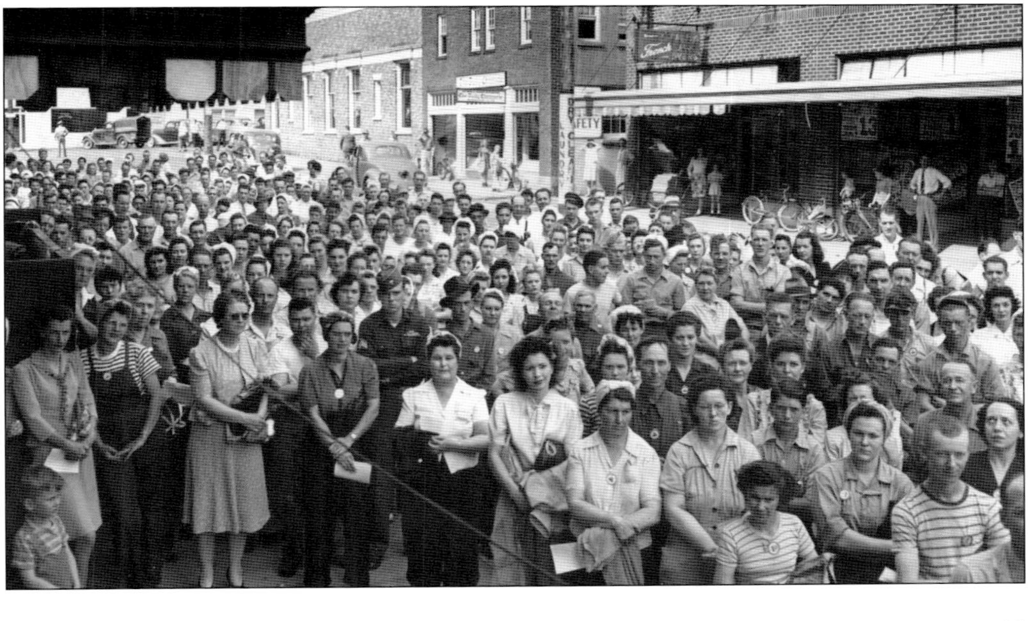

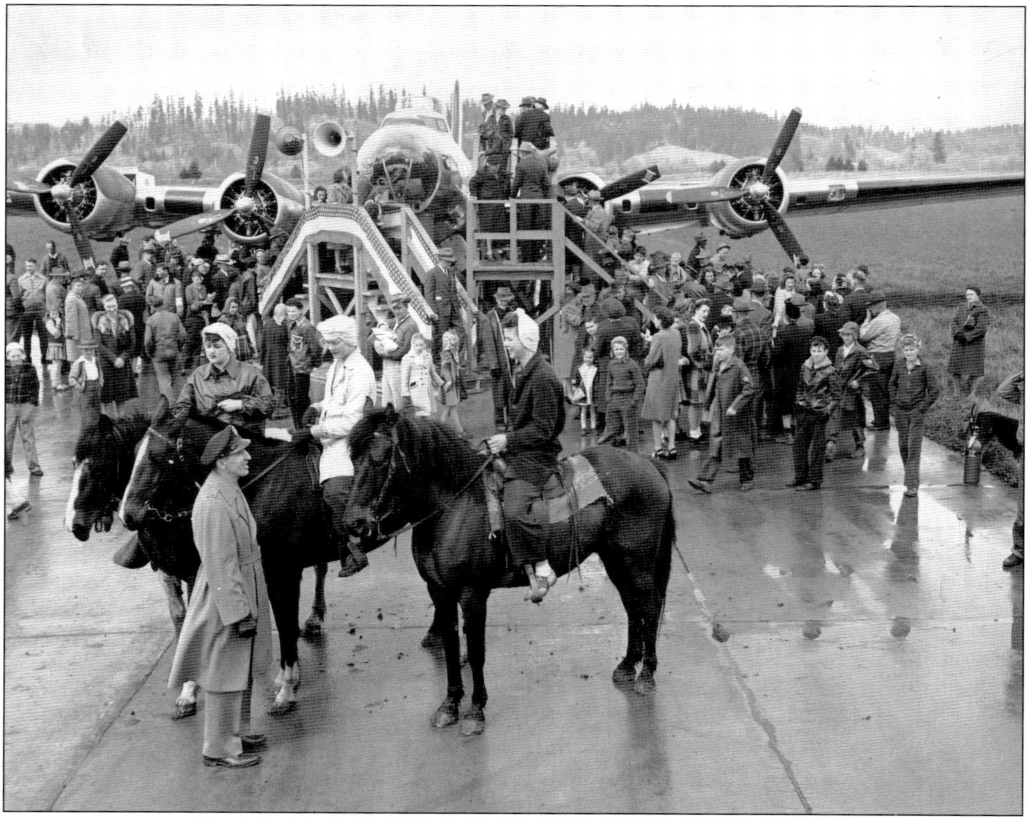

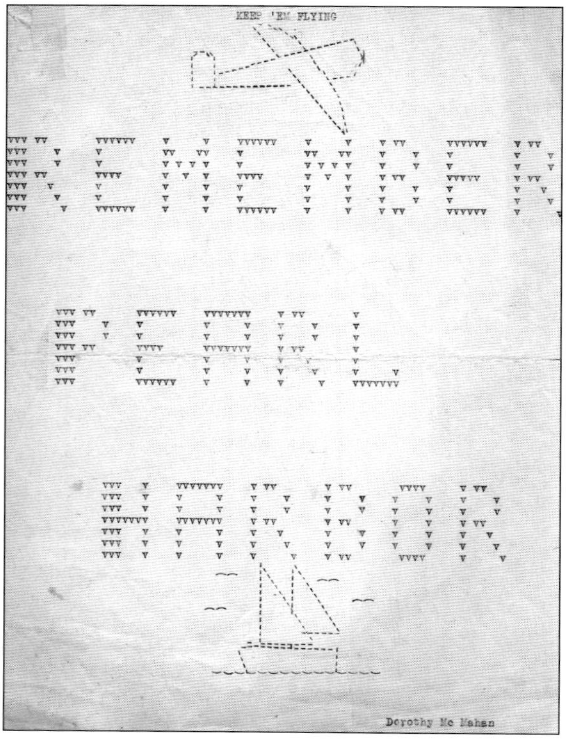

Eloise Nugent Evans, right, Rose Ormbrek Menish, center, and Ruby Savage were riding horses after school when they saw a B-17 Flying Fortress at the airport and rode over to view it. Because of rationing, they had little gas and few tires, so Eloise said they often rode horses to get around. During visits to branch plant cities in western Washington, more than 65,000 people turned out to view the Flying Fortress. Chehalis people defied heavy rains April 16, 1944, to come to the Twin City Airport to inspect the new Flying Fortress. Dorothy (McMahan) Powell, a student at Mossyrock High School, used a typewriter to create this depiction of the American rallying cry after December 7, 1941: "Remember Pearl Harbor," with small print reading "Keep 'em flying." Powell worked at the Chehalis plant from May 1944 to August 1945, initially as a bucker and, later, in the office. (Above, courtesy of Boeing.)

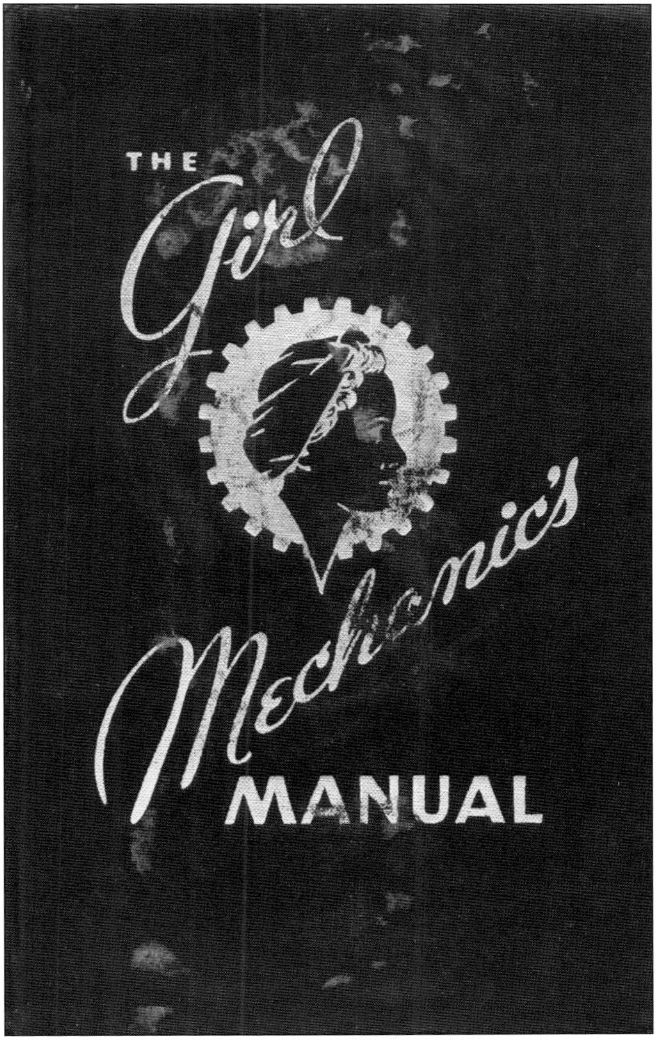

The Girl Mechanic's Manual, published in 1944, specifically for Rosie the Riveters working on the home front, speaks clearly about how women were perceived in the 1940s. For example, the authors talk about clothes being a subject that should interest any woman and emphasize the importance of safety around equipment to prevent losing an arm, "for after all, arms are nice things to have—both on and around you." When Eva Perona Hauck started working at Boeing, she earned 80.5¢ an hour as a C mechanic but saw her pay increase to 92.5¢ an hour after she made B mechanic. She said her highest check was for $78.62. In the pay stub shown below, she earned 82.5¢ an hour and worked 95.8 hours. She also contributed 90¢ per paycheck for a war bond. (Both, courtesy of Eva Perona Hauck.)

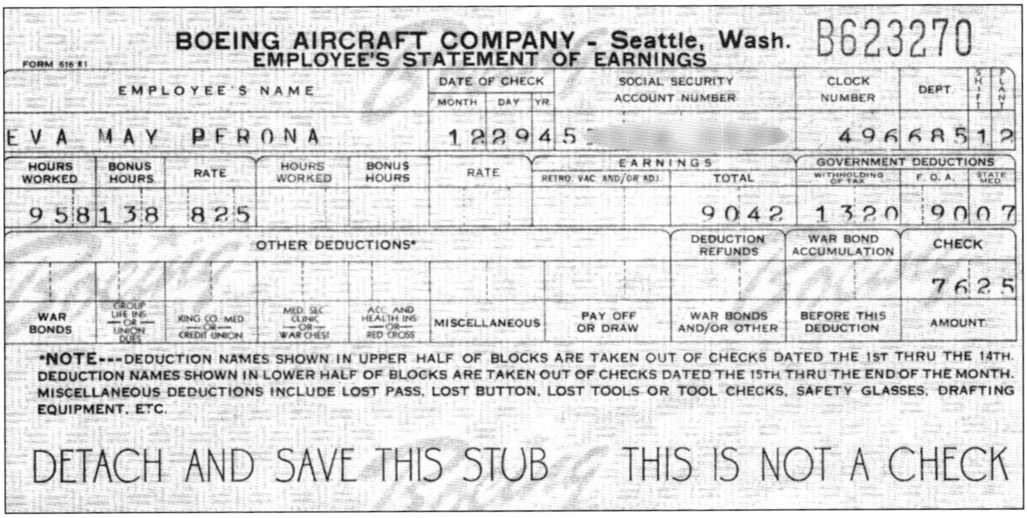

BOEING AIRCRAFT COMPANY - Seattle, Wash. B623270
EMPLOYEE'S STATEMENT OF EARNINGS
FORM 616 R1

EMPLOYEE'S NAME	DATE OF CHECK MONTH	DAY	YR	SOCIAL SECURITY ACCOUNT NUMBER	CLOCK NUMBER	DEPT	SHIFT	PLANT
EVA MAY PERONA	12	29	45		4966	85	1	2

HOURS WORKED	BONUS HOURS	RATE	HOURS WORKED	BONUS HOURS	RATE	EARNINGS RETRO. VAC. AND/OR ADJ.	EARNINGS TOTAL	GOVERNMENT DEDUCTIONS WITHHOLDING OF TAX	F. O. A.	STATE MED
958	138	825					9042	1320	90	07

OTHER DEDUCTIONS* WAR BONDS	GROUP LIFE INS —OR— UNION DUES	KING CO. MED —OR— CREDIT UNION	MED. SEC. CLINIC —OR— WAR CHEST	ACC. AND HEALTH INS —OR— RED CROSS	MISCELLANEOUS	PAY OFF OR DRAW	DEDUCTION REFUNDS WAR BONDS AND/OR OTHER	WAR BOND ACCUMULATION BEFORE THIS DEDUCTION	CHECK AMOUNT
									7625

*NOTE---DEDUCTION NAMES SHOWN IN UPPER HALF OF BLOCKS ARE TAKEN OUT OF CHECKS DATED THE 1ST THRU THE 14TH. DEDUCTION NAMES SHOWN IN LOWER HALF OF BLOCKS ARE TAKEN OUT OF CHECKS DATED THE 15TH THRU THE END OF THE MONTH. MISCELLANEOUS DEDUCTIONS INCLUDE LOST PASS, LOST BUTTON, LOST TOOLS OR TOOL CHECKS, SAFETY GLASSES, DRAFTING EQUIPMENT, ETC.

DETACH AND SAVE THIS STUB THIS IS NOT A CHECK

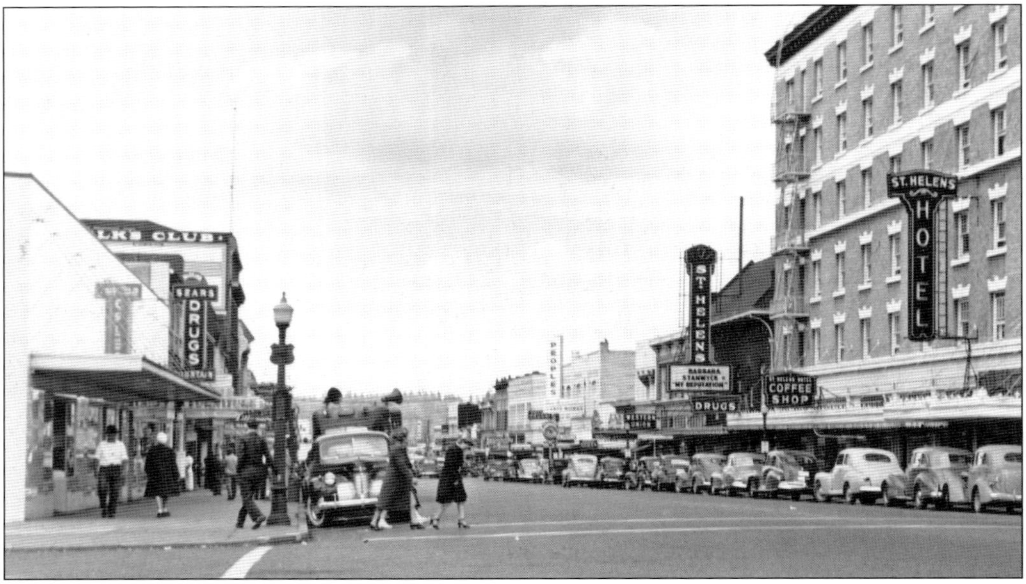

Ecstatic celebrations greeted the end of the war on August 14, 1945, and shortly afterward, Boeing closed its branch plants. Servicemen returned from the war front, and people resumed life in Chehalis. This photograph shows Market Street in Chehalis from the south end. At left are the St. Helens Hotel, St. Helens Coffee Shop, and St. Helens Fox Theatre, featuring Barbara Stanwyck in 1946's *My Deportation*. In the image below, a large crowd gathers in front of the Sears Roebuck store on Market Street in Chehalis in October 1945. The occasion was a large sale marking the store's reopening after a fire. The building later became the Ben Franklin store. Visible are the Shoe Hospital, Fred's Tavern, and the Washington Hotel.

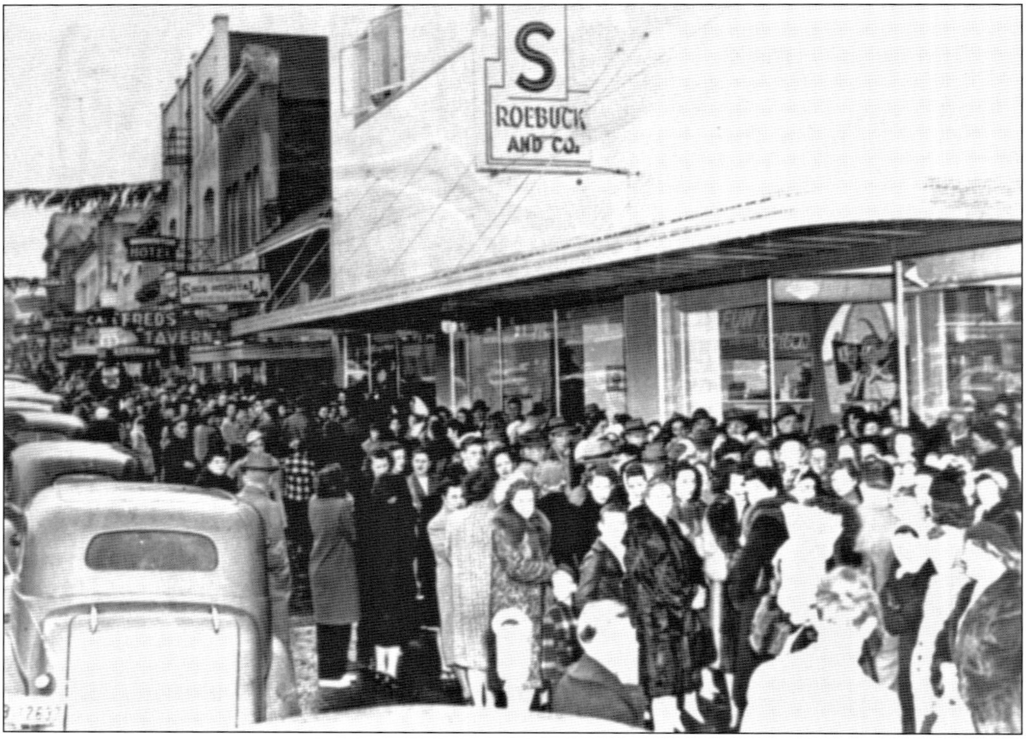

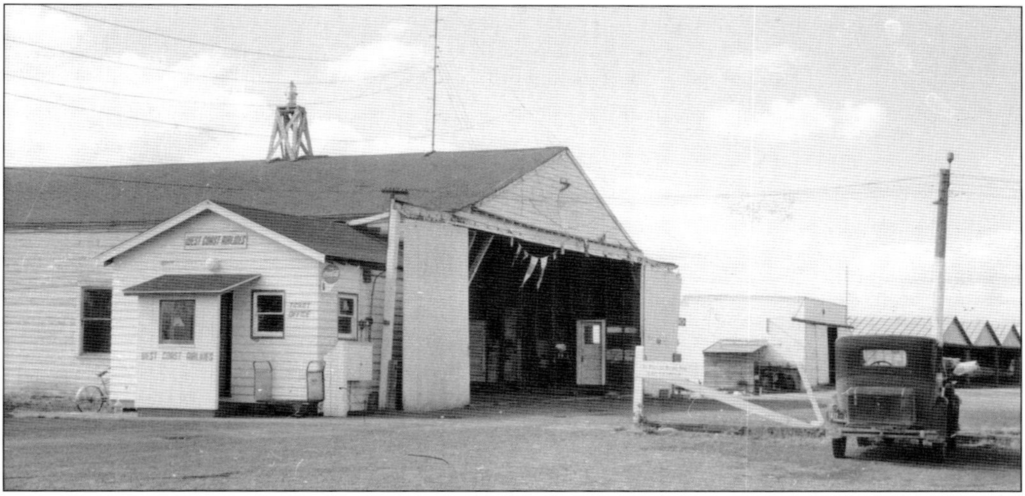

Soon after World War II ended, the Chehalis-Lewis County Airport Board once again oversaw the airport, and the first commercial air service began with the opening of West Coast Airlines, which operated from 1947 through 1956. This c. 1946 photograph shows the ticket office attached to the original hangar, with John Twiss's car parked by the fence. Below, local business leaders pose by a West Coast Airlines plane before a Chamber of Commerce trip to Seattle in 1947. Pictured from left to right are C.C. White, E. Newgard, George Literal, Arthur C. St. John, Ray Severns, Chuck Downie, L. Givens, George Hayden, two unidentified men, Lloyd Sullivan, Joe Chytil, Bob Todd, Bill West, Tobe Willms, John Edinger, Louis Pemerl, Spence Shoemaker, George Sears, and (on the top steps) Kenneth Chase, Alex Coburn, and Louis Vimont. Arnold James is behind Louis Pemerl, to the right. The airport, which purchased another 200 acres nearby, was annexed by the City of Chehalis in the late 1950s. Centralia became a partner in 1961 but pulled out in 2004.

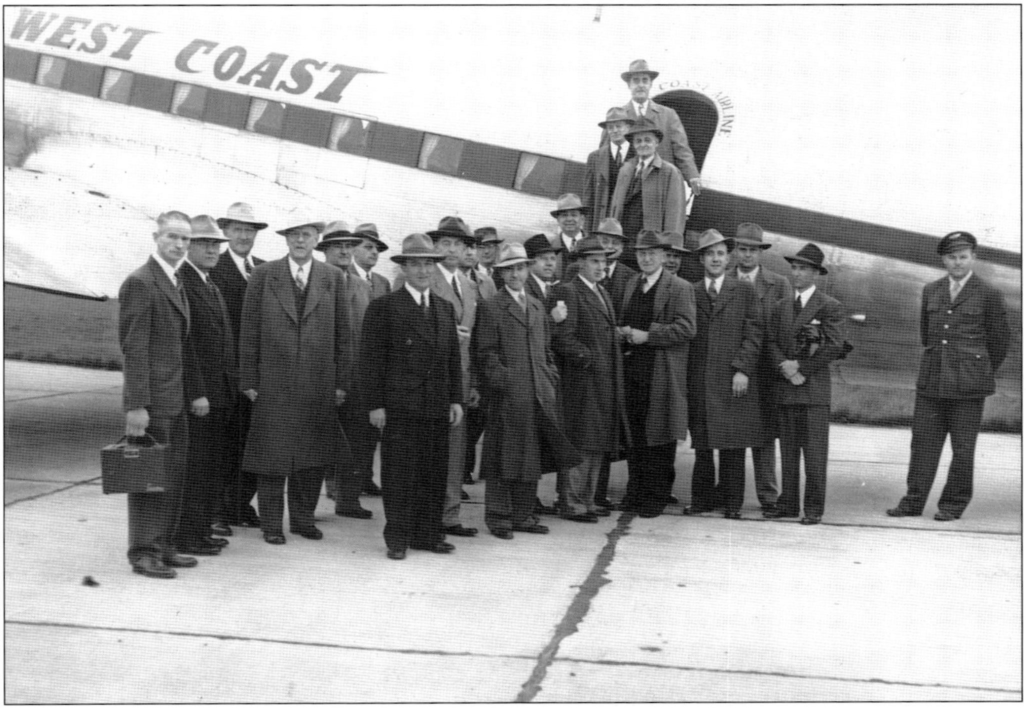

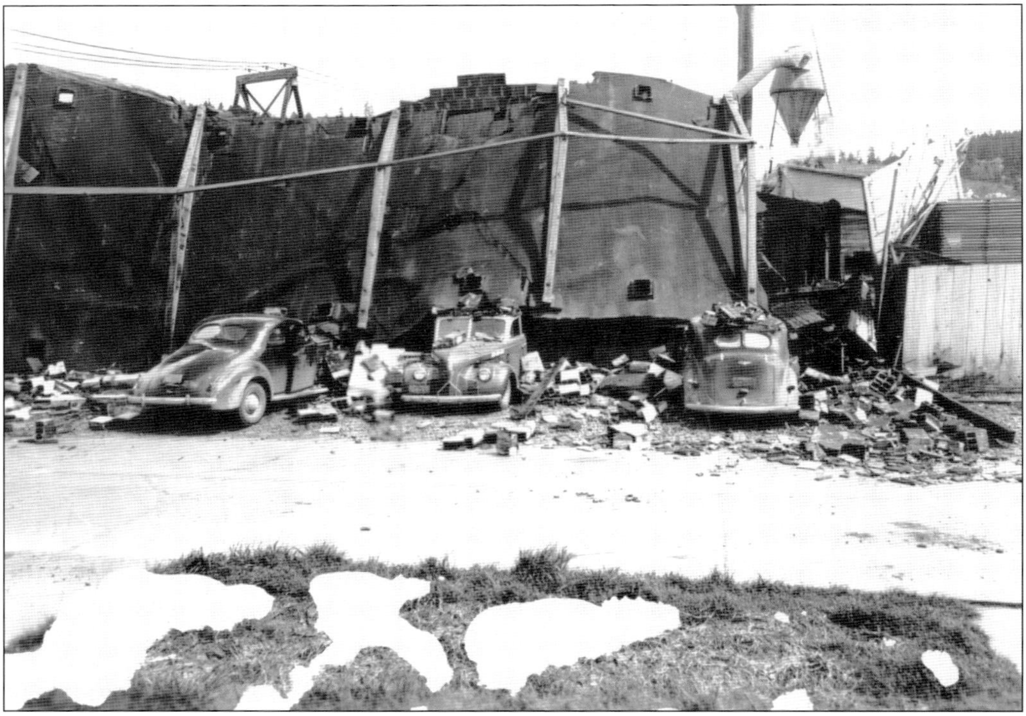

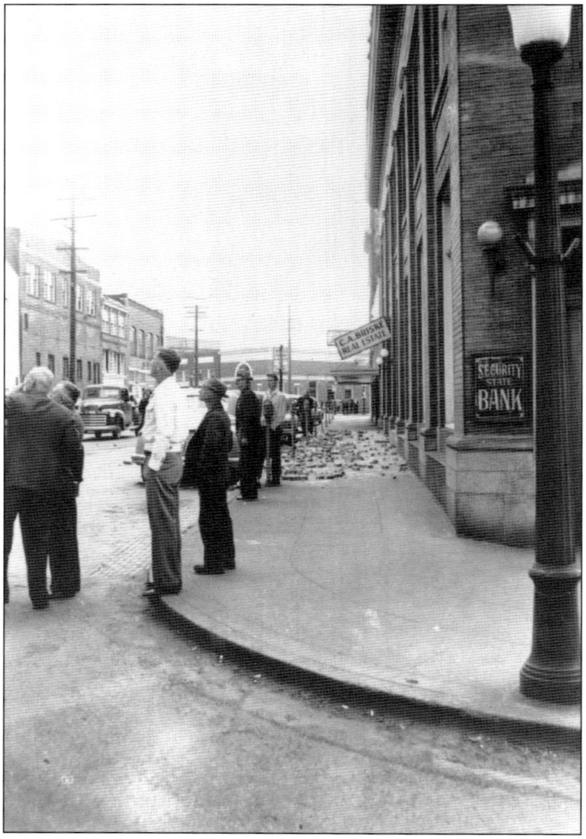

At 11:55 a.m. on April 13, 1949, an earthquake centered at Littlerock, north of Centralia, shook western Washington communities for up to 45 seconds. The quake, which measured 7.1 on the Richter scale, toppled bricks from buildings, crushing a 69-year-old Centralia man, an 11-year-old school crossing guard in Tacoma, the 18-year-old Castle Rock High School senior class president, and a pipe fitter at an Olympia veneer plant. An Olympia woman also suffered a fatal heart attack. Three others also died in the quake that caused an estimated $100 million in damage throughout the region. These photographs show crushed cars at Palmer Lumber and Manufacturing Company in Chehalis and men standing at the corner of Chehalis and Pacific Avenues. Fire chief Ernie Kuehner is the second man from the left. Bricks shaken loose by the earthquake are visible on the sidewalk.

Nine

Moving Forward

Wicked winds, a frigid blizzard, and recurrent flooding in Chehalis marked the latter half of the 20th century. January 1950 saw up to three feet of snow dumped on the community in a Friday the 13th blizzard ranked by the National Weather Service as Washington state's third-worst weather event of the 20th century.

The worst event took place on October 12, 1962, when the infamous Columbus Day windstorm swept through the region, with winds gusting up to 100 miles per hour, uprooting trees and destroying property in the Chehalis area. And the eruption of Mount St. Helens on May 18, 1980, made international headlines, yet it was the May 25 eruption that spewed ash throughout the Twin Cities.

But it's the flooding that has most affected Chehalis, where floodwaters close Interstate 5, hindering passage along the main north-south route today—just as when the area was known as Saunders Bottom. Devastating floods swamped the region in 1972, 1986, 1990, 1996, and 2007, with the last three completely closing Interstate 5, which opened in 1955. A 72-year-old Winlock man driving around freeway barriers drowned in 1990. Flooding has caused millions of dollars in damage to Chehalis roads and bridges, private homes, the Southwest Washington Fairgrounds, and a gem in Chehalis—the Veterans Memorial Museum that opened in 2005. City and county officials are still working with the US Army Corps of Engineers (as they've been doing since the 1930s) to curtail flood damage.

The community saw growth in the ensuing decades, in large part because of companies that settled in the Industrial Park south of town. In the early 1950s, more than 500 Chehalis residents working in a collaborative Adventure in Cooperation divided into committees to evaluate the town and determine its needs. That effort spawned the Chehalis Industrial Commission, which formed in 1956 to purchase land and encourage companies to build there.

Volunteers have once again banded together to improve the community through the Chehalis Community Renaissance Team. Retail development has burgeoned west of Interstate 5 near the northern part of Chehalis. In 2007, the historic city hall and Carnegie Library were demolished to make way for the Vernetta Smith Chehalis Timberland Library, which opened in 2008 and features the first drive-through library window in Washington.

Today, Chehalis, so rich in history, is known as a community of museums—the Lewis County Historical Museum in the 1912 Chehalis train depot, the Vintage Motorcycle Museum in the renovated 1889 Washington Hotel, the Chehalis-Centralia Railroad and Museum, and the Veterans Memorial Museum built near Interstate 5, where military men and women are honored for their service and sacrifices, and where, as the motto states, "They Shall Not Be Forgotten."

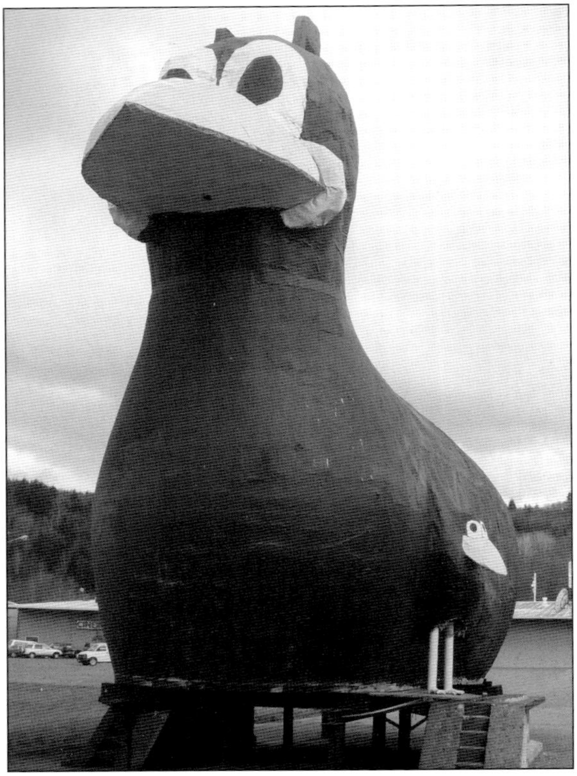

A goofy giant black crow sits in front of the 305,000-square-foot Yard Birds Mall on the one-way couplet between Chehalis and Centralia. The infamous Yard Birds resemble cartoonlike crows with yellow claws and personality. In 1947, Bill Jones and Richard Gillingham opened a surplus store in a tent in Centralia, subsequently moving the business to a gas station and auto garage in Chehalis, where Sunbird Shopping Center is today. The men referred to themselves as "The Two Yard Birds." Expanding in 1971 to the current location, they erected a 70-foot fiberglass Yard Bird motorists could drive under. Fire from a car destroyed the bird in 1976, and a new Yard Bird was reconstructed. The photograph below shows flames devouring the original bird in 1976. Both Yard Birds and the nearby Sunbird store have been flooded time and again, often leaving the Yard Bird seemingly afloat amid a sea of murky waters. (Both, courtesy of the *Chronicle* in Centralia.)

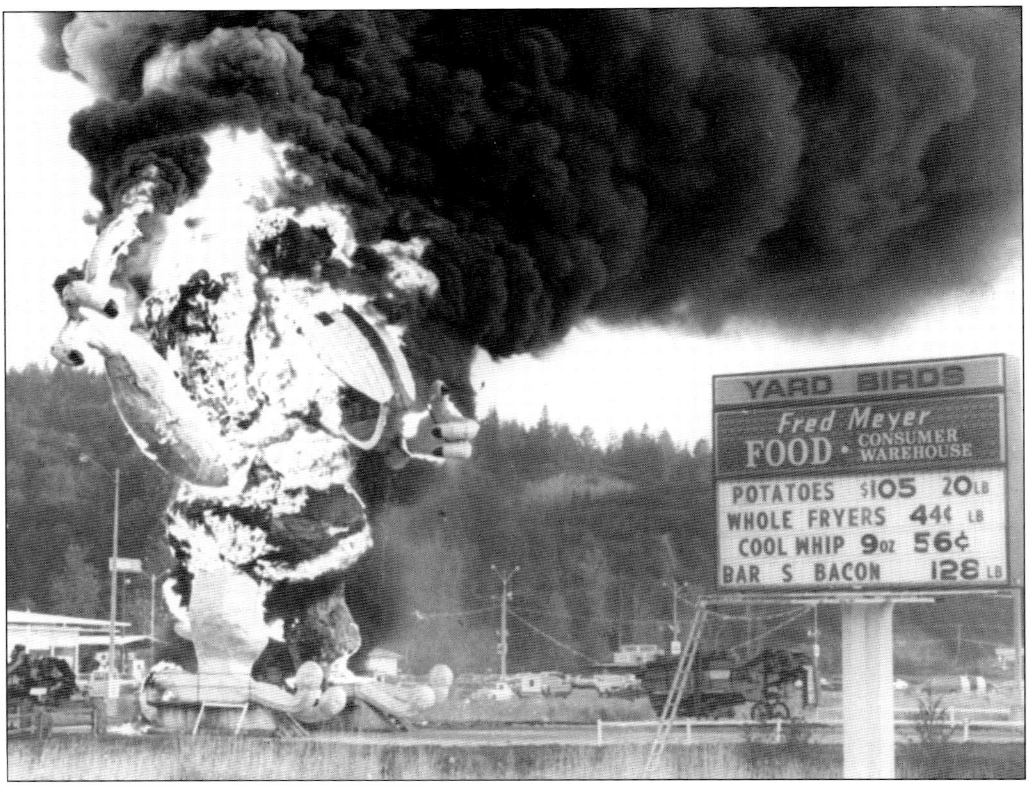

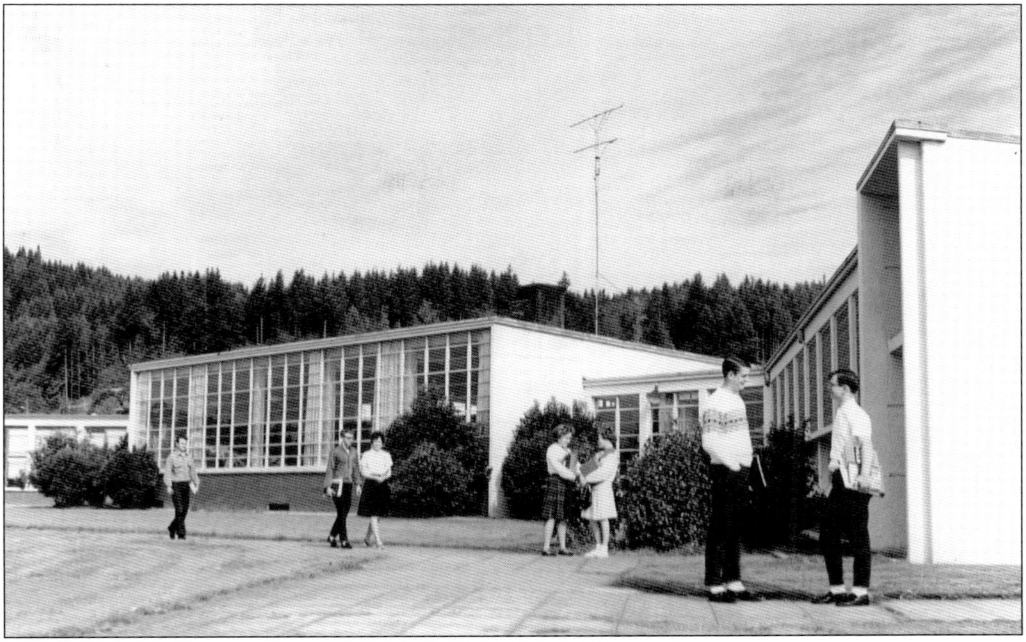

The Chehalis High School at Main and Market Streets was damaged extensively in the 1949 earthquake, so it needed to be replaced. William F. West (right), youngest child of the pioneer who helped build the city, donated land to the Chehalis School District for a new school, which opened as Chehalis High School in 1951. On September 19, 1957, the district changed the school's name to W.F. West High School, seen above in 1964. From left to right are two unidentified boys, Kathy Pemerl, an unidentified girl, Janie Wirta, Benny Ames, and Mike Rasmussen. West, longtime owner and operator of St. Helens Hotel, and his wife, Blanche, gave the school district more than $40,000 between 1950 and Bill's death in 1963, when he was 87. After his wife passed away in 1969 at 88, the district received money to establish the William F. and Blanche E. West scholarship trust. Les Schwab Tire Center is on the old school site.

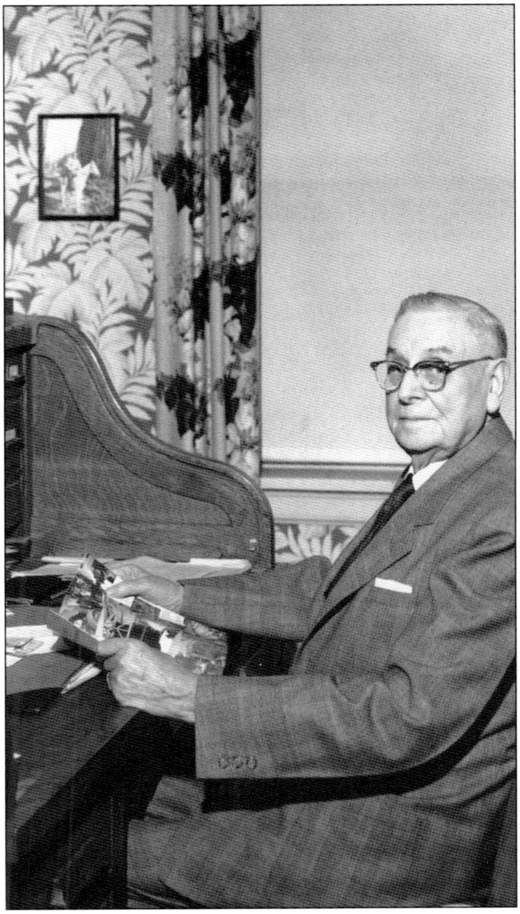

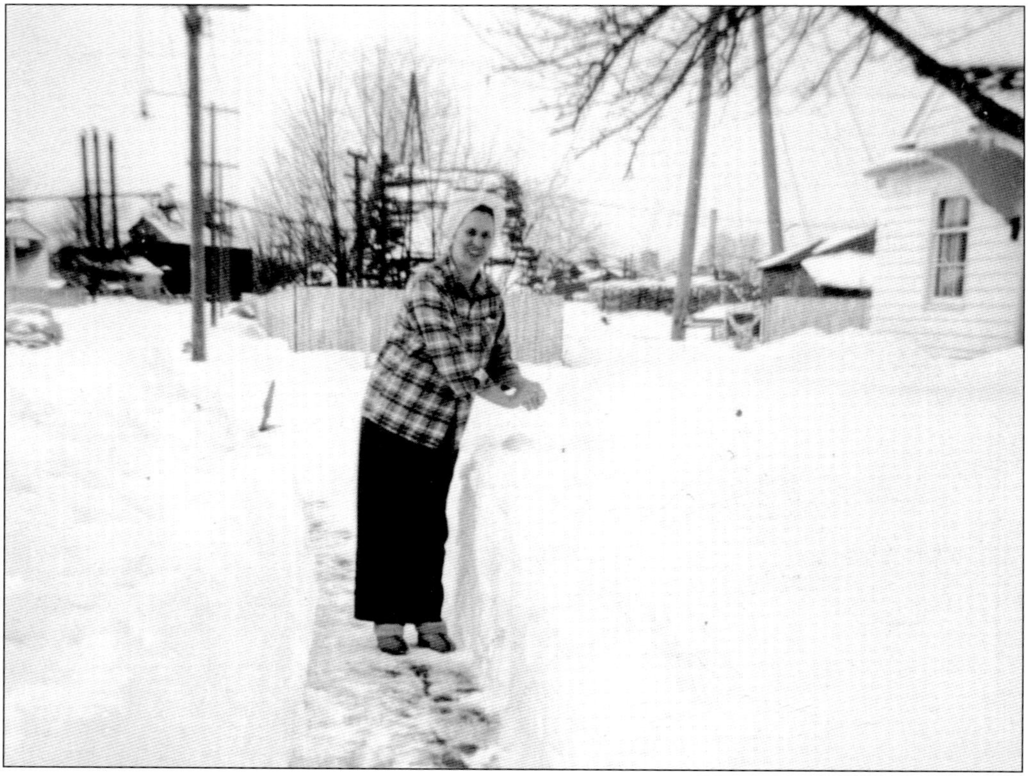

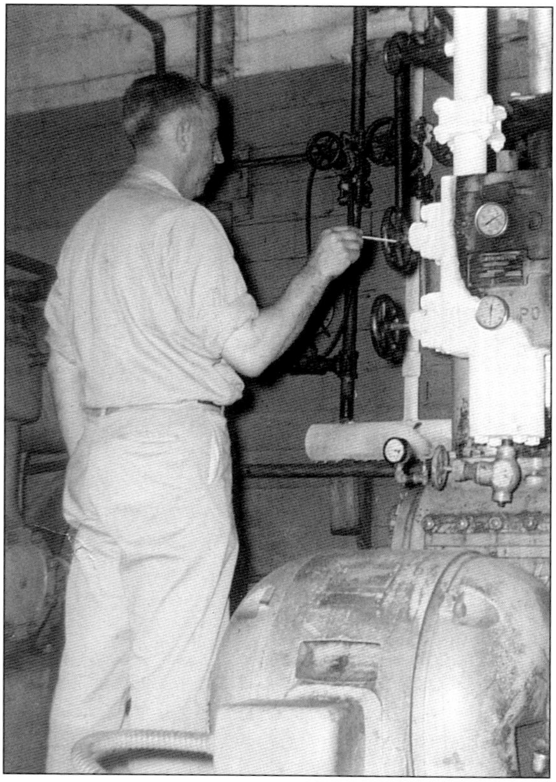

Sarah Ciranny Zopolos, pregnant with her first child, stands outside her home on Chehalis Avenue after the January 1950 blizzard, which piled deep snow on Chehalis and left four-foot-long icicles hanging from roofs. The fierce wind blew snow through the keyhole in the heavy mahogany door of the Zopolos' unfinished home, creating "a white, wet anthill on the wood floor," Sarah Zopolos recalled. Harry Zopolos, whose parents emigrated from Greece, graduated from Chehalis High School in 1939 and began working for the Forget-Me-Not Ice Cream Company on the west side of Chehalis. He is seen working in 1959, two decades after the company's original plant was destroyed by the devastating Palmer Lumber fire. (Both, courtesy of Sarah Ciranny Zopolos.)

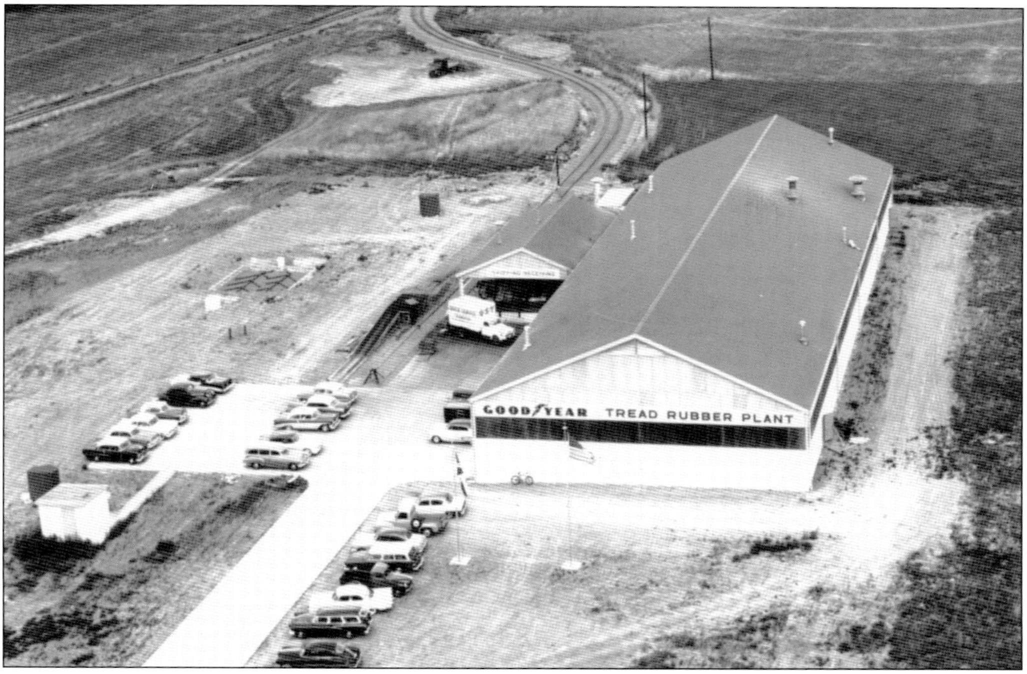

In 1955, the Chehalis Industrial Park became a reality when 221 investors formed the Industrial Commission, which bought land south of town in 1956. Volunteers known as Gandy Dancers spent two weekends laying 3,500 feet of railroad track for a spur line to serve the park's first client—Goodyear Tire and Rubber Co., which opened a $1 million plant in 1957. The park has grown to more than 700 acres.

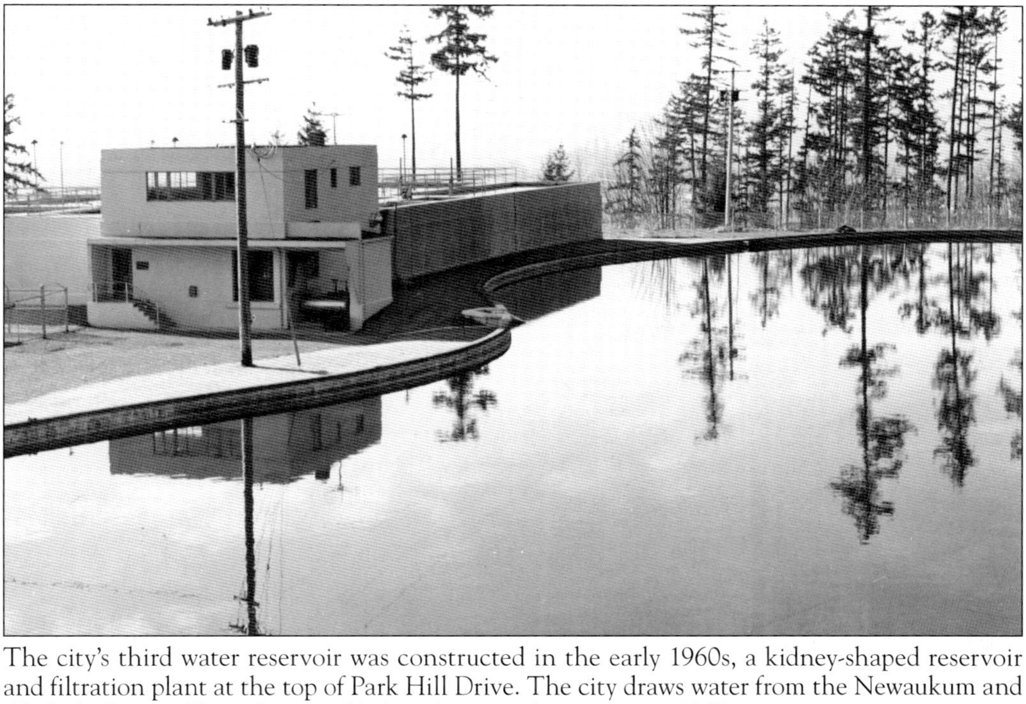

The city's third water reservoir was constructed in the early 1960s, a kidney-shaped reservoir and filtration plant at the top of Park Hill Drive. The city draws water from the Newaukum and Chehalis Rivers. Fluoride was added to the water beginning in 1968.

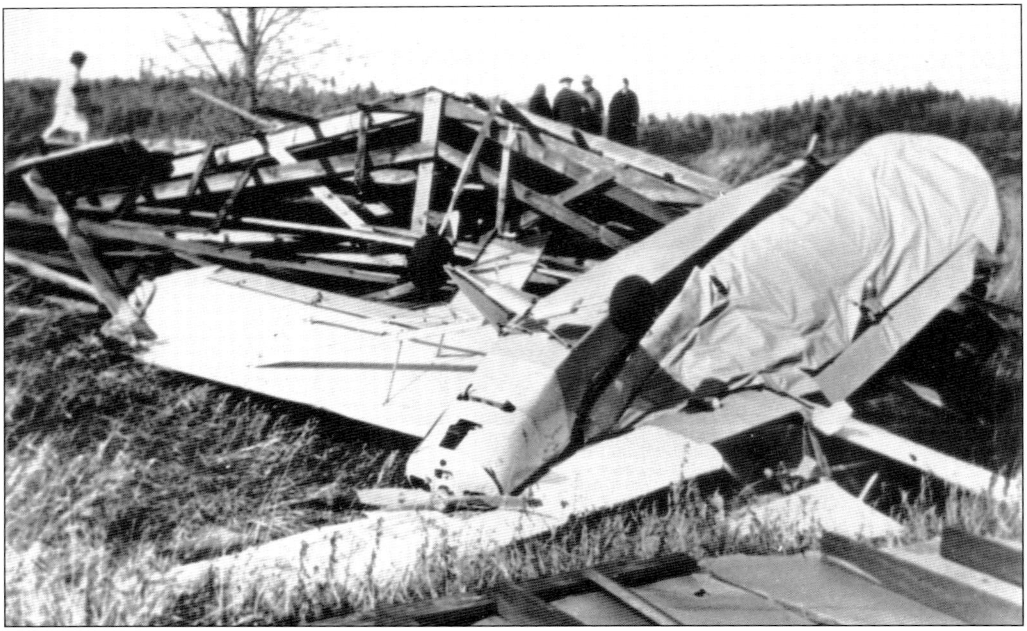

Natural disasters left Chehalis residents reeling. The Columbus Day storm of 1962 brought ferocious 100-mile-per-hour winds that pummeled the Pacific Northwest, toppling trees, ripping off roofs, knocking out electricity, and killing 46 people. The above photograph by Ray Spears shows an airplane at the Chehalis airport mangled by the storm that was described by the National Weather Service as "the mother of all windstorms this century, the windstorm all others are compared to." Then, a week after the May 18, 1980, eruption of Mount St. Helens, which killed 57 people, a second eruption spewed ash throughout Lewis County. Below, Harry Zopolos covers his nose and mouth with a bandana while shoveling ash from the sidewalk leading to his Chehalis Avenue home. (Below, courtesy of Sarah Ciranny Zopolos.)

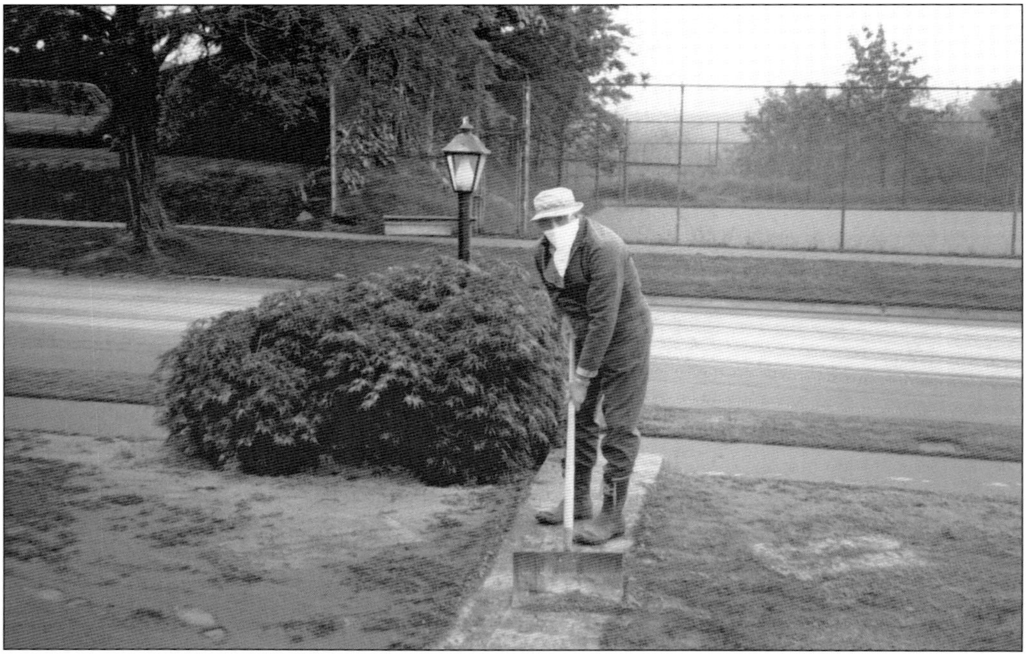

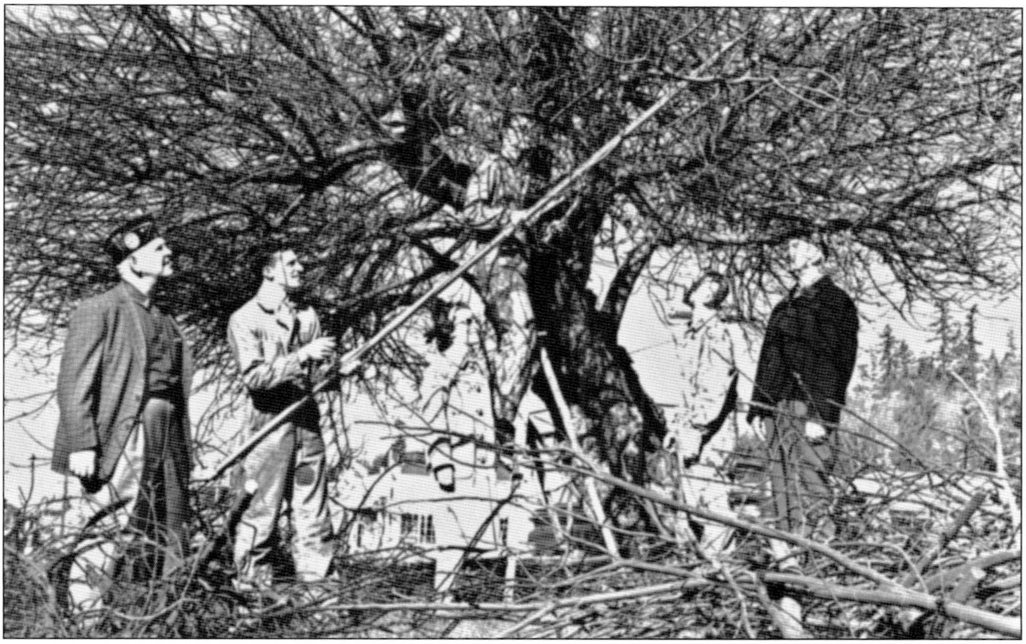

Around 1964 and 1965, Future Farmers of America students wearing coveralls prune the historic Saunders Tree while supervised by educator F.B. Smith, at left, and Jackie Morgan. Joseph Saunders and Billy Jobe, a Native American, grafted a Gravenstein apple tree to an old crab apple stump in 1870. The knotted and scarred tree bore apples at Fourth and Market Streets for years. During street widening in 1968, the Lewis County Historical Society moved the tree to Henderson Park, but it didn't survive.

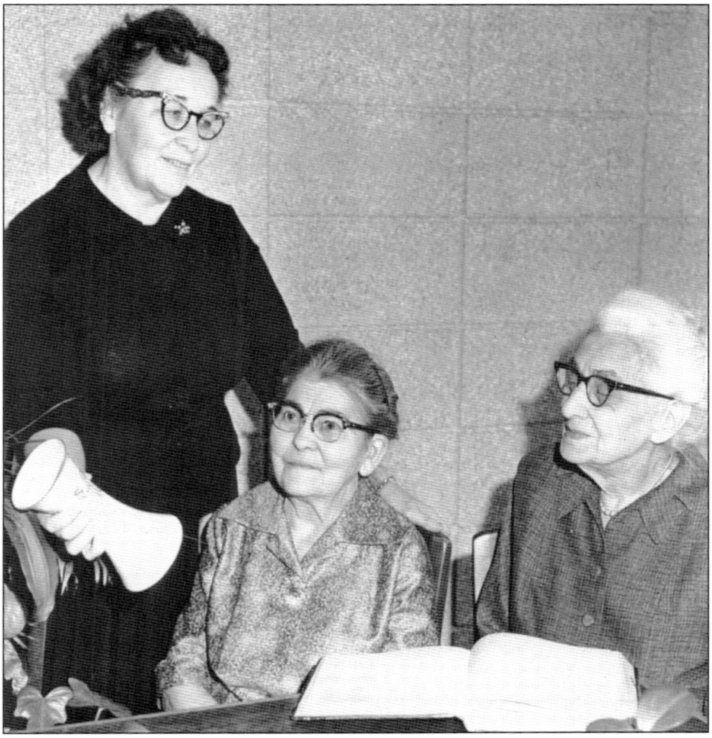

St. Helens Club members pictured around 1960 are, from left to right, Margaret Steck, Emily Jane Burrows, and Anna Koontz, granddaughter of John R. Jackson. The club formed in February 1895 "to promote interest in literature, art, science and the vital issues of the day." In the past, it spearheaded civic projects to clean up Chehalis, restore the historic Jackson Courthouse, plant shade trees, and pay for a restroom on Chehalis Avenue.

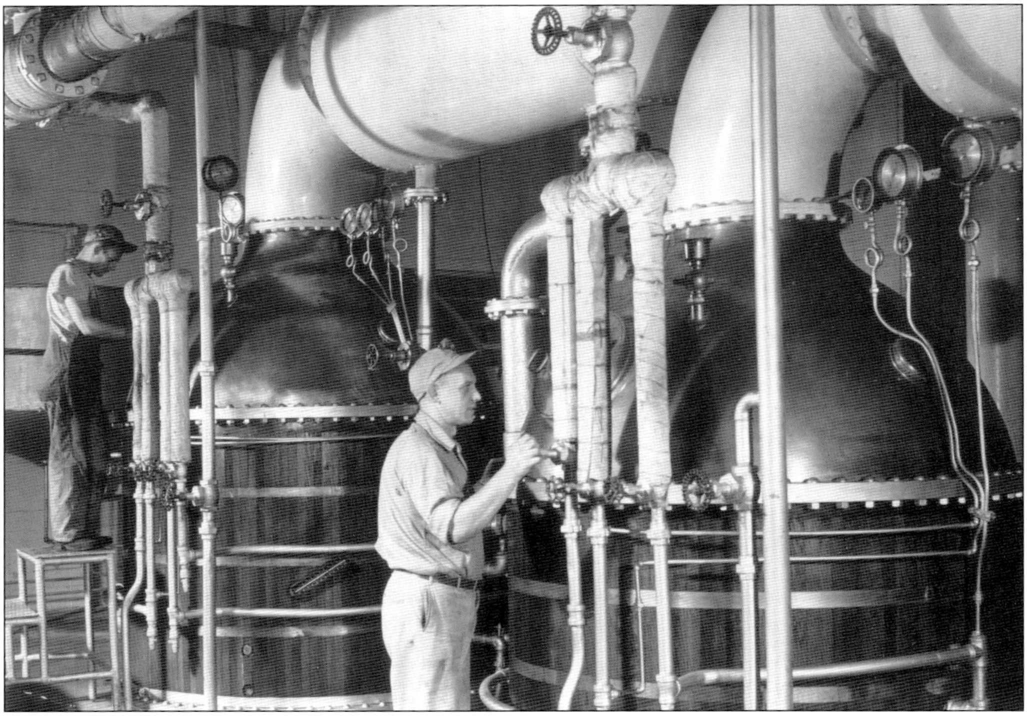

This 1960s photograph shows Jim Lund, at left, and an unidentified employee in the distilling room at the I.P Callison and Sons plant on National Avenue. In 1900, Callison, a schoolteacher who published a weekly newspaper, worked with a stranger to fulfill an order from drug manufacturers for two train carloads of cascara bark. Afterward, Callison launched a company that expanded in 1916 to provide digitalis and, later, the processing and marketing of peppermint and other essential oils.

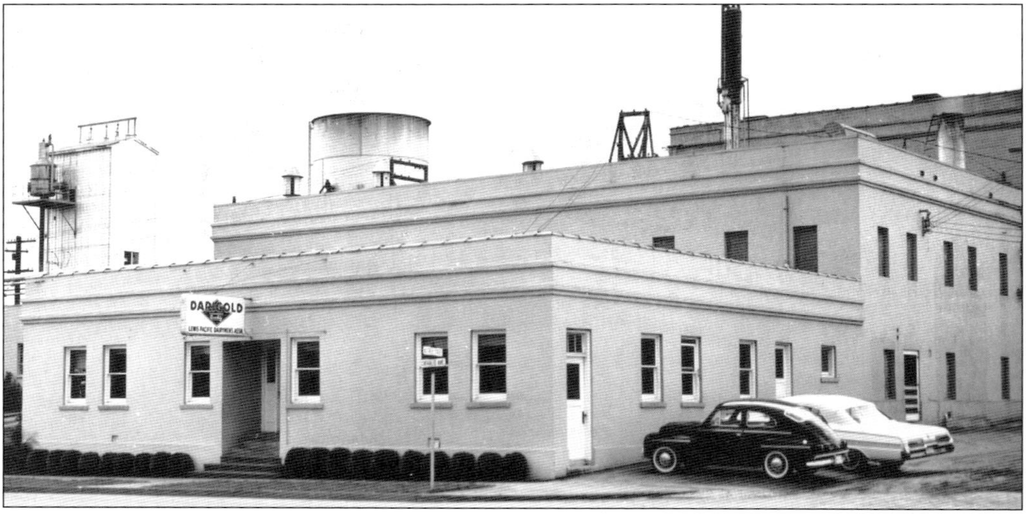

Seen here is the front entrance of the Darigold milk processing plant in Chehalis in the 1950s. The plant, located on the corner of Alfred Street and Chehalis Avenue, has served local dairy farmers and provided jobs for the community. The company is one of the nation's largest agricultural cooperatives, processing and packaging 2 million gallons of milk a day, as well as producing butter, cheese, milk powder, and whey.

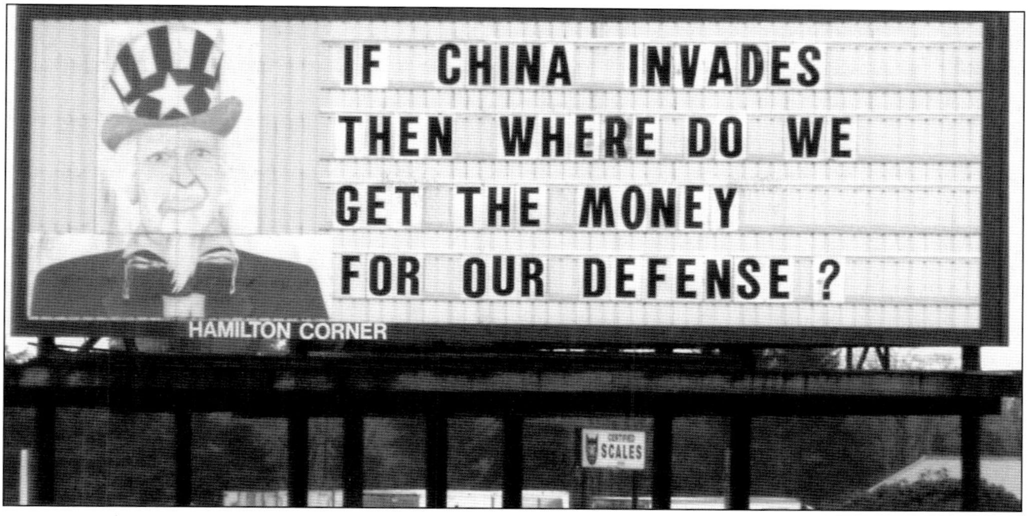

For more than four decades, Chehalis has been the home of the Hamilton Farms billboard along Interstate 5, which displays conservative messages and has provided motorists with entertainment or angst, depending on their political persuasion. The sign—in recent years located near Exit 72, south of Chehalis—has outlived its founder, turkey farmer Alfred Hamilton of Chehalis, who died November 9, 2004, at 84.

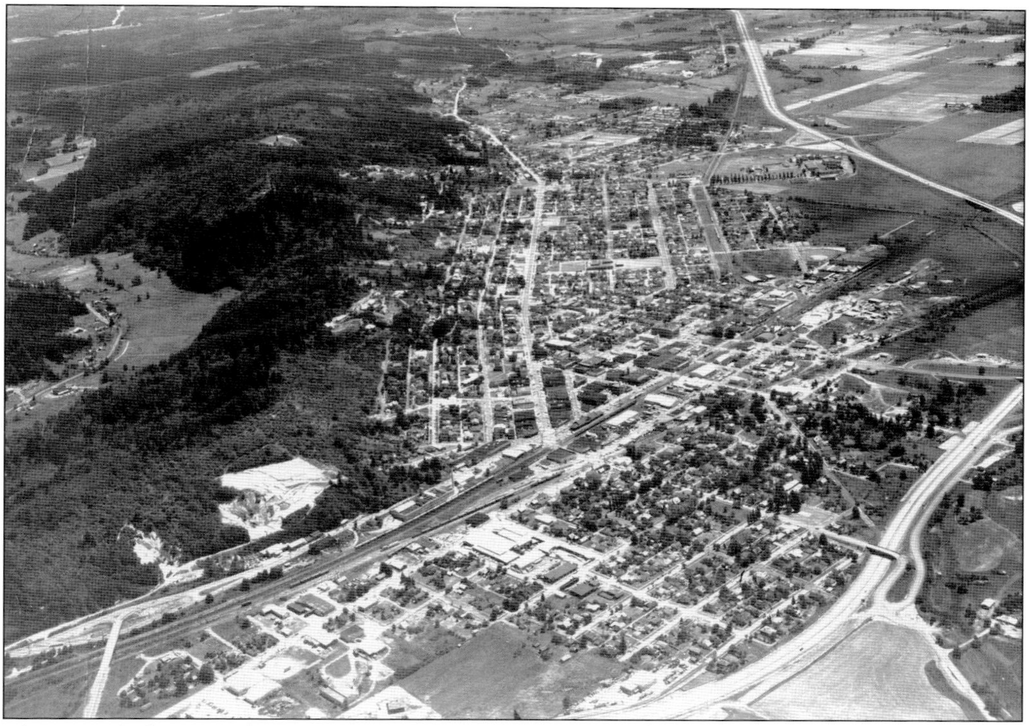

This aerial photograph shows Chehalis around 1970. The overpass in the left corner is the National Avenue exit from Interstate 5, now called Chamber Way. To the right are the diggings of the Brick and Tile Company, which appears across the highway and the railroad spur. Kostick Brothers Scrap Metal and Welding was between North National Avenue and the diggings. Market Street runs from mid-bottom to the top. Interstate 5 runs through the right corner. Coal Creek is at center left.

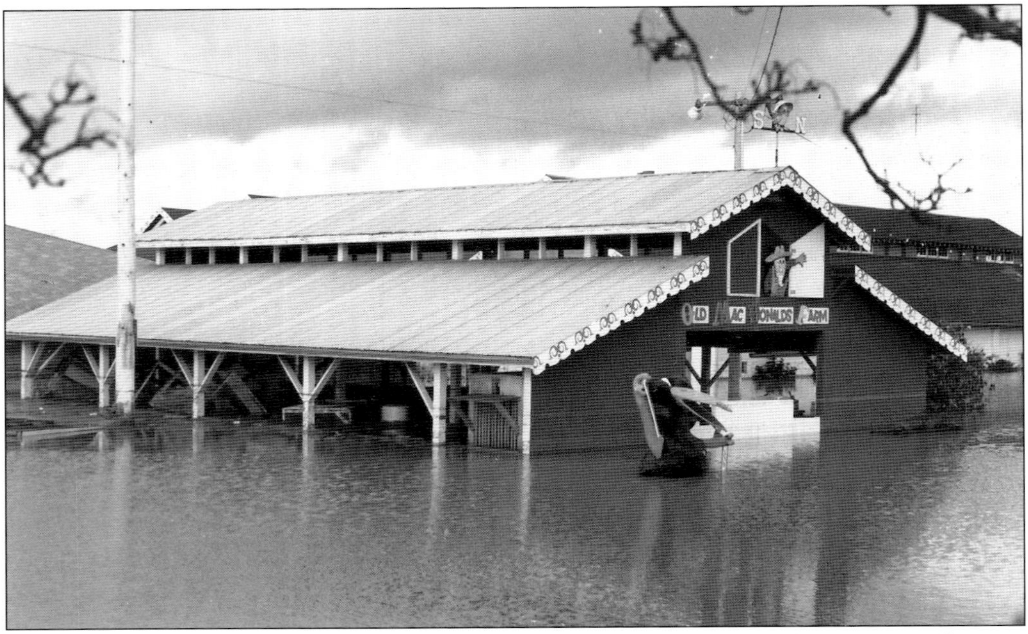

The Southwest Washington Fair, frequently inundated when the Chehalis River overflows its banks, is seen during the 1972 flood. The fairgrounds sustained extensive damage of $250,000 when water rose to the eaves of the concession stands, ruining food preparation equipment. A dike around the fairgrounds, constructed in 1952, washed out January 21 "during the worst flooding in county history," according to a February 1, 1972, *Daily Chronicle* article.

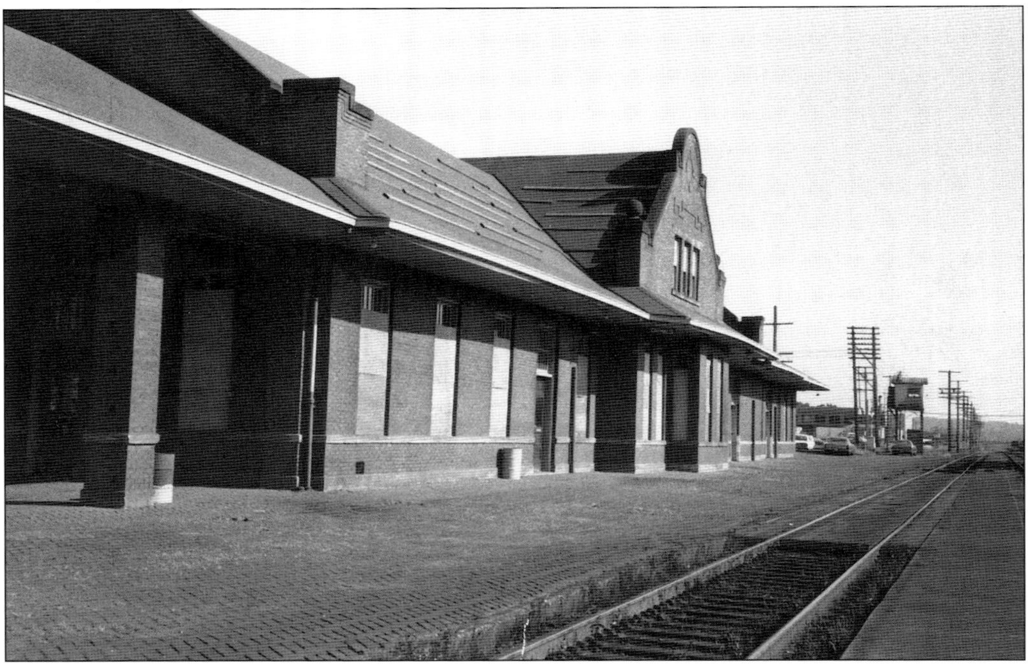

The historic Chehalis train depot is seen in September 1979, just before the grand opening of the Lewis County Historical Museum. The Lewis County Historical Society organized in 1965 as a tax-exempt nonprofit group. The museum officially opened in 1967 in the donated Washington Avenue home of Arthur Cory and was moved to the renovated Chehalis depot in 1979.

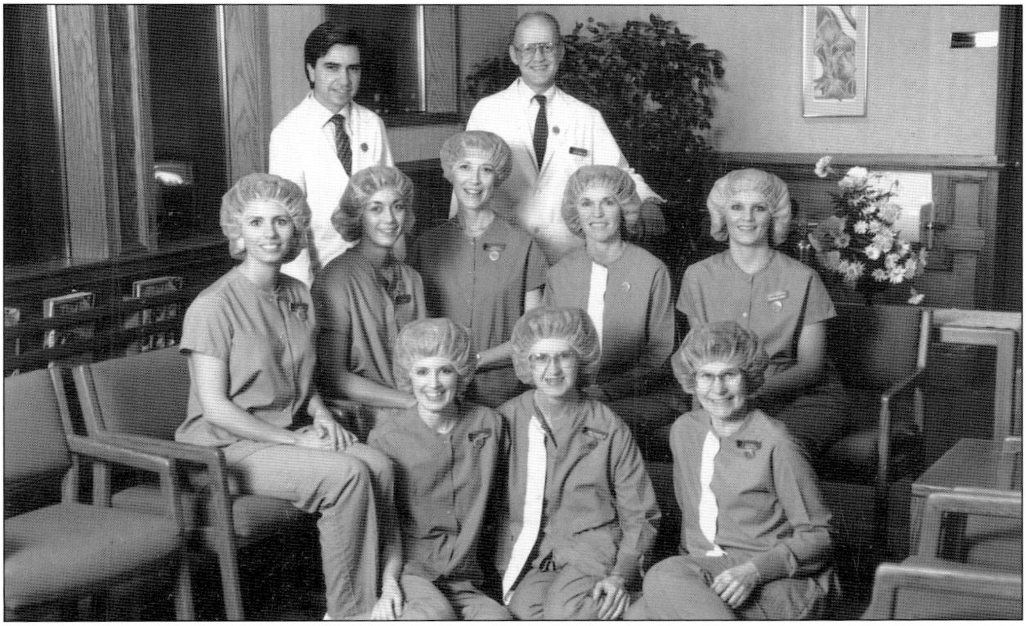

This photograph shows eye surgeons Dr. Robert O. Ford (left) and Dr. Helgi Heider and nurses. In 1985, they formed the Pacific Cataract and Laser Institute in Chehalis. It has become a renowned outpatient center with clinics in the Washington cities of Bellevue, Bellingham, Kennewick, Olympia, Silverdale, Spokane, Tacoma, Vancouver, and Yakima, as well as Portland and Tualatin in Oregon and Anchorage, Boise, Lewiston, Great Falls, and Albuquerque. Physicians have performed more than 300,000 micro eye surgeries.

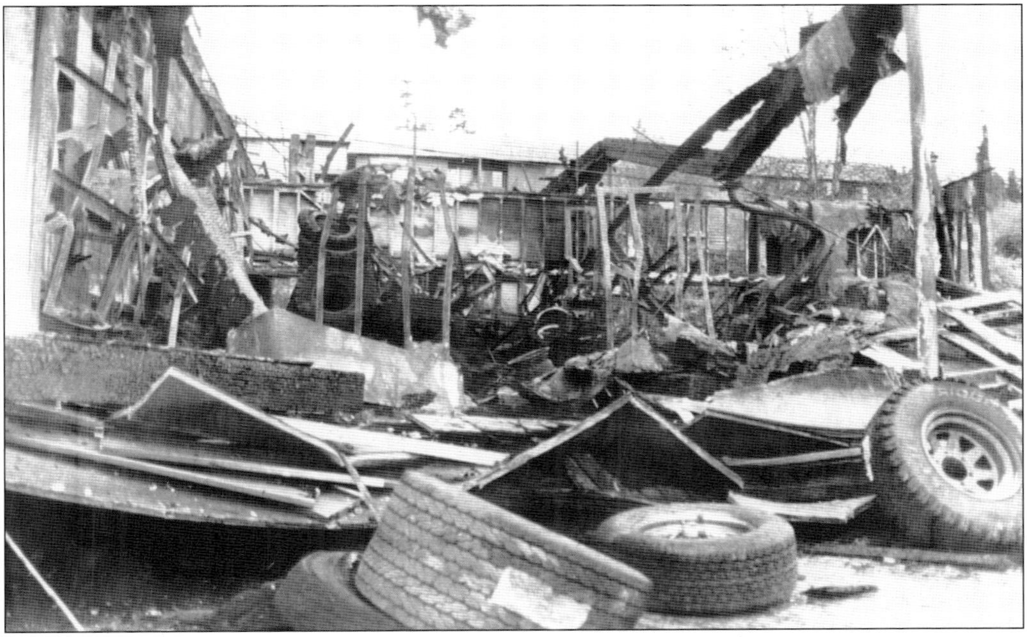

A spectacular fire engulfed the Les Schwab Tire Center in Chehalis in 1981, leaving only piles of rubble. This photograph shows the burnt tires and wall braces remaining after the fire at Main and Market Streets. The Kleene Apartments are in the background. The store reopened six months later, after rebuilding with cement blocks. (Courtesy of the *Daily Chronicle*.)

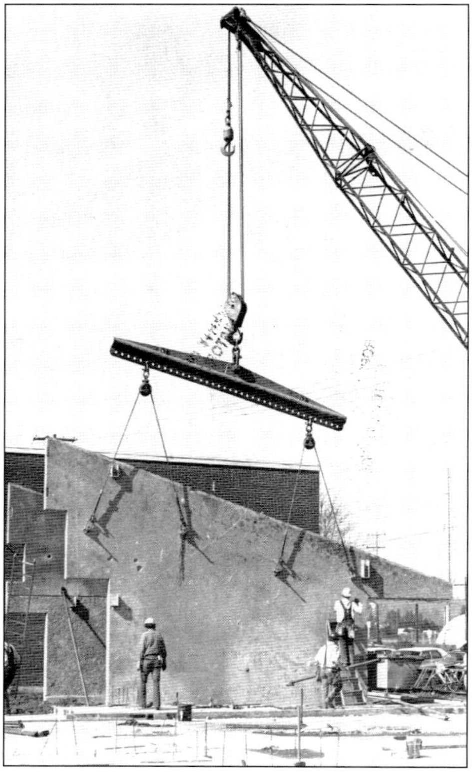

This c. 1978 photograph shows a crane putting a concrete wall into place for the National Frozen Foods cold storage building. The company, founded in 1912 as the National Fruit Canning Company, was renamed after discontinuing its canning operations in 1974. The company has plants in Chehalis, Moses Lake, and Quincy in Washington, and in Albany, Oregon. The Chehalis plant processes 110 million pounds a year of frozen corn, carrots, and peas. (Courtesy of the *Daily Chronicle*.)

Mary McCrank, born in 1900 in Vancouver, British Columbia, couldn't cook when she started what remains a charming Chehalis area restaurant known for good homemade food. She lost her secretarial job when the Automobile Club of Washington closed during the Depression. In 1935, she bought the Dutch Mill Tavern on busy Highway 99 and named her business the Shamrock Inn to honor her Irish ancestry. It later became Mary McCrank's, seen here in 1984, the year she died.

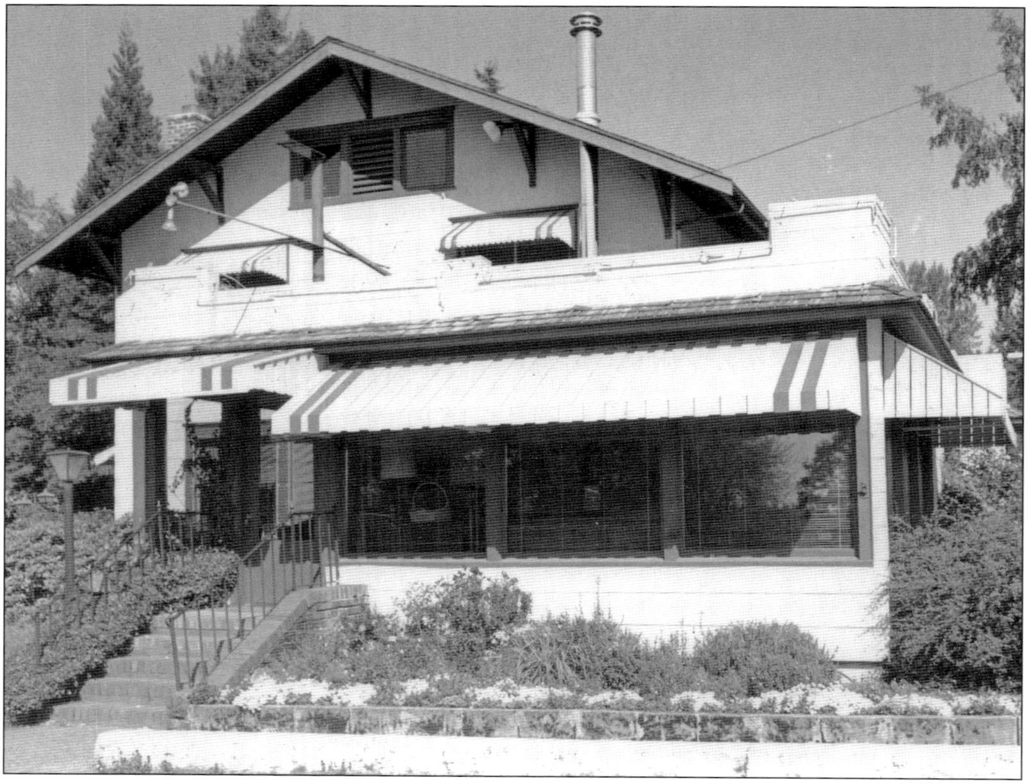

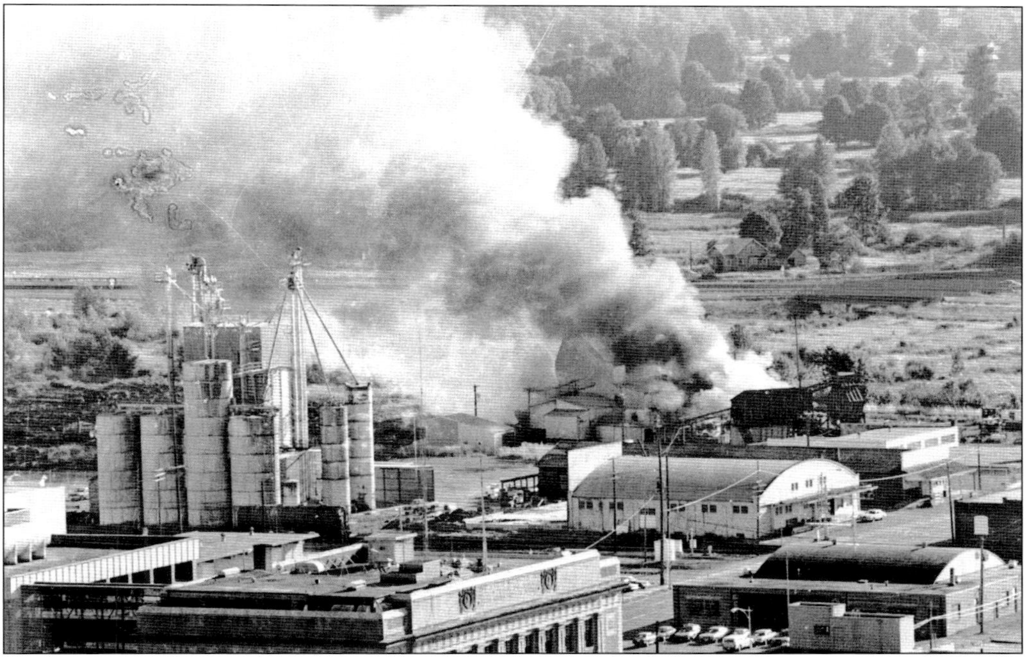

Smoke billows into the Chehalis sky from a raging fire at the former Hemphill-O'Neill Company's Date mill on July 16, 1984. Hemphill-O'Neill had just sold the mill to three of its managers when the fire occurred on a hot July day. As prices for lumber dropped and timber grew harder to come by, mills in Chehalis and throughout the Northwest shut down. (Courtesy of the *Daily Chronicle*.)

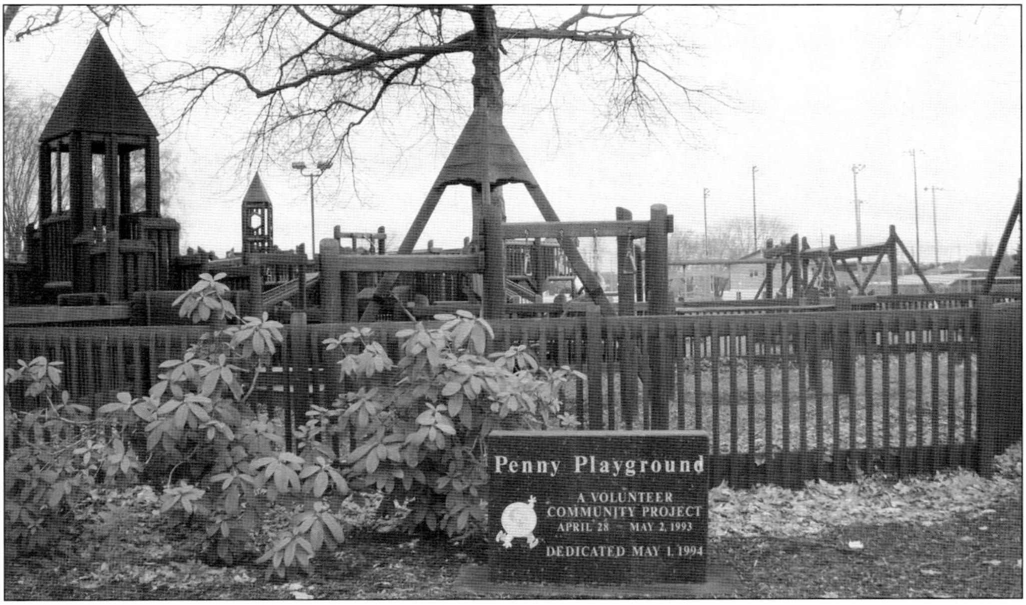

The Penny Playground, with its wooden play structures in the city's 12-acre Recreation Park, earned its name from fundraising efforts that preceded its construction. People dropped loose change into collection barrels, and schoolchildren held penny drives. In 1993, two-thousand people devoted 8,000 hours over five days to erect the $80,000 playground. The nearby Stan Hedwall Park opened in 1975 after citizens contributed $117,000 in matching funds and labor to construct the $511,000 park with ball fields, picnic tables, bike trails, and overnight camping.

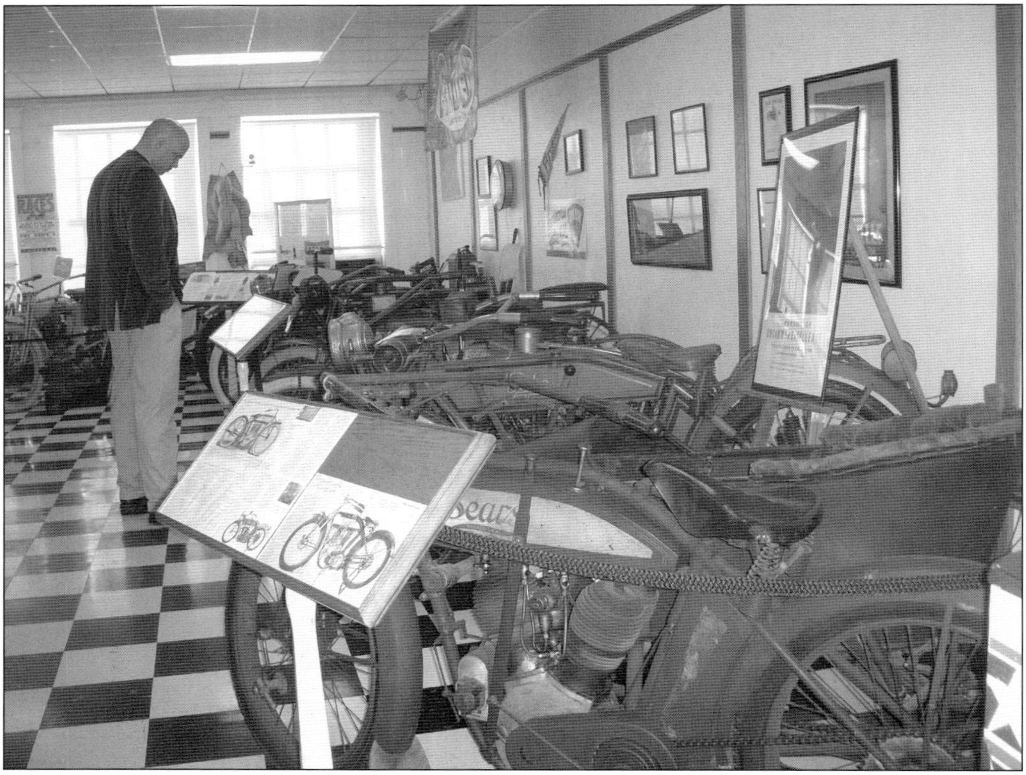

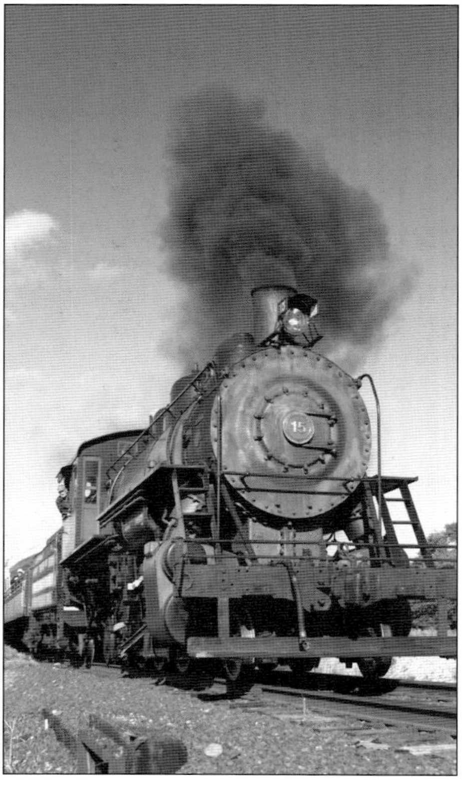

The Vintage Antique Motorcycle Museum at the Washington Hotel on Market Street is an example of a hobby shared for the enjoyment of others, such as Terry Knapp, pictured. Frank and Barbara Mason, who collected antique motorcycles, bought and restored the 1889 brick hotel after a fire raged through downtown Chehalis businesses on July 11, 1997. The Masons, owners of Mason Construction, renovated the brick archway, entry, and interior of the building to its original state. They also remodeled the St. Helens Inn into 42 apartments in 1970.

Engineer Harold Borovec drives the 1916 Cowlitz, Chehalis & Cascade Railroad No. 15 steam locomotive, restored by the Chehalis-Centralia Railroad Association after sitting in a Chehalis park for 30 years. The nonprofit corporation, formed in 1986, began offering train rides along old tracks in 1989. The 95-year-old locomotive still pulls trains for holidays, school field trips, and special lunch and dinner events sponsored by the Chehalis-Centralia Railroad and Museum, a name adopted in 2006. (Courtesy of the Chehalis-Centralia Railroad Association.)

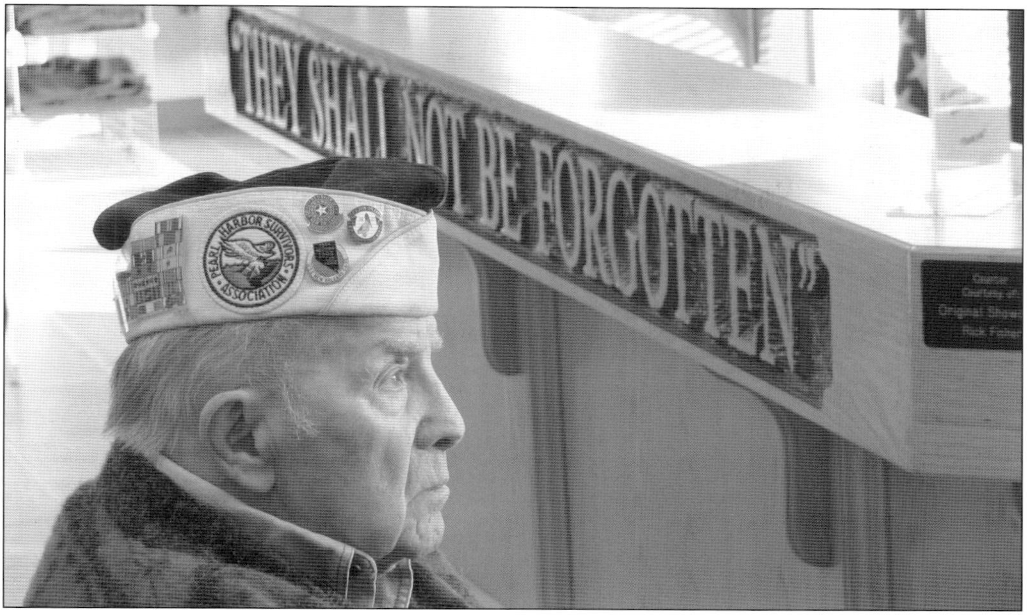

The Veterans Memorial Museum off Interstate 5, Exit 77, in Chehalis features a 9,000-square-foot gallery with 85 display cases that tell the stories of military men and women who served and sacrificed for the United States. This photograph shows Bud Fox—a veteran of World War II, Korea, and Vietnam—sitting in his wheelchair near the sign declaring the museum's motto: "They Shall Not Be Forgotten." (Courtesy of Charles Duncan.)

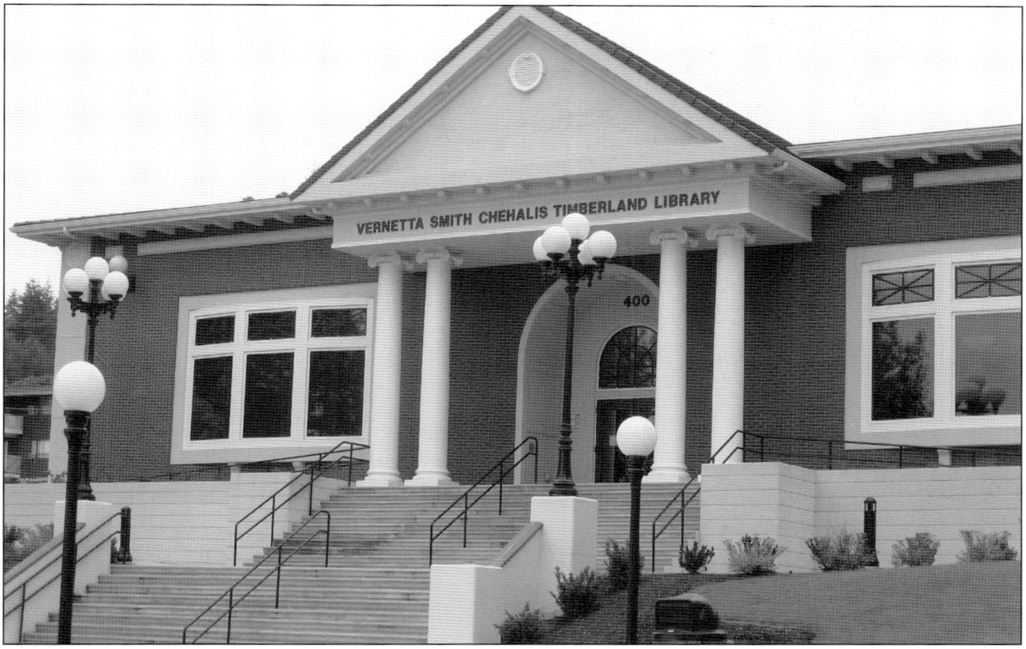

The Vernetta Smith Chehalis Timberland Library, which opened November 4, 2008, replaced the 1910 Carnegie Library. The 9,000-square-foot building features the state's first drive-through window. The library was built much the way early pioneers constructed the city, through private donations. It is named for the mother of Orin Smith, the chief donor. Chehalis became part of the five-county Timberland Regional Library system in January 1970. (Courtesy of the City of Chehalis.)

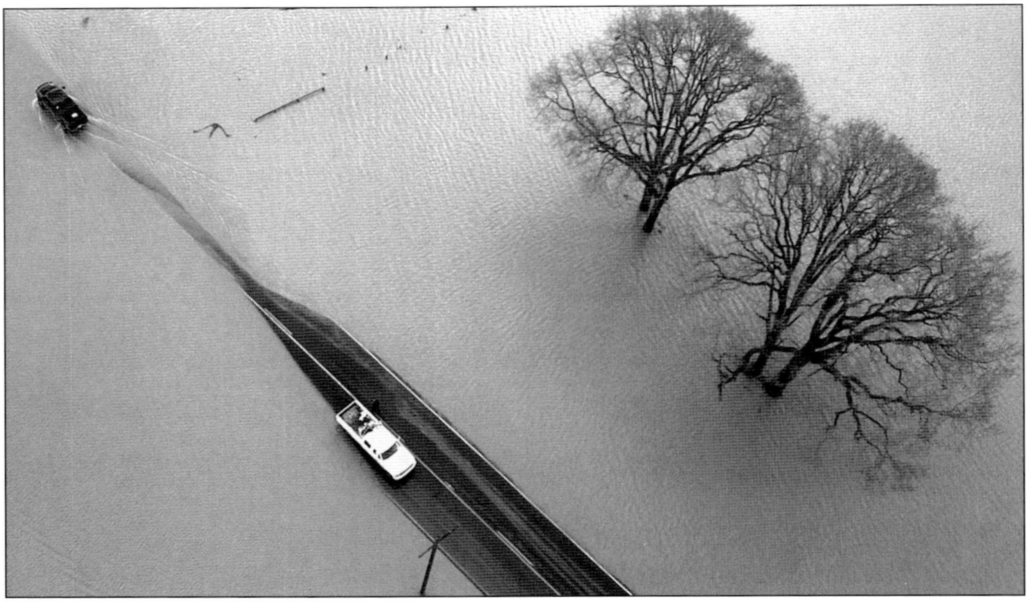

This photograph shows a flooded Interstate 5 between Centralia and Chehalis during the devastating December 2007 flood, which closed the highway and caused an estimated $500 million in damage in Lewis County. Rescuers evacuated about 500 people. Water damaged 638 homes, and 100 had to be demolished. At the new Veterans Memorial Museum, erected several feet above the 100-year floodplain, floodwaters inundated the building, soaking carpets, display items on lower shelves, and—most heartbreaking—tapes of oral history interviews conducted by museum executive director and founder Lee Grimes with veterans over the years. Mike Gregoire, husband to Gov. Christine Gregoire, offered to restore the tapes, which he did. Learning the hard way, museum officials created emergency plans to stay overnight when high water threatens so that they can remove items from lower display cases. In the image below, an exhausted Grimes poses with a fishing pole in 2009 after waiting and worrying all night while water levels rose outside—but stopped just short of entering the building. (Above, courtesy of the *Chronicle*; below, courtesy of Charles Duncan.)

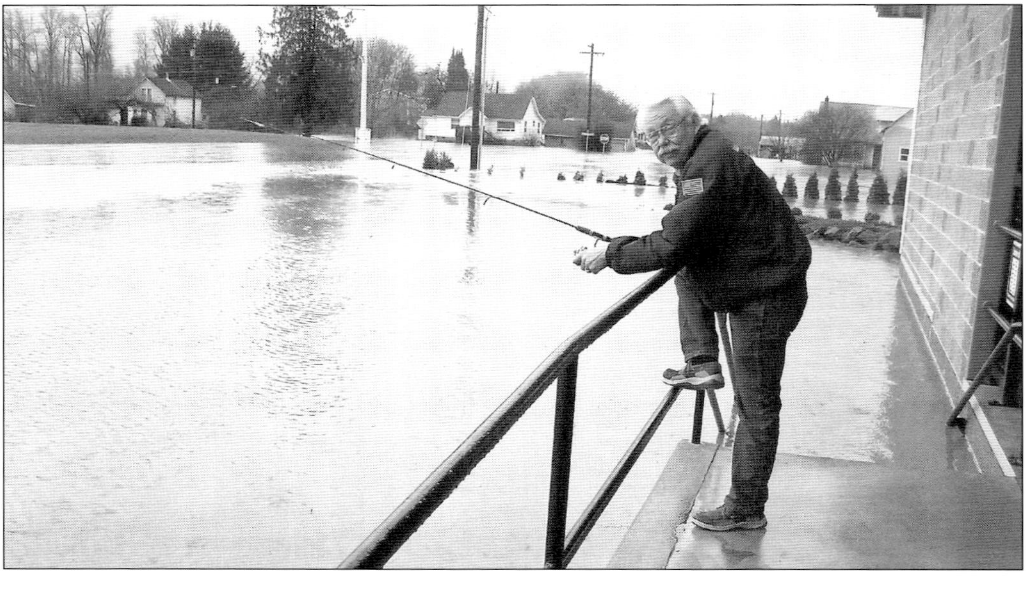

Bibliography

Chronicle, The (formerly the *Daily Chronicle*). Centralia, WA.

Clemens, Shelly, Debbie Knapp, and Caryn Foley. *Historic Downtown Chehalis Walking Tour.* July 2010. Brochure.

Crowell, Sandra A. *The Land Called Lewis: A History of Lewis County, Washington.* Chehalis, WA: Panesko Publishing, 2007.

Lewis County Historical Museum. Photo caption cards, 1965–2011.

Ott, Jen. *Chehalis—Thumbnail History.* HistoryLink.org Essay 8645. www.historylink.org/index.cfm?DisplayPage=output.cfm&file_id=8645. July 2008.

Pearson, Flaval, ed., and the Adventure in Cooperation History Committee. *A History of Chehalis.* Chehalis, WA: Chehalis Community Development Programs, 1956 and 1976.

Smith, Herndon, ed. *Centralia: The First Fifty Years, 1845–1900.* Centralia, WA: The *Daily Chronicle* and F.H. Cole Printing Co., 1975.

Toledo History Committee. *The Toledo Community Story.* Toledo, WA: Chapters of Life, 2008.

Zander, Julie McDonald. *Chapters of Life in 1915 Chehalis: The Chehalis Bee-Nugget Historical Souvenir Edition May 14, 1915, Illustrated and Republished.* Toledo, WA: Chapters of Life, 2011.

———. *Bucoda: The Little Town with a Million Memories.* Toledo, WA: Chapters of Life, 2010.

———. *Legacy of Two Lumbermen: The Hemphill-O'Neill Company History.* Toledo, WA: Chapters of Life, 2006.

———. *Life on the Home Front: Stories of Those Who Worked, Waited, and Worried during WWII.* Toledo, WA: Chapters of Life, 2005.

Zopolos, Sarah Ciranny. *Laboring in Love: Angelo and Teresa Ciranny—From Italy to Tono to Centralia.* Toledo, WA: Chapters of Life, 2007.